Year 3C

A Guide to Teaching for Mastery

Series Editor: Tony Staneff

Contents

Introduction   page 4
What is *Power Maths*?   page 5
Introduction to the author team   page 6
Your *Power Maths* resources   page 7
The *Power Maths* teaching model   page 10
The *Power Maths* lesson sequence   page 12
Using the *Power Maths* Teacher Guide   page 15
Power Maths Year 3, yearly overview   page 16
Mindset: an introduction   page 20
The *Power Maths* characters   page 21
Mathematical language   page 22
The role of talk and discussion   page 23
Assessment strategies   page 24
Power Maths unit assessment grid   page 26
Keeping the class together   page 27
Depth and breadth   page 28
Same-day intervention   page 29
The role of practice   page 30
Structures and representations   page 31
Practical aspects of *Power Maths*   page 32
List of practical resources   page 34
Variation helps visualisation   page 36
Getting started with *Power Maths*   page 37

Unit 10 – Fractions (2)   page 38
Lesson 1 – Equivalent fractions (1)   page 40
Lesson 2 – Equivalent fractions (2)   page 44
Lesson 3 – Equivalent fractions (3)   page 48
Lesson 4 – Comparing fractions   page 52
Lesson 5 – Comparing and ordering fractions   page 56
Lesson 6 – Adding fractions   page 60
Lesson 7 – Subtracting fractions   page 64
Lesson 8 – Problem solving – adding and subtracting fractions   page 68
Lesson 9 – Problem solving – fractions of measures   page 72
End of unit check   page 76

Unit 11 – Time   page 78
Lesson 1 – Months and years   page 80
Lesson 2 – Hours in a day   page 84
Lesson 3 – Estimating time   page 88
Lesson 4 – Telling time to 5 minutes   page 92
Lesson 5 – Telling time to the minute (1)   page 96
Lesson 6 – Telling time to the minute (2)   page 100
Lesson 7 – Telling time to the minute (3)   page 104

Lesson 8 – Finding the duration   page 108
Lesson 9 – Comparing duration   page 112
Lesson 10 – Finding start and end times   page 116
Lesson 11 – Measuring time in seconds   page 120
End of unit check   page 124

Unit 12 – Angles and properties of shapes   page 126
Lesson 1 – Turns and angles   page 128
Lesson 2 – Right angles in shapes   page 132
Lesson 3 – Comparing angles   page 136
Lesson 4 – Drawing accurately   page 140
Lesson 5 – Types of line (1)   page 144
Lesson 6 – Types of line (2)   page 148
Lesson 7 – Recognising and describing 2D shapes   page 152
Lesson 8 – Recognising and describing 3D shapes   page 156
Lesson 9 – Constructing 3D shapes   page 160
End of unit check   page 164

Unit 13 – Mass   page 166
Lesson 1 – Measuring mass (1)   page 168
Lesson 2 – Measuring mass (2)   page 172
Lesson 3 – Measuring mass (3)   page 176
Lesson 4 – Comparing masses   page 180
Lesson 5 – Adding and subtracting masses   page 184
Lesson 6 – Problem solving – mass   page 188
End of unit check   page 192

Unit 14 – Capacity   page 194
Lesson 1 – Measuring capacity (1)   page 196
Lesson 2 – Measuring capacity (2)   page 200
Lesson 3 – Measuring capacity (3)   page 204
Lesson 4 – Comparing capacities   page 208
Lesson 5 – Adding and subtracting capacities   page 212
Lesson 6 – Problem solving – capacity   page 216
End of unit check   page 220

Introduction

Foreword by the series editor and author, Tony Staneff

For far too long in the UK, maths has been feared by learners – and by many teachers, too. As a result, most learners consistently underachieve. More crucially, negative beliefs about ability, aptitude and the nature of maths are entrenched in children's thinking from an early age.

Yet, as someone who has loved maths all my life, I've always believed that every child has the capacity to succeed in maths. I've also had the great pleasure of leading teams and departments who share that belief and passion. Teaching for mastery, as practised in China and other South-East Asian jurisdictions since the 1980s, has confirmed my conviction that maths really is for everyone and not just those who have a special talent. In recent years, my team and I at Trinity Academy, Halifax, have had the privilege of researching with and working alongside some of the finest mastery practitioners from the UK and beyond, whose impact on learners' confidence, achievement and attitude is an inspiration.

The mastery approach recognises the value of developing the power to think rather than just do. It also recognises the value of making a coherent journey in which whole-class groups tackle concepts in very small steps, one by one. You cannot build securely on loose foundations – and it is just the same with maths: by creating a solid foundation of deep understanding, our children's skills and confidence will be strong and secure. What's more, the mindset of learner and teacher alike is fundamental: everyone can do maths … EVERYONE CAN!

I am proud to have been part of the extensive team responsible for turning the best of the world's practice, research, insights, and shared experiences into *Power Maths*, a unique teaching and learning resource developed especially for UK classrooms. *Power Maths* embodies our vision to help and support primary maths teachers to transform every child's mathematical and personal development. 'Everyone can!' has become our mantra and our passion, and we hope it will be yours, too.

Now, explore and enjoy all the resources you need to teach for mastery, and please get back to us with your *Power Maths* experiences and stories!

What is *Power Maths*?

Created especially for UK primary schools, and aligned with the new National Curriculum, *Power Maths* is a whole-class, textbook-based mastery resource that empowers every child to understand and succeed. *Power Maths* rejects the notion that some people simply 'can't' do maths. Instead, it develops growth mindsets and encourages hard work, practice and a willingness to see mistakes as learning tools.

Best practice consistently shows that mastery of small, cumulative steps builds a solid foundation of deep mathematical understanding. *Power Maths* combines interactive teaching tools, high-quality textbooks and continuing professional development (CPD) to help you equip children with a deep and long lasting understanding. Based on extensive evidence, and developed in partnership with practising teachers, *Power Maths* ensures that it meets the needs of children in the UK.

Power Maths and Mastery

Power Maths makes mastery practical and achievable by providing the structures, pathways, content, tools and support you need to make it happen in your classroom.

To develop mastery in maths children need to be enabled to acquire a deep understanding of maths concepts, structures and procedures, step by step. Complex mathematical concepts are built on simpler conceptual components and when children understand every step in the learning sequence, maths becomes transparent and makes logical sense. Interactive lessons establish deep understanding in small steps, as well as effortless fluency in key facts such as tables and number bonds. The whole class works on the same content and no child is left behind.

Power Maths

- Builds every concept in small, progressive steps.
- Is built with interactive, whole-class teaching in mind.
- Provides the tools you need to develop growth mindsets.
- Helps you check understanding and ensure that every child is keeping up.
- Establishes core elements such as intelligent practice and reflection.

The *Power Maths* approach

Everyone can!

Founded on the conviction that every child can achieve, *Power Maths* enables children to build number fluency, confidence and understanding, step by step.

Child-centred learning

Children master concepts one step at a time in lessons that embrace a Concrete-Pictorial-Abstract (C-P-A) approach, avoid overload, build on prior learning and help them see patterns and connections. Same-day intervention ensures sustained progress.

Continuing professional development

Embedded teacher support and development offer every teacher the opportunity to continually improve their subject knowledge and manage whole-class teaching for mastery.

Whole-class teaching

An interactive, whole-class teaching model encourages thinking and precise mathematical language and allows children to deepen their understanding as far as they can.

Introduction to the author team

Power Maths arises from the work of maths mastery experts who are committed to proving that, given the right mastery mindset and approach, **everyone can do maths**. Based on robust research and best practice from around the world, *Power Maths* was developed in partnership with a group of UK teachers to make sure that it not only meets our children's wide-ranging needs but also aligns with the National Curriculum in England.

Tony Staneff, Series Editor and author

Vice Principal at Trinity Academy, Halifax, Tony also leads a team of mastery experts who help schools across the UK to develop teaching for mastery via nationally recognised CPD courses, problem-solving and reasoning resources, schemes of work, assessment materials and other tools.

✚ A team of experienced authors, including:

⚡ **Josh Lury** – a specialist maths teacher, author and maths consultant with a passion for innovative and effective maths education

⚡ **Trinity Academy Halifax** (Michael Gosling CEO, Tony Staneff, Emily Fox, Kate Henshall, Rebecca Holland, Stephanie Kirk, Stephen Monaghan and Rachel Webster)

⚡ **David Board, Belle Cottingham, Jonathan East, Tim Handley, Derek Huby, Neil Jarrett, Stephen Monaghan, Beth Smith, Tim Weal, Paul Wrangles** – skilled maths teachers and mastery experts

⚡ **Cherri Moseley** – a maths author, former teacher and professional development provider

✚ Professors Liu Jian and Zhang Dan, Series Consultants and authors, and their team of mastery expert authors:

⚡ **Wei Huinv, Huang Lihua, Zhu Dejiang, Zhu Yuhong, Hou Huiying, Yin Lili, Zhang Jing, Zhou Da and Liu Qimeng**

Used by over 20 million children, Professor Liu Jian's textbook programme is one of the most popular in China. He and his author team are highly experienced in intelligent practice and in embedding key maths concepts using a C-P-A approach.

✚ A group of 15 teachers and maths co-ordinators

We have consulted our teacher group throughout the development of *Power Maths* to ensure we are meeting their real needs in the classroom.

Your *Power Maths* resources

To help you teach for mastery, *Power Maths* comprises a variety of high-quality resources.

Pupil Textbooks

Discover, Share, and Think together sections promote discussion and introduce mathematical ideas logically, so that children understand more easily.

Using a Concrete-Pictorial-Abstract approach, clear mathematical models help children to make connections and grasp concepts.

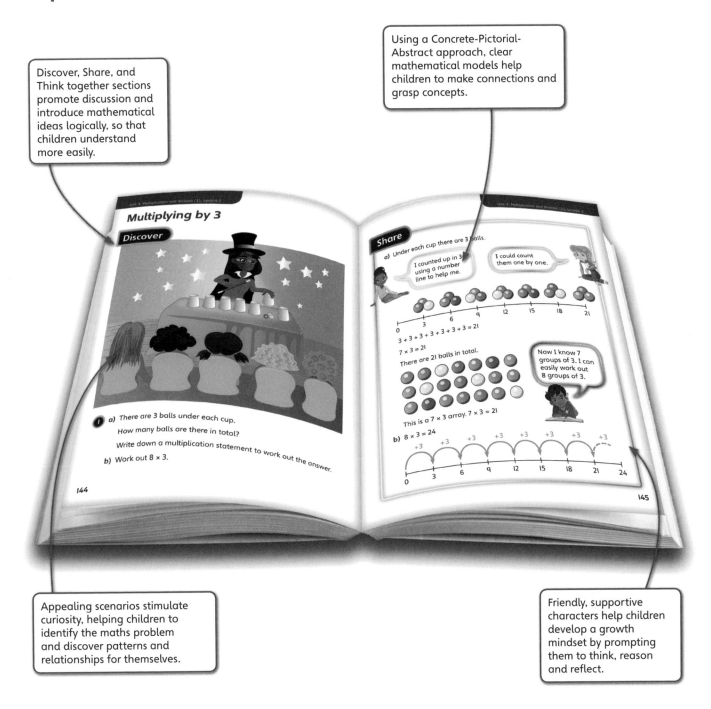

Appealing scenarios stimulate curiosity, helping children to identify the maths problem and discover patterns and relationships for themselves.

Friendly, supportive characters help children develop a growth mindset by prompting them to think, reason and reflect.

The coherent *Power Maths* lesson structure carries through into the vibrant, high-quality textbooks. Setting out the core learning objectives for each class, the lesson structure follows a carefully mapped journey through the curriculum and supports children on their journey to deeper understanding.

Pupil Practice Books

The Practice Books offer just the right amount of intelligent practice for children to complete independently in the final section of each lesson.

The practice questions are for everyone – each question varies one small element to move children on in their thinking. Look at the different parts in question ❶!

Calculations are connected so that children think about the underlying concept. In question ❸, children have to write out the calculation to find the answer. Concepts are presented differently again in question ❹ to challenge children.

Practice questions are finely tuned to move children forward in their thinking and to reveal misconceptions.

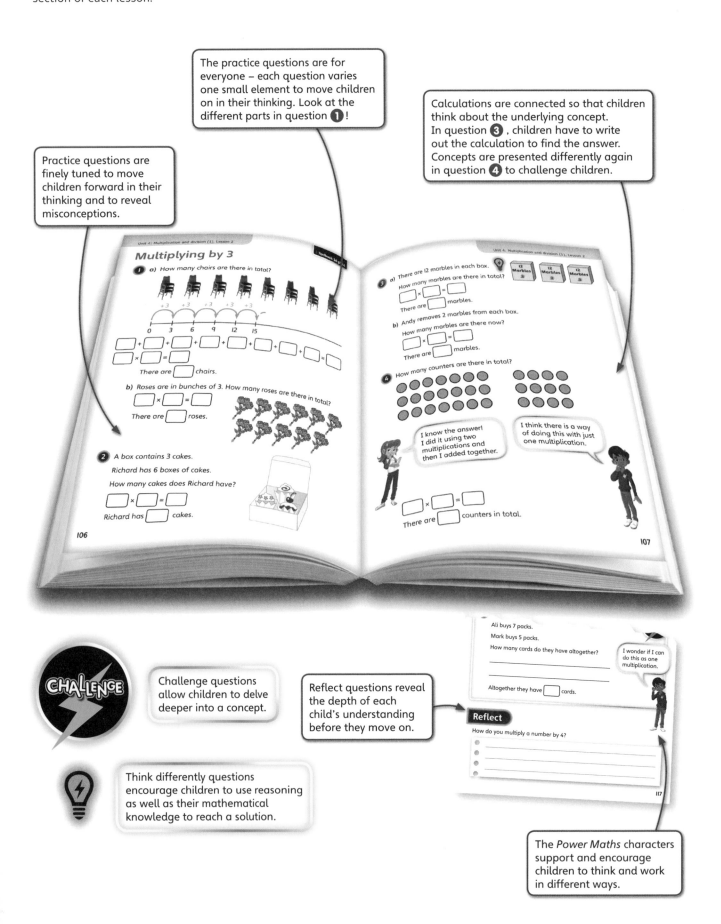

Challenge questions allow children to delve deeper into a concept.

Reflect questions reveal the depth of each child's understanding before they move on.

Think differently questions encourage children to use reasoning as well as their mathematical knowledge to reach a solution.

The *Power Maths* characters support and encourage children to think and work in different ways.

Online subscriptions

The online subscription will give you access to additional resources.

eTextbooks

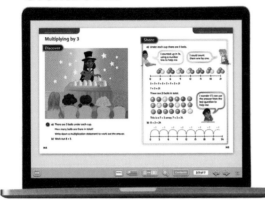

Digital versions of *Power Maths* Textbooks allow class groups to share and discuss questions, solutions and strategies. They allow you to project key structures and representations at the front of the class, to ensure all children are focusing on the same concept.

Teaching tools

Here you will find interactive versions of key *Power Maths* structures and representations.

Power Ups

Use this series of daily activities to promote and check number fluency.

Online versions of Teacher Guide pages

PDF pages give support at both unit and lesson levels. You will also find help with key strategies and templates for tracking progress.

Unit videos

Watch the professional development videos at the start of each unit to help you teach with confidence. The videos explore common misconceptions in the unit, and include intervention suggestions as well as suggestions on what to look out for when assessing mastery in your children.

End of unit Strengthen and Deepen materials

Each Strengthen activity at the end of every unit addresses a key misconception and can be used to support children who need it. The Deepen activities are designed to be 'Low Threshold High Ceiling' and will challenge those children who can understand more deeply. These resources will help you ensure that every child understands and will help you keep the class moving forward together. These printable activities provide an optional resource bank for use after the assessment stage.

Underpinning all of these resources, *Power Maths* is infused throughout with continual professional development, supporting you at every step.

The *Power Maths* teaching model

At the heart of *Power Maths* is a clearly structured teaching and learning process that helps you make certain that every child masters each maths concept securely and deeply. For each year group, the curriculum is broken down into core concepts, taught in units. A unit divides into smaller learning steps – lessons. Step by step, strong foundations of cumulative knowledge and understanding are built.

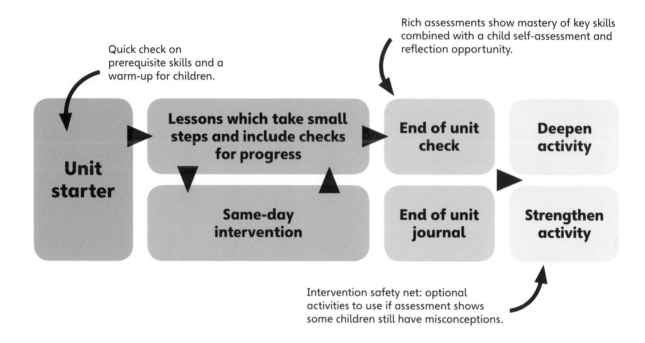

Quick check on prerequisite skills and a warm-up for children.

Rich assessments show mastery of key skills combined with a child self-assessment and reflection opportunity.

Intervention safety net: optional activities to use if assessment shows some children still have misconceptions.

Unit starter

Each unit begins with a unit starter, which introduces the learning context along with key mathematical vocabulary, structures and representations.

- The Textbooks include a check on readiness and a warm-up task for children to complete.

- Your Teacher Guide gives support right from the start on important structures and representations, mathematical language, common misconceptions and intervention strategies.

- Unit-specific videos develop your subject knowledge and insights so you feel confident and fully equipped to teach each new unit. These are available via the online subscription.

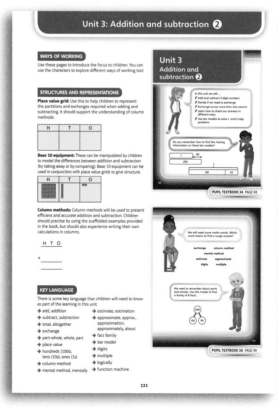

Lesson

Once a unit has been introduced, it is time to start teaching the series of lessons.

- Each lesson is scaffolded with Textbook and Practice Book activities and always begins with a Power Up activity (available via online subscription).

- *Power Maths* identifies lesson by lesson what concepts are to be taught.

- Your Teacher Guide offers lots of support for you to get the most from every child in every lesson. As well as highlighting key points, tricky areas and how to handle them, you will also find question prompts to check on understanding and clarification on why particular activities and questions are used.

Same-day intervention

Same-day interventions are vital in order to keep the class progressing together. Therefore, *Power Maths* provides plenty of support throughout the journey.

- Intervention is focused on keeping up now, not catching up later, so interventions should happen as soon as they are needed.

- Practice questions are designed to bring misconceptions to the surface, allowing you to identify these easily as you circulate during independent practice time.

- Child-friendly assessment questions in the Teacher Guide help you identify easily which children need to strengthen their understanding.

End of unit check and journal

At the end of a unit, summative assessment tasks reveal essential information on each child's understanding. An End of unit check in the Pupil Textbook lets you see which children have mastered the key concepts, which children have not and where their misconceptions lie. The Practice Book includes an End of unit journal in which children can reflect on what they have learned.
Each unit also offers Strengthen and Deepen activities, available via the online subscription.

The Teacher Guide offers support with handling misconceptions.

The End of unit check presents six to nine multiple-choice questions. These questions are designed to reveal misconceptions and help you target areas that need strengthening.

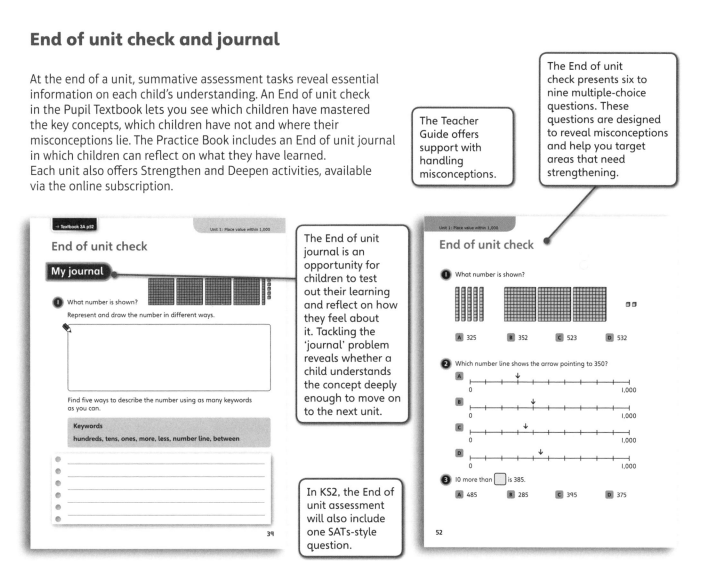

The End of unit journal is an opportunity for children to test out their learning and reflect on how they feel about it. Tackling the 'journal' problem reveals whether a child understands the concept deeply enough to move on to the next unit.

In KS2, the End of unit assessment will also include one SATs-style question.

The *Power Maths* lesson sequence

At the heart of *Power Maths* is a unique lesson sequence designed to empower children to understand core concepts and grow in confidence. Embracing the National Centre for Excellence in the Teaching of Mathematics' (NCETM's) definition of mastery, the sequence guides and shapes every *Power Maths* lesson you teach.

Flexibility is built into the *Power Maths* programme so there is no one-to-one mapping of lessons and concepts meaning you can pace your teaching according to your class. While some children will need to spend longer on a particular concept (through interventions or additional lessons), others will reach deeper levels of understanding. However, it is important that the class moves forward together through the termly schedules.

Power Up 🕑 5 minutes

Each lesson begins with a Power Up activity (available via the online subscription) which supports fluency in key number facts.

The whole-class approach depends on fluency, so the Power Up is a powerful and essential activity.

TOP TIP
If the class is struggling with the task, revisit it later and check understanding.

Power Ups reinforce key skills such as times-tables, number bonds and working with place value.

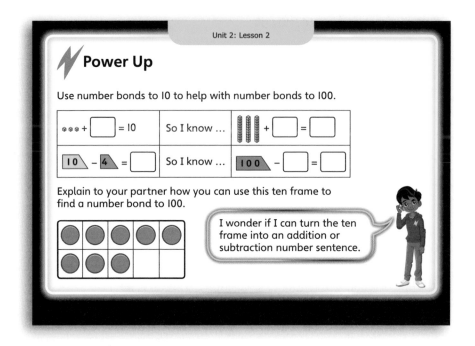

Discover 🕑 10 minutes

A practical, real-life problem arouses curiosity. Children find the maths through story-telling.

A real-life scenario is provided for the Discover section but feel free to build upon these with your own examples that are more relevant to your class.

TOP TIP
Discover works best when run at tables, in pairs with concrete objects.

Question **1** a) tackles the key concept and question **1** b) digs a little deeper. Children have time to explore, play and discuss possible strategies.

Share ⏱ 10 minutes

Teacher-led, this interactive section follows the Discover activity and highlights the variety of methods that can be used to solve a single problem.

TOP TIP

Bring children to the front (or onto the carpet if you have this area) to discuss their methods. Pairs sharing a textbook is a great format for this!

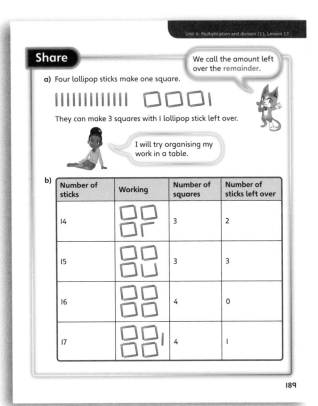

Your Teacher Guide gives target questions for children. The online toolkit provides interactive structures and representations to link concrete and pictorial to abstract concepts.

TOP TIP

Bring children to the front to share and celebrate their solutions and strategies.

Think together

⏱ 10 minutes

Children work in groups on the carpet or at tables, using their textbooks or eBooks.

TOP TIP

Make sure children have mini whiteboards or pads to write on if they are not at their tables.

Think together

1. Lexi and Zac use more lollipop sticks.

   How would you complete the table?

Number of sticks	Working	Number of squares	Number of sticks left over
18		4	
19			
20			

2. a) Describe the pattern that Lexi can see.

   > I can see a pattern in the number of lollipop sticks left over.

   Lexi

   b) Is Zac correct?

   > I don't think you can have more than 3 lollipop sticks left over.

   Zac

190

Using the Teacher Guide, model question ① for your class.

Question ② is less structured. Children will need to think together in their groups, then discuss their methods and solutions as a class.

In questions ③ and ④ children try working out the answer independently. The openness of the challenge question helps to check depth of understanding.

Using their Practice Books, children work independently while you circulate and check on progress.

Questions follow small steps of progression to deepen learning.

TOP TIP

Some children could work separately with a teacher or assistant.

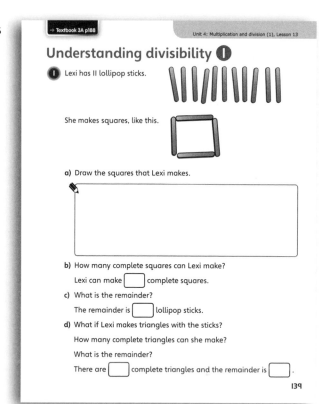

Are some children struggling? If so, work with them as a group, using mathematical structures and representations to support understanding as necessary.

There are no set routines: for real understanding, children need to think about the problem in different ways.

'Spot the mistake' questions are great for checking misconceptions.

The Reflect section is your opportunity to check how deeply children understand the target concept.

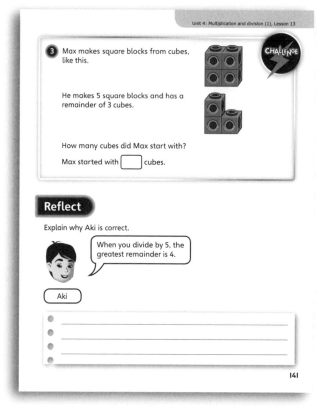

The Practice Books use various approaches to check that children have fully understood each concept.

Looking like they understand is not enough! It is essential that children can show they have grasped the concept.

Using the *Power Maths* Teacher Guide

Think of your Teacher Guides as *Power Maths* handbooks that will guide, support and inspire your day-to-day teaching. Clear and concise, and illustrated with helpful examples, your Teacher Guides will help you make the best possible use of every individual lesson. They also provide wrap-around professional development, enhancing your own subject knowledge and helping you to grow in confidence about moving your children forward together.

There is a Teacher Guide per year group for every term with unit and lesson level guidance and support.

Tips and advice on key elements such as C-P-A approaches, misconceptions, language, modelling growth mindsets and same-day intervention.

Annotations for every Pupil Textbook and Practice Book page, providing prompts for key questions to ask to expose understanding and explanations as to why key questions have been chosen.

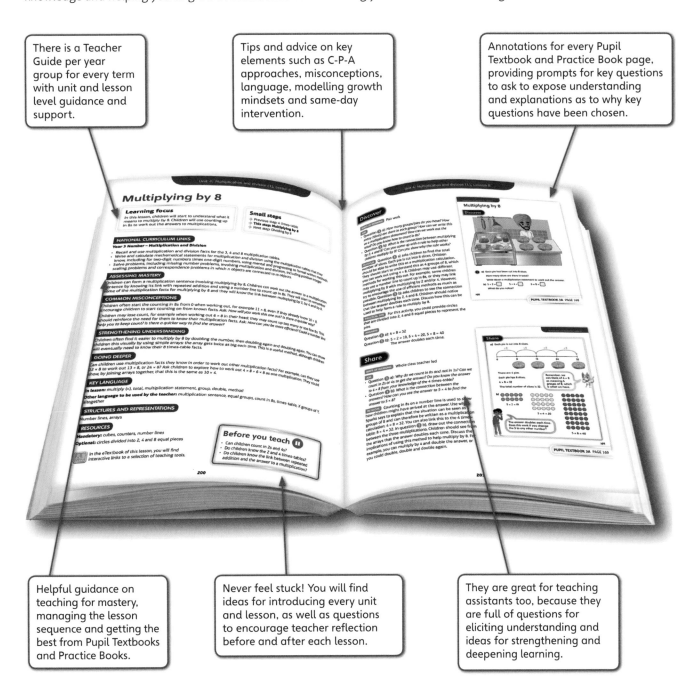

Helpful guidance on teaching for mastery, managing the lesson sequence and getting the best from Pupil Textbooks and Practice Books.

Never feel stuck! You will find ideas for introducing every unit and lesson, as well as questions to encourage teacher reflection before and after each lesson.

They are great for teaching assistants too, because they are full of questions for eliciting understanding and ideas for strengthening and deepening learning.

At the end of each unit, your Teacher Guide helps you identify who has fully grasped the concept, who has not and how to move every child forward. This is covered later in the Assessment strategies section.

Power Maths Year 3, yearly overview

Textbook	Strand	Unit		Number of Lessons
Textbook A / Practice Book A (Term 1)	Number – number and place value	1	Place value within 1,000	11
	Number – addition and subtraction	2	Addition and subtraction (1)	10
	Number – addition and subtraction	3	Addition and subtraction (2)	9
	Number – multiplication and division	4	Multiplication and division (1)	15
Textbook B / Practice Book B (Term 2)	Number – multiplication and division	5	Multiplication and division (2)	14
	Measurement	6	Money	5
	Statistics	7	Statistics	5
	Measurement	8	Length	11
	Number – fractions	9	Fractions (1)	11
Textbook C / Practice Book C (Term 3)	Number – fractions	10	Fractions (2)	9
	Measurement	11	Time	11
	Geometry – properties of shapes	12	Angles and properties of shapes	9
	Measurement	13	Mass	6
	Measurement	14	Capacity	6

Power Maths Year 3, Textbook 3C (Term 3) Overview

Strand 1	Strand 2	Unit		Lesson number	Lesson title	NC Objective 1	NC Objective 2	NC Objective 3
Number – fractions		Unit 10	Fractions (2)	1	Equivalent fractions (1)	Recognise and show, using diagrams, equivalent fractions with small denominators		
Number – fractions		Unit 10	Fractions (2)	2	Equivalent fractions (2)	Recognise and show, using diagrams, equivalent fractions with small denominators	Compare and order unit fractions, and fractions with the same denominators	
Number – fractions		Unit 10	Fractions (2)	3	Equivalent fractions (3)	Recognise and show, using diagrams, equivalent fractions with small denominators	Solve problems that involve all of the above	
Number – fractions		Unit 10	Fractions (2)	4	Comparing fractions	Recognise and show, using diagrams, equivalent fractions with small denominators	Compare and order unit fractions, and fractions with the same denominators	
Number – fractions		Unit 10	Fractions (2)	5	Comparing and ordering fractions	Compare and order unit fractions, and fractions with the same denominators		
Number – fractions		Unit 10	Fractions (2)	6	Adding fractions	Add and subtract fractions with the same denominator within one whole (for example, $\frac{5}{7} + \frac{1}{7} = \frac{6}{7}$)		
Number – fractions		Unit 10	Fractions (2)	7	Subtracting fractions	Add and subtract fractions with the same denominator within one whole (for example, $\frac{5}{7} + \frac{1}{7} = \frac{6}{7}$)		
Number – fractions		Unit 10	Fractions (2)	8	Problem solving – adding and subtracting fractions	Solve problems that involve all of the above	Add and subtract fractions with the same denominator within one whole (for example, $\frac{5}{7} + \frac{1}{7} = \frac{6}{7}$)	

Strand 1	Strand 2	Unit		Lesson number	Lesson title	NC Objective 1	NC Objective 2	NC Objective 3
Number – fractions		Unit 10	Fractions (2)	9	Problem solving – fractions of measures	Solve problems that involve all of the above	Recognise and use fractions as numbers: unit fractions and non-unit fractions with small denominators	Recognise, find and write fractions of a discrete set of objects: unit fractions and non-unit fractions with small denominators
Measurement		Unit 11	Time	1	Months and years	Know the number of seconds in a minute and the number of days in each month, year and leap year		
Measurement		Unit 11	Time	2	Hours in a day	Estimate and read time with increasing accuracy to the nearest minute; record and compare time in terms of seconds, minutes and hours; use vocabulary such as o'clock, am/pm, morning, afternoon, noon and midnight	Tell and write the time from an analogue clock, including using Roman numerals from I to XII, and 12-hour and 24-hour clocks	
Measurement		Unit 11	Time	3	Estimating time	Tell and write the time from an analogue clock, including using Roman numerals from I to XII, and 12-hour and 24-hour clocks		
Measurement		Unit 11	Time	4	Telling time to 5 minutes	Tell and write the time from an analogue clock, including using Roman numerals from I to XII, and 12-hour and 24-hour clocks		
Measurement		Unit 11	Time	5	Telling time to the minute (1)	Estimate and read time with increasing accuracy to the nearest minute; record and compare time in terms of seconds, minutes and hours; use vocabulary such as o'clock, am/pm, morning, afternoon, noon and midnight		
Measurement		Unit 11	Time	6	Telling time to the minute (2)	Estimate and read time with increasing accuracy to the nearest minute; record and compare time in terms of seconds, minutes and hours; use vocabulary such as o'clock, am/pm, morning, afternoon, noon and midnight		
Measurement		Unit 11	Time	7	Telling time to the minute (3)	Tell and write the time from an analogue clock, including using Roman numerals from I to XII, and 12-hour and 24-hour clocks	Estimate and read time with increasing accuracy to the nearest minute; record and compare time in terms of seconds, minutes and hours; use vocabulary such as o'clock, am/pm, morning, afternoon, noon and midnight	
Measurement		Unit 11	Time	8	Finding the duration	Estimate and read time with increasing accuracy to the nearest minute; record and compare time in terms of seconds, minutes and hours; use vocabulary such as o'clock, am/pm, morning, afternoon, noon and midnight		
Measurement		Unit 11	Time	9	Comparing duration	Compare durations of events (for example to calculate the time taken by particular events or tasks)	Estimate and read time with increasing accuracy to the nearest minute; record and compare time in terms of seconds, minutes and hours; use vocabulary such as o'clock, am/pm, morning, afternoon, noon and midnight	

Strand 1	Strand 2	Unit		Lesson number	Lesson title	NC Objective 1	NC Objective 2	NC Objective 3
Measurement		Unit 11	Time	10	Finding start and end times	Estimate and read time with increasing accuracy to the nearest minute; record and compare time in terms of seconds, minutes and hours; use vocabulary such as o'clock, am/pm, morning, afternoon, noon and midnight	Compare durations of events (for example to calculate the time taken by particular events or tasks)	
Measurement		Unit 11	Time	11	Measuring time in seconds	Estimate and read time with increasing accuracy to the nearest minute; record and compare time in terms of seconds, minutes and hours; use vocabulary such as o'clock, am/pm, morning, afternoon, noon and midnight	Compare durations of events (for example to calculate the time taken by particular events or tasks)	
Geometry – properties of shapes		Unit 12	Angles and properties of shapes	1	Turns and angles	Recognise angles as a property of shape or a description of a turn	Identify right angles, recognise that two right angles make a half-turn, three make three quarters of a turn and four a complete turn; identify whether angles are greater than or less than a right angle	
Geometry – properties of shapes		Unit 12	Angles and properties of shapes	2	Right angles in shapes	Recognise angles as a property of shape or a description of a turn	Identify right angles, recognise that two right angles make a half-turn, three make three quarters of a turn and four a complete turn; identify whether angles are greater than or less than a right angle	
Geometry – properties of shapes		Unit 12	Angles and properties of shapes	3	Comparing angles	Identify right angles, recognise that two right angles make a half-turn, three make three quarters of a turn and four a complete turn; identify whether angles are greater than or less than a right angle	Recognise angles as a property of shape or a description of a turn	
Geometry – properties of shapes		Unit 12	Angles and properties of shapes	4	Drawing accurately	Draw 2D shapes and make 3D shapes using modelling materials; recognise 3D shapes in different orientations and describe them	Identify horizontal and vertical lines and pairs of perpendicular and parallel lines	
Geometry – properties of shapes		Unit 12	Angles and properties of shapes	5	Types of line (1)	Identify horizontal and vertical lines and pairs of perpendicular and parallel lines		
Geometry – properties of shapes		Unit 12	Angles and properties of shapes	6	Types of line (2)	Identify horizontal and vertical lines and pairs of perpendicular and parallel lines		
Geometry – properties of shapes		Unit 12	Angles and properties of shapes	7	Recognising and describing 2D shapes	Draw 2D shapes and make 3D shapes using modelling materials; recognise 3D shapes in different orientations and describe them		
Geometry – properties of shapes		Unit 12	Angles and properties of shapes	8	Recognising and describing 3D shapes	Draw 2D shapes and make 3D shapes using modelling materials; recognise 3D shapes in different orientations and describe them		
Geometry – properties of shapes		Unit 12	Angles and properties of shapes	9	Constructing 3D shapes	Draw 2D shapes and make 3D shapes using modelling materials; recognise 3D shapes in different orientations and describe them		
Measurement		Unit 13	Mass	1	Measuring mass (1)	Measure, compare, add and subtract: lengths (m/cm/mm); mass (kg/g); volume/capacity (l/ml)		

Strand 1	Strand 2	Unit		Lesson number	Lesson title	NC Objective 1	NC Objective 2	NC Objective 3
Measurement		Unit 13	Mass	2	Measuring mass (2)	Measure, compare, add and subtract: lengths (m/cm/mm); mass (kg/g); volume/capacity (l/ml)		
Measurement		Unit 13	Mass	3	Measuring mass (3)	Measure, compare, add and subtract: lengths (m/cm/mm); mass (kg/g); volume/capacity (l/ml)		
Measurement		Unit 13	Mass	4	Comparing masses	Measure, compare, add and subtract: lengths (m/cm/mm); mass (kg/g); volume/capacity (l/ml)		
Measurement		Unit 13	Mass	5	Adding and subtracting masses	Measure, compare, add and subtract: lengths (m/cm/mm); mass (kg/g); volume/capacity (l/ml)		
Measurement		Unit 13	Mass	6	Problem solving – mass	Measure, compare, add and subtract: lengths (m/cm/mm); mass (kg/g); volume/capacity (l/ml)		
Measurement		Unit 14	Capacity	1	Measuring capacity (1)	Measure, compare, add and subtract: lengths (m/cm/mm); mass (kg/g); volume/capacity (l/ml)		
Measurement		Unit 14	Capacity	2	Measuring capacity (2)	Measure, compare, add and subtract: lengths (m/cm/mm); mass (kg/g); volume/capacity (l/ml)		
Measurement		Unit 14	Capacity	3	Measuring capacity (3)	Measure, compare, add and subtract: lengths (m/cm/mm); mass (kg/g); volume/capacity (l/ml)		
Measurement		Unit 14	Capacity	4	Comparing capacities	Measure, compare, add and subtract: lengths (m/cm/mm); mass (kg/g); volume/capacity (l/ml)		
Measurement		Unit 14	Capacity	5	Adding and subtracting capacities	Measure, compare, add and subtract: lengths (m/cm/mm); mass (kg/g); volume/capacity (l/ml)		
Measurement		Unit 14	Capacity	6	Problem solving – capacity	Measure, compare, add and subtract: lengths (m/cm/mm); mass (kg/g); volume/capacity (l/ml)		

Mindset: an introduction

Global research and best practice deliver the same message: learning is greatly affected by what learners perceive they can or cannot do. What is more, it is also shaped by what their parents, carers and teachers perceive they can do. Mindset – the thinking that determines our beliefs and behaviours – therefore has a fundamental impact on teaching and learning.

Everyone can!

Power Maths and mastery methods focus on the distinction between 'fixed' and 'growth' mindsets (Dweck, 2007).[1] Those with a fixed mindset believe that their basic qualities (for example, intelligence, talent and ability to learn) are pre-wired or fixed: 'If you have a talent for maths, you will succeed at it. If not, too bad!' By contrast, those with a growth mindset believe that hard work, effort and commitment drive success and that 'smart' is not something you are or are not, but something you become. In short, everyone can do maths!

Key mindset strategies

A growth mindset needs to be actively nurtured and developed. *Power Maths* offers some key strategies for fostering healthy growth mindsets in your classroom.

It is okay to get it wrong

Mistakes are valuable opportunities to re-think and understand more deeply. Learning is richer when children and teachers alike focus on spotting and sharing mistakes as well as solutions.

Praise hard work

Praise is a great motivator, and by focusing on praising effort and learning rather than success, children will be more willing to try harder, take risks and persist for longer.

Mind your language!

The language we use around learners has a profound effect on their mindsets. Make a habit of using growth phrases, such as, 'Everyone can!', 'Mistakes can help you learn' and 'Just try for a little longer'. The king of them all is one little word, 'yet ... I cannot solve this ... yet!' Encourage parents and carers to use the right language too.

Build in opportunities for success

The step-by-small-step approach enables children to enjoy the experience of success. In addition, avoid ability grouping and encourage every child to answer questions and explain or demonstrate their methods to others.

[1]Dweck, C (2007) *The New Psychology of Success*, Ballantine Books: New York

The *Power Maths* characters

The *Power Maths* characters model the traits of growth mindset learners and encourage resilience by prompting and questioning children as they work. Appearing frequently in the Textbooks and Practice Books, they are your allies in teaching and discussion, helping to model methods, alternatives and misconceptions, and to pose questions. They encourage and support your children, too: they are all hardworking, enthusiastic and unafraid of making and talking about mistakes.

Meet the team!

Creative Flo is open-minded and sometimes indecisive. She likes to think differently and come up with a variety of methods or ideas.

Determined Dexter is resolute, resilient and systematic. He concentrates hard, always tries his best and he'll never give up – even though he doesn't always choose the most efficient methods!

'Let's try again.'

'Mistakes are cool!'

'Have I found all of the solutions?'

'Let's try it this way ...'

'Can we do it differently?'

'I've got another way of doing this!'

'I'm going to try this!'

'I know how to do that!'

'Want to share my ideas?'

Curious Ash is eager, interested and inquisitive, and he loves solving puzzles and problems. Ash asks lots of questions but sometimes gets distracted.

'What if we tried this ...?'

'I wonder ...'

'Is there a pattern here?'

Miaow!   Sparks the Cat

Brave Astrid is confident, willing to take risks and unafraid of failure. She is never scared to jump straight into a problem or question, and although she often makes simple mistakes she is happy to talk them through with others.

Mathematical language

Traditionally, we in the UK have tended to try simplifying mathematical language to make it easier for young children to understand. By contrast, evidence and experience show that by diluting the correct language, we actually mask concepts and meanings for children. We then wonder why they are confused by new and different terminology later down the line! *Power Maths* is not afraid of 'hard' words and avoids placing any barriers between children and their understanding of mathematical concepts. As a result, we need to be planned, precise and thorough in building every child's understanding of the language of maths. Throughout the Teacher Guides you will find support and guidance on how to deliver this, as well as individual explanations throughout the Pupil Textbooks.

Use the following key strategies to build children's mathematical vocabulary, understanding and confidence.

Precise and consistent

Everyone in the classroom should use the correct mathematical terms in full, every time. For example, refer to 'equal parts', not 'parts'. Used consistently, precise maths language will be a familiar and non-threatening part of children's everyday experience.

Full sentences

Teachers and children alike need to use full sentences to explain or respond. When children use complete sentences, it both reveals their understanding and embeds their knowledge.

Stem sentences

These important sentences help children express mathematical concepts accurately, and are used throughout the *Power Maths* books. Encourage children to repeat them frequently, whether working independently or with others. Examples of stem sentences are:

'4 is a part, 5 is a part, 9 is the whole.'

'There are … groups. There are … in each group.'

Key vocabulary

The unit starters highlight essential vocabulary for every lesson. In the Pupil Textbooks, characters flag new terminology and the Teacher Guide lists important mathematical language for every unit and lesson. New terms are never introduced without a clear explanation.

Mathematical signs

Mathematical signs are used early on so that children quickly become familiar with them and their meaning. Often, the *Power Maths* characters will highlight the connection between language and particular signs.

The role of talk and discussion

When children learn to talk purposefully together about maths, barriers of fear and anxiety are broken down and they grow in confidence, skills and understanding. Building a healthy culture of 'maths talk' empowers their learning from day one.

Explanation and discussion are integral to the *Power Maths* structure, so by simply following the books your lessons will stimulate structured talk. The following key 'maths talk' strategies will help you strengthen that culture and ensure that every child is included.

Sentences, not words

Encourage children to use full sentences when reasoning, explaining or discussing maths. This helps both speaker and listeners to clarify their own understanding. It also reveals whether or not the speaker truly understands, enabling you to address misconceptions as they arise.

Working together

Working with others in pairs, groups or as a whole class is a great way to support maths talk and discussion. Use different group structures to add variety and challenge. For example, children could take timed turns for talking, work independently alongside a 'discussion buddy', or perhaps play different *Power Maths* character roles within their group.

Think first – then talk

Provide clear opportunities within each lesson for children to think and reflect, so that their talk is purposeful, relevant and focused.

Give every child a voice

Where the 'hands up' model allows only the more confident child to shine, *Power Maths* involves everyone. Make sure that no child dominates and that even the shyest child is encouraged to contribute – and are praised when they do.

Assessment strategies

Teaching for mastery demands that you are confident about what each child knows and where their misconceptions lie: therefore, practical and effective assessment is vitally important.

Formative assessment within lessons

The Think together section will often reveal any confusions or insecurities: try ironing these out by doing the first Think together question as a class. For children who continue to struggle, you or your teaching assistant should provide support and enable them to move on.

Performance in Practice can be very revealing: check Practice Books and listen out both during and after practice to identify misconceptions.

The Reflect section is designed to check on the all-important depth of understanding. Be sure to review how children performed in this final stage before you teach the next lesson.

End of unit check – Textbook

Each unit concludes with a summative check to help you assess quickly and clearly each child's understanding, fluency, reasoning and problem-solving skills. In KS2 this check also contains a SATs-style question to help children become familiar with answering this type of question.

In KS2 we would suggest the End of unit check is completed independently in children's exercise books, but you can adapt this to suit the needs of your class.

End of unit check – Practice Book

The Practice Book contains further opportunities for assessment, and can be completed by children independently whilst you are carrying out diagnostic assessment with small groups. Your Teacher Guide will advise you on what to do if children struggle to articulate an explanation – or perhaps encourage you to write down something they have explained well. It will also offer insights into children's answers and their implications for the next learning steps. It is split into three main sections, outlined below.

My journal

My journal is designed to allow children to show their depth of understanding of the unit. It can also serve as a way of checking that children have grasped key mathematical vocabulary. Children should have some time to think about how they want to answer the question, and you could ask them to talk to a partner about their ideas. Then children should write their answer in their Practice Book.

Power check

The Power check allows children to self-assess their level of confidence on the topic by colouring in different smiley faces. You may want to introduce the faces as follows:

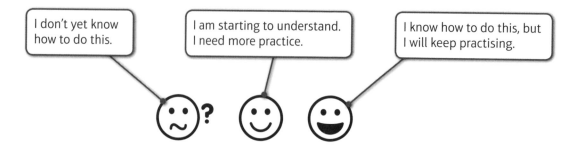

I don't yet know how to do this.

I am starting to understand. I need more practice.

I know how to do this, but I will keep practising.

Power play or Power puzzle

Each unit ends with either a Power play or a Power puzzle. This is an activity, puzzle or game that allows children to use their new knowledge in a fun, informal way. In Key Stage 2 we have also included a deeper level to each game to help challenge those children who have grasped a concept quickly.

How to use diagnostic questions

The diagnostic questions provided in *Power Maths* Textbooks are carefully structured to identify both understanding and misconceptions (if children answer in a particular way, you will know why). The simple procedure below may be helpful:

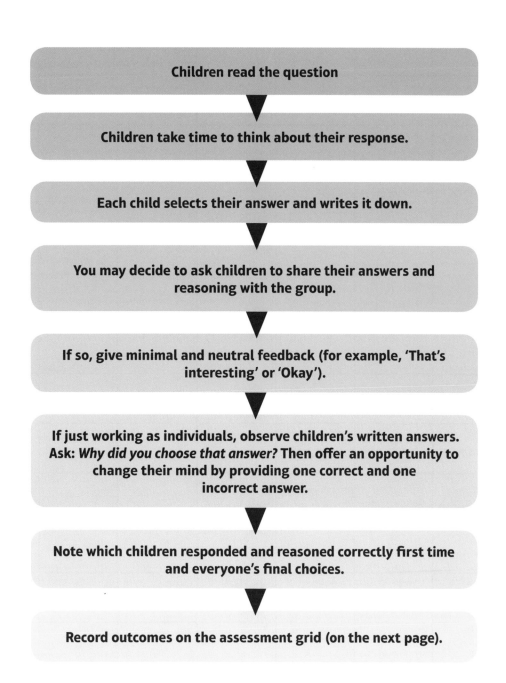

Children read the question

▼

Children take time to think about their response.

▼

Each child selects their answer and writes it down.

▼

You may decide to ask children to share their answers and reasoning with the group.

▼

If so, give minimal and neutral feedback (for example, 'That's interesting' or 'Okay').

▼

If just working as individuals, observe children's written answers. Ask: *Why did you choose that answer?* Then offer an opportunity to change their mind by providing one correct and one incorrect answer.

▼

Note which children responded and reasoned correctly first time and everyone's final choices.

▼

Record outcomes on the assessment grid (on the next page).

Power Maths unit assessment grid

Year ___   **Unit** ___ _____

Record only as much information as you judge appropriate for your assessment of each child's mastery of the unit and any steps needed for intervention.

Name	Diagnostic questions	SATs - style question	My journal	Power check	Power play/puzzle	Mastery	Intervention/ Strengthen

Keeping the class together

Traditionally, children who learn quickly have been accelerated through the curriculum. As a consequence, their learning may be superficial and will lack the many benefits of enabling children to learn with and from each other.

By contrast, *Power Maths'* mastery approach values real understanding and richer, deeper learning above speed. It sees all children learning the same concept in small, cumulative steps, each finding and mastering challenge at their own level. Remember that when you teach for mastery, EVERYONE can do maths! Those who grasp a concept easily have time to explore and understand that concept at a deeper level. The whole class therefore moves through the curriculum at broadly the same pace via individual learning journeys.

For some teachers, the idea that a whole class can move forward together is revolutionary and challenging. However, the evidence of global good practice clearly shows that this approach drives engagement, confidence, motivation and success for all learners, and not just the high flyers. The strategies below will help you keep your class together on their maths journey.

Mix it up

Do not stick to set groups at each table. Every child should be working on the same concept, and mixing up the groupings widens children's opportunities for exploring, discussing and sharing their understanding with others.

Recycling questions

Reuse the Pupil Textbook and Practice Book questions with concrete materials to allow children to explore concepts and relationships and deepen their understanding. This strategy is especially useful for reinforcing learning in same-day interventions.

Strengthen at every opportunity

The next lesson in a *Power Maths* sequence always revises and builds on the previous step to help embed learning. These activities provide golden opportunities for individual children to strengthen their learning with the support of teaching assistants.

Prepare to be surprised!

Children may grasp a concept quickly or more slowly. The 'fast graspers' won't always be the same individuals, nor does the speed at which a child understands a concept predict their success in maths. Are they struggling or just working more slowly?

Depth and breadth

Just as prescribed in the National Curriculum, the goal of *Power Maths* is never to accelerate through a topic but rather to gain a clear, deep and broad understanding.

"Pupils who grasp concepts rapidly should be challenged through being offered rich and sophisticated problems before any acceleration through new content. Those who are not sufficiently fluent with earlier material should consolidate their understanding, including through additional practice, before moving on."

National Curriculum: Mathematics programmes of study: KS1 & 2, 2013

The lesson sequence offers many opportunities for you to deepen and broaden children's learning, some of which are suggested below.

Discover

As well as using the questions in the Teacher Guide, check that children are really delving into why something is true. It is not enough to simply recite facts, such as '6 + 3 = 9'. They need to be able to see why, explain it, and to demonstrate the solution in several ways.

Share

Make sure that every child is given chances to offer answers and expand their knowledge and not just those with the greatest confidence.

Think together

Encourage children to think about how they found the solution and explain it to their partner. Be sure to make concrete materials available on group tables throughout the lesson to support and reinforce learning.

Practice

Avoid any temptation to select questions according to your assessment of ability: practice questions are presented in a logical sequence and it is important that each child works through every question.

Reflect

Open-ended questions allow children to deepen their understanding as far as they can by discovering new ways of finding answers. For example, *Give me another way of working out how high the wall is … And another way?*

Online materials

For each unit you will find additional strengthening activities to support those children who need it and to deepen the understanding of those who need the additional challenge.

Same-day intervention

Since maths competence depends on mastering concepts one-by-one in a logical progression, it is important that no gaps in understanding are ever left unfilled. Same-day interventions – either within or after a lesson – are a crucial safety net for any child who has not fully made the small step covered that day. In other words, intervention is always about keeping up, not catching up, so that every child has the skills and understanding they need to tackle the next lesson. That means presenting the same problems used in the lesson, with a variety of concrete materials to help children model their solutions.

We offer two intervention strategies below, but you should feel free to choose others if they work better for your class.

Within-lesson intervention

The Think together activity will reveal those who are struggling, so when it is time for Practice, bring these children together to work with you on the first Practice questions. Observe these children carefully, ask questions, encourage them to use concrete models and check that they reach and can demonstrate their understanding.

After-lesson intervention

You might like to use Think together before an assembly, giving you or teaching assistants time to recap and expand with slow graspers during assembly time. Teaching assistants could also work with strugglers at other convenient points in the school day.

The role of practice

Practice plays a pivotal role in the *Power Maths* approach. It takes place in class groups, smaller groups, pairs and independently, so that children always have the opportunities for thinking as well as the models and support they need to practise meaningfully and with understanding.

Intelligent practice

In *Power Maths*, practice never equates to the simple repetition of a process. Instead we embrace the concept of intelligent practice, in which all children become fluent in maths through varied, frequent and thoughtful practice that deepens and embeds conceptual understanding in a logical, planned sequence. To see the difference, take a look at the following examples.

Traditional practice

- Repetition can be rote – no need for a child to think hard about what they are doing.

- Praise may be misplaced.

- Does this prove understanding?

Intelligent practice

- Varied methods – concrete, pictorial and abstract.

- Calculations expressed in different ways, requiring thought and understanding.

- Constructive feedback.

All practice questions are designed to move children on and reveal misconceptions.

Simple, logical steps build onto earlier learning.

C-P-A runs throughout – different ways of modelling and understanding the same concept.

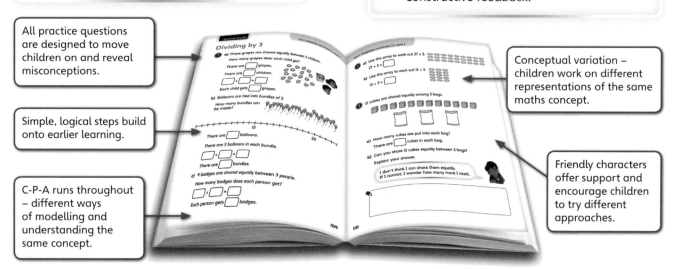

Conceptual variation – children work on different representations of the same maths concept.

Friendly characters offer support and encourage children to try different approaches.

A carefully designed progression

The Practice Books provide just the right amount of intelligent practice for children to complete independently in the final sections of each lesson. It is really important that all children are exposed to the Practice questions, and that children are not directed to complete different sections. That is because each question is different and has been designed to challenge children to think about the maths they are doing. The questions become more challenging so children grasping concepts more quickly will start to slow down as they progress. Meanwhile, you have the chance to circulate and spot any misconceptions before they become barriers to further learning.

Homework and the role of carers

While *Power Maths* does not prescribe any particular homework structure, we acknowledge the potential value of practice at home. For example, practising fluency in key facts, such as number bonds and times-tables, is an ideal homework task, and carers could work through uncompleted Practice Book questions with children at either primary stage.

However, it is important to recognise that many parents and carers may themselves lack confidence in maths, and few, if any, will be familiar with mastery methods. A Parents' and Carers' Evening that helps them understand the basics of mindsets, mastery and mathematical language is a great way to ensure that children benefit from their homework. It could be a fun opportunity for children to teach their families that everyone can do maths!

Structures and representations

Unlike most other subjects, maths comprises a wide array of abstract concepts – and that is why children and adults so often find it difficult. By taking a Concrete-Pictorial-Abstract (C-P-A) approach, *Power Maths* allows children to tackle concepts in a tangible and more comfortable way.

Non-linear stages

Concrete

Replacing the traditional approach of a teacher working through a problem in front of the class, the concrete stage introduces real objects that children can use to 'do' the maths – any familiar object that a child can manipulate and move to help bring the maths to life. It is important to appreciate, however, that children must always understand the link between models and the objects they represent. For example, children need to first understand that three cakes could be represented by three pretend cakes, and then by three counters or bricks. Frequent practice helps consolidate this essential insight. Although they can be used at any time, good concrete models are an essential first step in understanding.

Pictorial

This stage uses pictorial representations of objects to let children 'see' what particular maths problems look like. It helps them make connections between the concrete and pictorial representations and the abstract maths concept. Children can also create or view a pictorial representation together, enabling discussion and comparisons. The *Power Maths* teaching tools are fantastic for this learning stage, and bar modelling is invaluable for problem solving throughout the primary curriculum.

Abstract

Our ultimate goal is for children to understand abstract mathematical concepts, signs and notation and, of course, some children will reach this stage far more quickly than others. To work with abstract concepts, a child needs to be comfortable with the meaning of, and relationships between, concrete, pictorial and abstract models and representations. The C-P-A approach is not linear, and children may need different types of models at different times. However, when a child demonstrates with concrete models and pictorial representations that they have grasped a concept, we can be confident that they are ready to explore or model it with abstract signs such as numbers and notation.

Use at any time and with any age to support understanding.

Practical aspects of *Power Maths*

One of the key underlying elements of *Power Maths* is its practical approach, allowing you to make maths real and relevant to your children, no matter their age.

Manipulatives are essential resources for both key stages and *Power Maths* encourages teachers to use these at every opportunity, and to continue the Concrete-Pictorial-Abstract approach right through to Year 6.

The Textbooks and Teacher Guides include lots of opportunities for teaching in a practical way to show children what maths means in real life.

Discover and Share

The Discover and Share sections of the Textbook give you scope to turn a real-life scenario into a practical and hands-on section of the lesson. Use these sections as inspiration to get active in the classroom. Where appropriate, use the Discover contexts as a springboard for your own examples that have particular resonance for your children – and allow them to get their hands dirty trying out the mathematics for themselves.

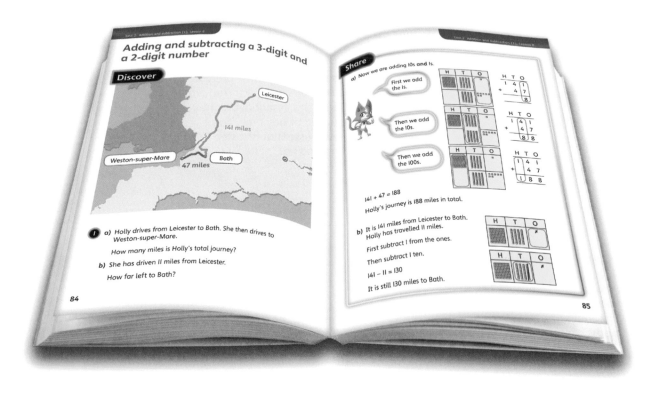

Unit videos

Every term has one unit video which incorporates real-life classroom sequences.

These videos show you how the reasoning behind mathematics can be carried out in a practical manner by showing real children using various concrete and pictorial methods to come to the solution. You can see how using these practical models, such as part-whole and bar models, helps them to find and articulate their answer.

Mastery tips

Mastery Experts give anecdotal advice on where they have used hands-on and real-life elements to inspire their children.

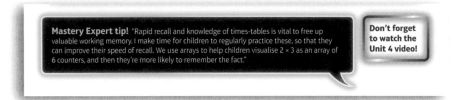

Mastery Expert tip! "Rapid recall and knowledge of times-tables is vital to free up valuable working memory. I make time for children to regularly practice these, so that they can improve their speed of recall. We use arrays to help children visualise 2 × 3 as an array of 6 counters, and then they're more likely to remember the fact."

Don't forget to watch the Unit 4 video!

Concrete-Pictorial-Abstract (C-P-A) approach

Each Share section uses various methods to explain an answer, helping children to access abstract concepts by using concrete tools, such as counters. Remember this isn't a linear process, so even children who appear confident using the more abstract method can deepen their knowledge by exploring the concrete representations. Encourage children to use all three methods to really solidify their understanding of a concept.

Pictorial representation – drawing the problem in a logical way that helps children visualise the maths

Concrete representation – using manipulatives to represent the problem. Encourage children to physically use resources to explore the maths.

Abstract representation – using words and calculations to represent the problem.

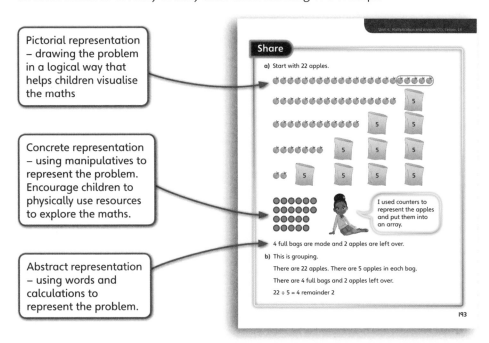

Practical tips

Every lesson suggests how to draw out the practical side of the Discover context.

You'll find these in the Discover section of the Teacher Guide for each lesson.

PRACTICAL TIPS You could use balls, counters or cubes under plastic cups to re-enact the artwork and help children get a feel for this activity.

Resources

Every lesson lists the practical resources you will need or might want to use. There is also a summary of all of the resources used throughout the term on page 34 to help you be prepared.

RESOURCES

Mandatory: cubes, counters, number lines

Optional: balls, plastic cups

List of practical resources

Year 3C Mandatory resources

Resource	Lesson
24-hour clocks	**Unit 11** lesson 7
3D shapes to handle (cuboid, cube, prisms, pyramids, sphere, cone, cylinder)	**Unit 12** lesson 8
A4 paper cut into 10 cm strips (landscape)	**Unit 12** lesson 4
Analogue clock and written time flash cards	**Unit 11** lessons 4, 6
Analogue clock manipulatives	**Unit 11** lessons 3, 4, 5, 6, 8, 9, 10, 11
Bar model	**Unit 10** lessons 1, 2
Calendars	**Unit 11** lesson 1
Construction materials	**Unit 12** lesson 9
Different value weights	**Unit 13** lesson 3
Digital clock	**Unit 11** lessons 6, 7, 8, 9, 10, 11
Flash cards (o'clock', 'half past', 'quarter past', 'quarter to')	**Unit 11** lessons 3, 4
Fraction cards	**Unit 10** lesson 3
Fraction strip (bars)	**Unit 10** lessons 1, 2, 3, 4, 5, 6, 7
Fraction walls	**Unit 10** lessons 2, 4
Laminated pictures of clock faces	**Unit 11** lesson 10
Modelling clay	**Unit 13** lessons 1, 2
Multilink cubes	**Unit 12** lesson 9
Number lines	**Unit 10** lessons 2, 3, 5, 6, 7 **Unit 14** lesson 5
Paper for folding	**Unit 12** lessons 2, 6
Paper strips	**Unit 10** lesson 3
Ruler	**Unit 12** lessons 2, 4, 6
Scissors	**Unit 12** lesson 4
Squared paper	**Unit 12** lesson 6
Square dotted paper	**Unit 12** lesson 6
Sticks or pencils of equal length	**Unit 12** lesson 7
Weighing scales	**Unit 13** lessons 1, 2, 3, 4, 5
Weights	**Unit 13** lessons 3, 4

Year 3C Optional resources

Resource	Lesson
24 pictures of activities linked to each hour in the day	**Unit 11** lesson 2
3d shape nets	**Unit 12** lesson 8
A pair of hinged rods	**Unit 12** lesson 3
Analogue clock and written time flash cards	**Unit 11** lessons 5, 7, 8, 9
Analogue clock manipulatives	**Unit 11** lessons 2, 7 **Unit 12** lesson 3
Bar models	**Unit 10** lessons 8, 9
Base 10 equipment	**Unit 14** lessons 3, 6

Resource	Lesson
Capacity measuring equipment	**Unit 10** lesson 9 **Unit 14** lessons 1, 2, 3, 4, 5, 6
Clear pictures of a flat and straight horizon	**Unit 12** lesson 5
Counters	**Unit 10** lesson 8
Diagrams of eight-point compass (or drawn on the playground)	**Unit 12** lesson 1
Dice	**Unit 14** lesson 4
Examples of modern art that contain parallel and perpendicular lines (Piet Mondrian); circles with 3–10 dots (see Practice Book question 5)	**Unit 12** lesson 6
Fraction rods	**Unit 10** lessons 2, 8, 9
Fraction tiles	**Unit 10** lesson 2
Fraction walls	**Unit 10** lesson 5
Geoboards and bands or dotted paper to represent geoboards	**Unit 12** lesson 3
Hoops	**Unit 11** lesson 5
Interlocking cubes	**Unit 10** lessons 6, 7
Laminated pictures of clock faces	**Unit 11** lessons 2, 10
Large pieces of paper	**Unit 11** lesson 5
Marbles	**Unit 12** lesson 5
Milk containers greater than 1 litre	**Unit 14** lesson 3
Mirrors	**Unit 12** lesson 5
Modelling clay	**Unit 12** lesson 9 **Unit 13** lessons 3, 4, 5, 6
Number cards	**Unit 10** lesson 3 **Unit 11** lesson 5
Number cards from 1 to 12	**Unit 10** lesson 3 **Unit 11** lesson 5
Number lines	**Unit 11** lesson 10 **Unit 13** lessons 1, 2, 3, 4, 5, 6 **Unit 14** lessons 1, 2, 3, 6
Paper circles (paper plates)	**Unit 10** lessons 6, 7
Paper strips	**Unit 10** lessons 1, 2, 4, 5
Parachutes	**Unit 13** lesson 1
Part-whole models	**Unit 10** lessons 8, 9
PE equipment	**Unit 12** lesson 5
Pictures of sunset and sunrise	**Unit 11** lesson 2
Pipe cleaners	**Unit 12** lesson 3
Place value cards	**Unit 14** lesson 3
Place value columns	**Unit 14** lesson 3
Place value counters	**Unit 13** lesson 2
Plastic or wooden 2D shapes	**Unit 12** lessons 4, 7
Plumb line	**Unit 12** lesson 5
Pre-cut 10 cm squares	**Unit 12** lesson 4
Range of cardboard boxes in different proportions	**Unit 12** lesson 8
Soft toys for role play	**Unit 11** lesson 2
Squared paper	**Unit 12** lesson 3
Sticks and marshmallows	**Unit 12** lesson 9
Stopwatch	**Unit 11** lesson 11
Toy figures	**Unit 12** lesson 1
Two rulers or folded card to make angles	**Unit 12** lesson 3
Weighing scales	**Unit 13** lesson 6

Variation helps visualisation

Children find it much easier to visualise and grasp concepts if they see them presented in a number of ways, so be prepared to offer and encourage many different representations.

For example, the number six could be represented in various ways:

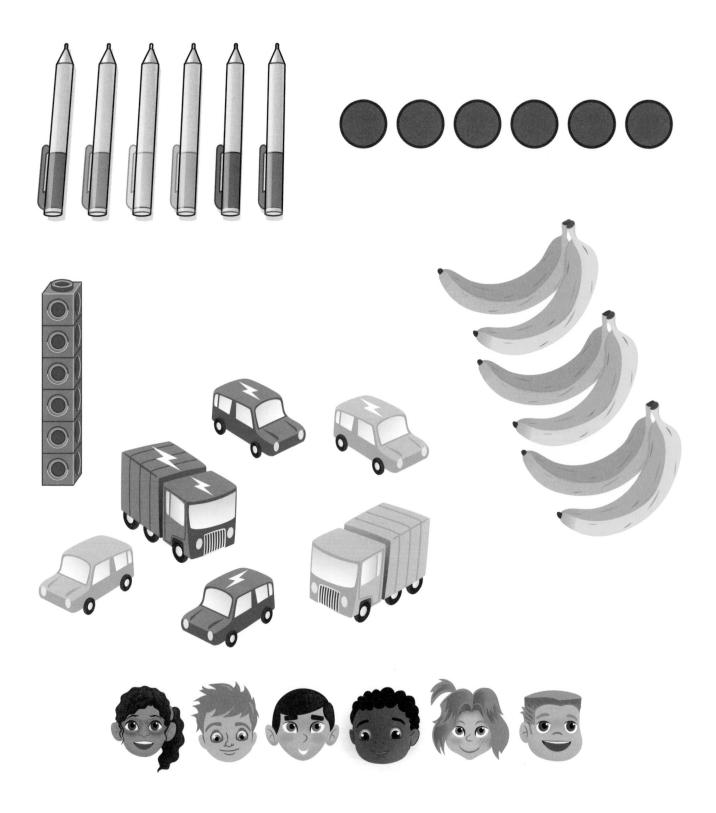

Getting started with *Power Maths*

As you prepare to put *Power Maths* into action, you might find the tips and advice below helpful.

STEP 1: Train up!

A practical, up-front full-day professional development course will give you and your team a brilliant head-start as you begin your *Power Maths* journey. You will learn more about the ethos, how it works and why.

STEP 2: Check out the progression

Take a look at the yearly and termly overviews. Next take a look at the unit overview for the unit you are about to teach in your Teacher Guide, remembering that you can match your lessons and pacing to your class.

STEP 3: Explore the context

Take a little time to look at the context for this unit: what are the implications for the unit ahead? (Think about key language, common misunderstandings and intervention strategies, for example.) If you have the online subscription, don't forget to watch the corresponding unit video.

STEP 4: Prepare for your first lesson

Familiarise yourself with the objectives, essential questions to ask and the resources you will need. The Teacher Guide offers tips, ideas and guidance on individual lessons to help you anticipate children's misconceptions and challenge those who are ready to think more deeply.

STEP 5: Teach and reflect

Deliver your lesson – and enjoy!

Afterwards, reflect on how it went… Did you cover all five stages? Does the lesson need more time? How could you improve it? What percentage of your class do you think mastered the concept? How can you help those that didn't?

Unit 10
Fractions 2

Mastery Expert tip! "Children need a rich experience of seeing, touching and creating simple fractions in order to gain a more secure understanding of what a fraction actually is. We created a fraction museum on a whiteboard and each lesson we added examples of our learning with lots of colourful resources and drawings. It really helped my class to embed what they learnt, recall what they already knew and ask questions where they were unsure.

Don't forget to watch the Unit 10 video!

WHY THIS UNIT IS IMPORTANT

In this unit, children will learn to recognise and show (using diagrams) equivalent fractions with small denominators. They will explore a fraction wall and use it to find equivalent fractions. Children will order fractions on a number line and compare two fractions using bar models and the comparison signs < > or =. They will learn to add and subtract two or more fractions with the same denominator, answering questions in more than one way and comparing the efficiency of each method. They will develop their understanding of solving fraction problems and learn to find fractions of measures.

WHERE THIS UNIT FITS

→ Unit 9: Fractions (1)
→ **Unit 10: Fractions (2)**
→ Unit 11: Time

Before they start this unit, it is expected that children:
• understand how to make a whole out of two fractional parts
• can recognise tenths
• understand fractions as a number
• can calculate a fraction of a set of objects
• can use a bar model to represent problems
• understand the concept of equal parts.

ASSESSING MASTERY

Children who have mastered this unit will be able to describe equivalent fractions and mark fractions with different denominators on a number line. They can compare pairs of unit fractions and fractions with small denominators and explain which is larger. Children can count in fraction steps of a constant size to help make sense of adding and subtracting fractions with the same denominator, and find pairs of fractions that total one. Children solve problems with confidence by adding and subtracting fractions, and reasoning mathematically.

COMMON MISCONCEPTIONS	STRENGTHENING UNDERSTANDING	GOING DEEPER
Children may find the concept of numerator and denominator confusing, particularly if the numerator is greater than 1.	Provide opportunities for children to use resources and model fractions, for example, using fraction rods, beads and fraction strips.	Encourage children to make a fraction wall from scratch to deepen their understanding.

Give children number lines labelled 0 to 1. Ask them to create their own questions regarding the position of different fractions on the number line.

Challenge children to find different ways to answer the same question. Often, more able children are less inclined to look for alternative options, but finding the answer is not as important as the way they find the answer! |
| Children may find it difficult to recognise fractions as points on a number line. | Revisit counting in fraction intervals by showing children pre-marked number lines with different denominators. Hide some of the fractions and ask children to find them. | |
| Children who find it difficult to solve problems may not know where to start and so may guess which method to use. | Offer real-life examples of problem solving situations. Encourage children to role-play the problem and sketch something that helps them make sense of it. | |

Use these pages to introduce the unit focus to children. You can use the characters to explore different ways of working too!

STRUCTURES AND REPRESENTATIONS

Fraction wall: This representation is crucial to allow children to find equivalent fractions. If children become confident using the fraction wall, it will increase their conceptual understanding of fractions. It can be used by itself or with a number line to compare fractions with different denominators.

Number line: This model helps children to understand fractions as numbers. Positioning fractions on a number line will require a secure understanding of the role of the numerator and denominator within a fraction.

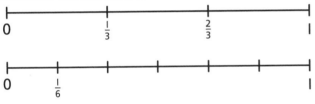

Fraction strip: This is a powerful representation that allows children to organise the information they are given visually, and understand how it should be manipulated in order to find the solution to a problem. It can be used alone, or with a number line to enhance understanding.

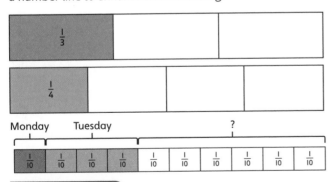

KEY LANGUAGE

There is some key language that children will need to know as part of the learning in this unit.

→ part, whole, equal parts, unit fraction, non-unit fraction, denominator, numerator, equivalent fraction

→ partition, split, share, count on, count back, compare, measure, calculate, method

→ whole number, add, subtract, difference, multiply, divide, equal to, greater than (>), less than (<)

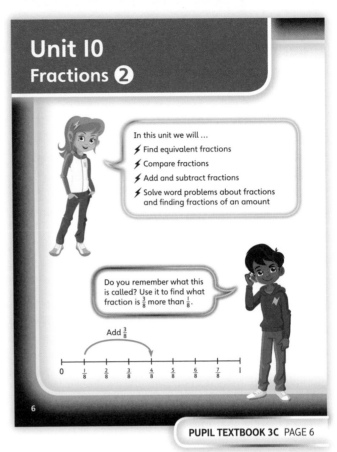

PUPIL TEXTBOOK 3C PAGE 6

PUPIL TEXTBOOK 3C PAGE 7

Equivalent fractions ❶

Learning focus

In this lesson, children will learn to recognise equivalent fractions with small denominators. They will use diagrams to represent equivalent fractions.

Small steps

→ Previous step: Problem solving – fractions
→ **This step: Equivalent fractions (1)**
→ Next step: Equivalent fractions (2)

NATIONAL CURRICULUM LINKS

Year 3 Number – Fractions

Recognise and show, using diagrams, equivalent fractions with small denominators.

ASSESSING MASTERY

Children can explain and demonstrate when two fractions are equivalent.

COMMON MISCONCEPTIONS

Some children may be unsure of the meaning of numerator and denominator, particularly if the denominator is greater than 1. When using resources, they may find it difficult to identify the fraction strips they need to use by referring to the denominator. Ask:

- *Show me a fraction strip that represents $\frac{3}{5}$. How many parts will the bar be split into? How many parts are shaded?*

Some children may find the concept of an equivalent fraction tricky, as they may have found a rule that works for some fractions but not for others. For example, to find an equivalent fraction, all you do is double the top and the bottom ($\frac{1}{2} = \frac{2}{4} = \frac{4}{8}$), but that rule cannot be used to complete the fractions $\frac{1}{2} = \frac{3}{?} = \frac{6}{?}$. Ask:

- *Tell me a fraction that is equivalent to $\frac{1}{2}$. How do you know? Are there others?*

STRENGTHENING UNDERSTANDING

Rather than simply learning a rule in order to solve a calculation, children need to know why the rule works as it does. Children should be given the opportunity to use fraction tiles, coloured rods and paper strips to show fractions in different ways. The more practical experience they have, the quicker they will understand the concept of equivalent fractions: that equivalent fractions are the same size, but can be split into different equal parts.

GOING DEEPER

Provide children with a fraction wall and ask them to create their own equivalent questions to show the depth of their understanding. How many equivalent fractions can they find?

KEY LANGUAGE

In lesson: whole, fraction, numerator, denominator, **equivalent fractions**, equal, equal parts

Other language to be used by the teacher: shared, multiply, divide

STRUCTURES AND REPRESENTATIONS

bar model, fraction wall

RESOURCES

Mandatory: fraction strips, bar model

Optional: paper strips

 In the eTextbook of this lesson, you will find interactive links to a selection of teaching tools.

Before you teach

- Do children know what the numerator and denominator represent?
- Are they familiar with resources such as fraction strips?
- What opportunities will you be providing for children to gain hands-on experience with fractions?

Discover

Equivalent fractions ❶

Discover

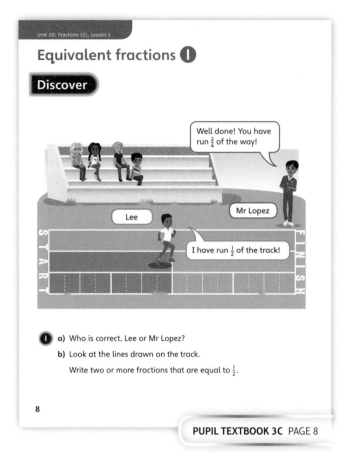

WAYS OF WORKING Pair work

ASK

- Question ❶ a): *What does the picture show? How far has Lee run?*
- Question ❶ b): *What markings can you see on the tracks above and below the track Lee is running on? What do you think these markings show?*

IN FOCUS Question ❶ a) brings attention to the fact that a fraction can be the same size, but split into a different number of equal parts. The picture should encourage children to see that $\frac{1}{2}$ and $\frac{2}{4}$ are equal.

PRACTICAL TIPS Give children the opportunity to use a variety of different resources to create $\frac{1}{2}$, such as coloured rods and paper fraction strips. Children should use these resources to establish that $\frac{1}{2}$ can be presented in different ways.

ANSWERS

Question ❶ a): Both Lee and Mr Lopez are correct.

Question ❶ b): $\frac{1}{2} = \frac{2}{4} = \frac{4}{8} = \frac{8}{16}$. These are all equivalent fractions.

❶ a) Who is correct, Lee or Mr Lopez?

   b) Look at the lines drawn on the track.

      Write two or more fractions that are equal to $\frac{1}{2}$.

8

PUPIL TEXTBOOK 3C PAGE 8

Share

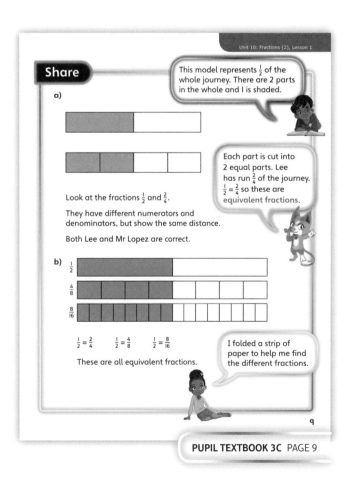

WAYS OF WORKING Whole class teacher led

ASK

- Question ❶ a): *How many parts is the first bar split into? How many of the parts are shaded? What fraction does the first model represent? What fraction does the second model represent? What do you notice about the size of the shaded part in each bar? How many $\frac{1}{4}$s do you think may be equivalent to $\frac{1}{2}$?*

IN FOCUS This may be a good opportunity to clarify any misconceptions children may have. Ensure they are confident that the first fraction represents $\frac{1}{2}$ and the second fraction represents $\frac{2}{4}$. Children should notice that both lengths are equal, and establish that $\frac{1}{2} = \frac{2}{4}$.

STRENGTHEN Discuss the relationship between the numerator and denominator. Ask: *What do you notice about the numerator and denominator of each fraction? What is the relationship between 1 and 2? 2 and 4? Are there other fractions that are equal to $\frac{1}{2}$? What is the relationship between the numerator and the denominator of these fractions?*

Provide children with two paper strips. Ask them to fold the first strip in half and the second strip into quarters. They then use scissors to cut the first strip into two parts, and the second strip into four parts. Ask children to align the two quarters below the half. What do they notice? How can they record their findings? Record that $\frac{1}{2} = \frac{2}{4}$ explaining that the = sign means 'equivalent' or 'the same as'.

PUPIL TEXTBOOK 3C PAGE 9

Think together

WAYS OF WORKING Whole class teacher led (I do, We do, You do)

ASK

- Question **1** : *How many parts are there? How many of them are coloured? If the paper is folded again, how many parts will there be? What do all the parts have in common? What happened to the original coloured parts? How many parts are coloured now?*
- Question **2** : *What fraction of the paper is coloured? How can the information be recorded?*

IN FOCUS In questions **1** and **2**, children may notice that $\frac{1}{6}$ is half of $\frac{1}{3}$, and $\frac{1}{10}$ is half of $\frac{1}{5}$. The questions highlight the fact that two $\frac{1}{6}$s are the same as $\frac{1}{3}$, and two $\frac{1}{10}$s are the same as $\frac{1}{5}$.

Question **3** asks children to use their knowledge of fractions to find the missing fractions on the fraction wall. They should then look for other fractions equivalent to $\frac{1}{2}$, $\frac{1}{3}$, $\frac{1}{4}$, $\frac{1}{6}$ and $\frac{1}{12}$.

STRENGTHEN When children are working on questions **1** and **2**, strengthen their understanding by giving them paper strips similar to the ones used in the questions. Encourage discussion on how the paper should be folded so that all the parts are equal. This may be an opportunity to clarify that in a fraction all the fraction-parts are of equal size. Encourage children to use the correct mathematical vocabulary to explain what they notice during this activity.

DEEPEN Deepen children's understanding by asking them to build their own fraction wall. Ask: *What fractions will they choose? How many of each unit fraction will they need to make a whole?* Encourage them to explain their reasoning clearly. Ask: *Write as many fractions equivalent to $\frac{1}{4}$ as you can.* They should try to be systematic in their approach.

ASSESSMENT CHECKPOINT At this point in the lesson, children understand what equivalent fractions are, and can recognise and show equivalent fractions by using paper fraction strips.

ANSWERS

Question **1** a): $\frac{1}{3}$ or $\frac{2}{6}$

Question **1** b): $\frac{1}{3} = \frac{2}{6}$

Question **2** a): $\frac{1}{5}$ or $\frac{2}{10}$

Question **2** b): $\frac{1}{5} = \frac{2}{10}$

Question **3** : $\frac{1}{3}, \frac{2}{6}$ or $\frac{4}{12}; \frac{1}{4}, \frac{2}{8}$ or $\frac{3}{12}; \frac{1}{6}$ or $\frac{2}{12}; \frac{1}{12}$

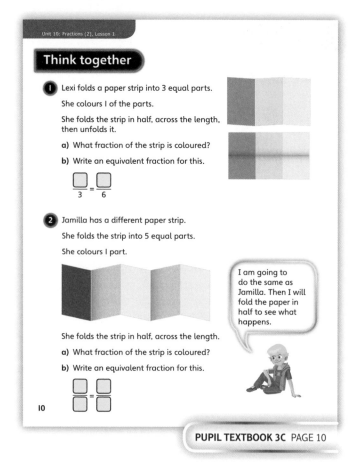

PUPIL TEXTBOOK 3C PAGE 10

PUPIL TEXTBOOK 3C PAGE 11

Practice

WAYS OF WORKING Independent thinking

IN FOCUS When working independently on the questions in this section, children should continue to secure their understanding of identifying equivalent fractions using diagrams. They use bar models to find the missing numerator or denominator from the equivalent fractions given.

STRENGTHEN Strengthen understanding by giving children paper fraction strips so they can see a concrete representation of the question. In question **1**, ask: *What is the same and what is different? Think of the example used in the lesson: what is the question asking? What does 'equivalent fraction' mean?*

DEEPEN Provide children with similar questions to question **4**, encouraging them to decide which representation they think best matches each part of the question. Ask: *Which bar represents the given fraction? How many parts should you shade? What will the numerator and denominator of the other fraction be, so that they are equal?* The more children have the opportunity to show a fraction in different ways, the deeper their understanding will be. Prompt children to explore the concept presented in question **5** in more depth. When discussing fractions, they need to pay attention not only to the number of parts shaded, but also to the size of each part. Ask: *Are they all equal? What is the numerator/denominator? What fraction is being represented?*

ASSESSMENT CHECKPOINT Children should be confident in identifying and showing equivalent fractions using diagrams. They can explain when two fractions are equal using the correct mathematical language. Successful answers and discussion around question **3** should offer an indication of the depth of their understanding.

ANSWERS Answers for the **Practice** part of the lesson appear in the separate **Practice and Reflect answer guide**.

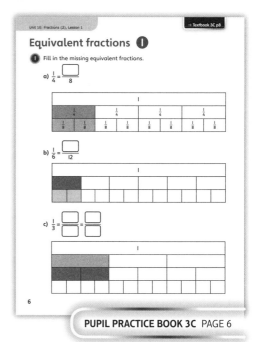

PUPIL PRACTICE BOOK 3C PAGE 6

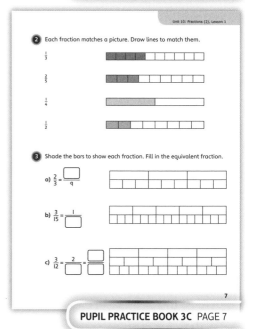

PUPIL PRACTICE BOOK 3C PAGE 7

Reflect

WAYS OF WORKING Pair work

IN FOCUS Begin this activity by giving children time to discuss with a partner how they can make equivalent fractions by folding a piece of paper. Once children have discussed their methods, give them time to write their explanations. Can they draw a diagram to support their reasoning?

ASSESSMENT CHECKPOINT Look for clarity in children's explanations. They should refer to the fact that equivalent fractions are the same size, but can be split into a different number of equal parts. Some children may want to model the activity with a piece of paper to cement their understanding.

ANSWERS Answers for the **Reflect** part of the lesson appear in the separate **Practice and Reflect answer guide**.

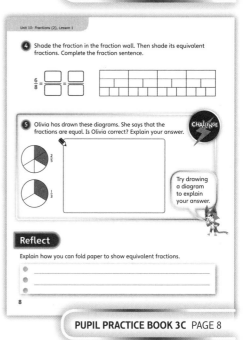

PUPIL PRACTICE BOOK 3C PAGE 8

After the lesson

- Do children know what equivalent fractions are?
- Can children explain how to make equivalent fractions?
- Which resources did children find most useful?

Equivalent fractions ②

Learning focus

In this lesson, children will learn to recognise and show equivalent fractions with small denominators, predominantly represented on number lines.

Small steps

→ Previous step: Equivalent fractions (1)
→ **This step: Equivalent fractions (2)**
→ Next step: Equivalent fractions (3)

NATIONAL CURRICULUM LINKS

Year 3 Number – Fractions
• Recognise and show, using diagrams, equivalent fractions with small denominators.
• Compare and order unit fractions, and fractions with the same denominators.

ASSESSING MASTERY

Children can show equivalent fractions on a number line. They can confidently describe how to use number lines to find equivalent fractions. Children use their knowledge of equivalence to mark fractions with different denominators on a number line. For example, on a number line labelled from 0 to 1, they can mark $\frac{1}{6}, \frac{1}{3}, \frac{1}{2}$.

COMMON MISCONCEPTIONS

Children may not have complete mastery of fractions – for example, they may find it difficult to place fractions on a number line. Some children may count the marks on a number line, rather than the intervals, and may be unsure of how to count in different fractional amounts. Ask:
• *How many equal parts has the number line been split into? What denominator will the fractions in this number line have?*

Some children may believe that to find equivalent fractions, you 'do the same to the top and the bottom', such as adding or subtracting the same number. For instance, some children may believe that $\frac{7}{8} = \frac{8}{9}$, since 7 + 1 = 8 and 8 + 1 = 9. Ask:
• *Can you think of a fraction that is equivalent to $\frac{1}{4}$? What did you do to find this equivalent fraction? What did you do to the numerator and the denominator?*

STRENGTHENING UNDERSTANDING

Allow time for all children to be confident when using a variety of resources. Revisit counting in fraction intervals, by showing children pre-marked number lines with different denominators. Hide some of the fractions and ask children to find them. If children generalise incorrectly, rather than telling them what is wrong, provide time for them to explain their findings. Ask: *Show me $\frac{7}{8}$. Show me $\frac{8}{9}$. Are they equal? How do you know?*

GOING DEEPER

Provide children with pairs of fractions that are equal and some that are not equal. Ask them to group them in 'equivalent fractions' and 'non-equivalent fractions'. Ask: *How can you prove your answers? What resources will you use?* By choosing their own resources and explaining their findings, children will gain a deeper understanding.

KEY LANGUAGE

In lesson: fraction, equivalent, equal, number line

Other language to be used by the teacher: whole, compare, intervals, shared, equal parts, numerator, denominator, multiply (×), divide (÷)

STRUCTURES AND REPRESENTATIONS

fraction wall, number line, bar model

RESOURCES

Mandatory: fraction wall, number line, fraction strips, bar model

Optional: paper strips, fraction tiles, fraction rods

 In the eTextbook of this lesson, you will find interactive links to a selection of teaching tools.

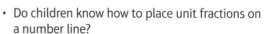

Before you teach ⏸

• Do children know how to place unit fractions on a number line?
• What other experiences can you offer children so they understand how to recognise equivalent fractions?

Discover

Pair work

ASK

- Question ① a): *What does the picture show? How many parts does the bracelet have? What fraction of the bracelet is blue? What fraction of the bracelet is pink? Which fraction strip on the wall is the same length as the blue part of the bracelet?*
- Question ① b): *Is there another fraction strip that is the same length? How can you show your results?*

IN FOCUS Question ① b) allows children to find pairs of equivalent fractions. The picture should encourage children to notice the fraction strips that are of equal length. Ask: *What does 'equivalent fraction' mean? What are you looking for on the fraction wall?*

PRACTICAL TIPS Give children the opportunity to recreate the question using concrete resources, such as fraction tiles or fraction rods, to build the fraction strips. They can use a string or paper strip to create a number line. They can measure the distance each bar represents and find the equivalent fractions. Moving from concrete to pictorial representations will deepen their understanding of equivalent fractions.

ANSWERS

Question ① a): $\frac{3}{4} = \frac{6}{8}$

Question ① b): $\frac{1}{4} = \frac{2}{8}, \frac{1}{2} = \frac{2}{4} = \frac{4}{8}, \frac{3}{4} = \frac{6}{8}$

PUPIL TEXTBOOK 3C PAGE 12

Share

Whole class teacher led

ASK

- Question ① a): *How many parts are there in total on the bar that shows $\frac{3}{4}$? What does the arrow show? What fraction do the top number line and fraction strip represent? What fraction do the second number line and fraction strip represent? Tell me a fraction that is equivalent to $\frac{1}{4}$. How do you know? Are there others?*
- Question ① b): *What are the coloured arrows pointing to? Can you see any other fractions that are equivalent?*

IN FOCUS Use this opportunity to recap the potential misconceptions listed in the **Common misconceptions** section. Allow children to show their understanding of using a number line to show equivalent fractions.

STRENGTHEN Discuss the different equivalent fractions that children may have found. Ask: *How do you know these fractions are equal? How did you use the number line and the fraction wall to find the equivalent fractions? Choose one pair of equivalent fractions. What do these fractions have in common? How do they differ?*

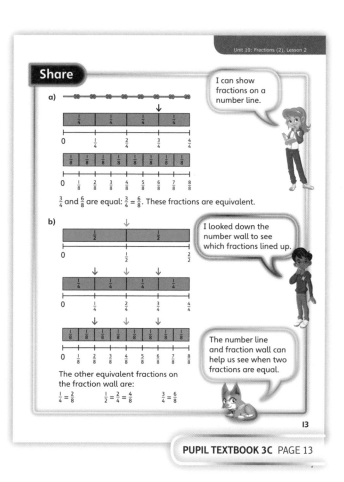

PUPIL TEXTBOOK 3C PAGE 13

Think together

WAYS OF WORKING Whole class teacher led (I do, We do, You do)

ASK

- Question ❶ : *How many equal parts are there in each of the number lines? What would the denominator in each of these fractions be?*
- Question ❷ : *How will you decide which of the number lines from question ❶ you can use to help you?*

IN FOCUS Question ❶ requires children to locate fractions with the same denominator on a number line.
In question ❷, children are required to use the number lines again, this time to find the missing numerators and denominators. Listen to children's reasoning for their answers, and encourage discussion of how the number lines can be used to identify equivalent fractions.

Question ❸ builds on the knowledge that children have gathered so far in the lesson and requires children to show how they can use number lines to find fractions equivalent to $\frac{2}{3}$. Children need to label the lines independently and use their understanding of equivalence to solve the question.

STRENGTHEN Question ❸ strengthens children's understanding, by revising one of the potential misconceptions highlighted in the lesson (that they have identified the fraction that is one mark before the end of each of the number lines). Encourage children to explain why Zac is wrong, using diagrams and the correct mathematical vocabulary.

DEEPEN Deepen children's understanding by asking them to compare $\frac{3}{4}$, $\frac{7}{8}$ and $\frac{11}{12}$. Ask: *Which fraction is the biggest? Which fraction is the smallest? Can you place all these fractions on the same number line labelled from 0 to 1?*

ASSESSMENT CHECKPOINT At this point in the lesson, children know how to order fractions on a number line. They understand how to use number lines to find equivalent fractions. For an indication of their understanding, observe their work as they attempt to solve question ❸ .

ANSWERS

Question ❶ a): $\frac{2}{4}$, $\frac{3}{4}$

Question ❶ b): $\frac{2}{8}$, $\frac{4}{8}$, $\frac{6}{8}$

Question ❶ c): $\frac{2}{6}$, $\frac{3}{6}$, $\frac{4}{6}$

Question ❶ d): $\frac{2}{3}$

Question ❷ : Possible answers include a) $\frac{1}{4} = \frac{2}{8}$ b) $\frac{1}{3} = \frac{2}{6}$
c) $\frac{2}{3} = \frac{6}{9}$ d) $\frac{3}{4} = \frac{6}{8}$ e) $\frac{2}{4} = \frac{3}{6} = \frac{4}{8}$

Question ❸ : $\frac{4}{6}$, $\frac{6}{9}$

Question ❹ a): Use the number lines to explain why the fractions are not equal.

Question ❹ b): Various correct answers, such as $\frac{2}{8}$, $\frac{3}{12}$ etc.

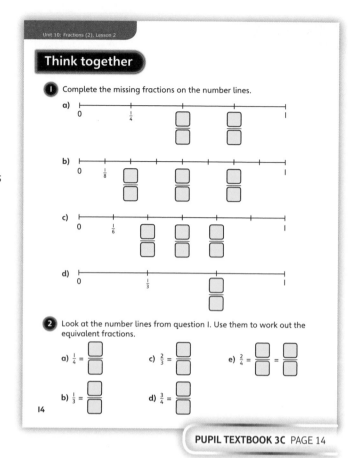

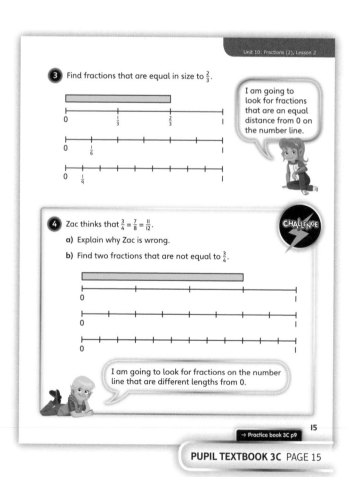

→ Practice book 3C p9

PUPIL TEXTBOOK 3C PAGE 14

PUPIL TEXTBOOK 3C PAGE 15

Practice

WAYS OF WORKING Independent thinking

IN FOCUS These questions will help children to secure their understanding of identifying equivalent fractions using diagrams. They use number lines to find the missing numerator and/or denominator from the given equivalent fractions.

STRENGTHEN If children are struggling, use paper fraction strips, so that they can see a concrete representation of the question. In question **1**, ask: *What is $\frac{1}{2}$ equal to (think of the example in the lesson)? How can you use the number lines to find equivalent fractions? What are you looking for? What does 'equivalent fraction' mean?*

DEEPEN Deepen children's understanding in question **4** by asking them: *How big is the interval from $\frac{1}{4}$ to $\frac{1}{2}$? How big is the interval from $\frac{1}{8}$ to $\frac{1}{2}$?* Ask them to demonstrate how they know they are correct.

Children could also explore the concept presented in question **6** in more depth. When discussing the fractions in the question, children need to think about how different parts of the whole are joined together to make one. Ask: *What does a whole look like in a diagram? How can it be represented as a fraction? What other equivalent fractions can you find?*

THINK DIFFERENTLY Question **5** encourages children to think differently by identifying the fractions that are not equivalent.

ASSESSMENT CHECKPOINT Children should be confident in identifying and showing equivalent fractions using diagrams. They can explain how number lines can be used to find equivalent fractions, using the correct mathematical language.

ANSWERS Answers for the **Practice** part of the lesson appear in the separate **Practice and Reflect answer guide**.

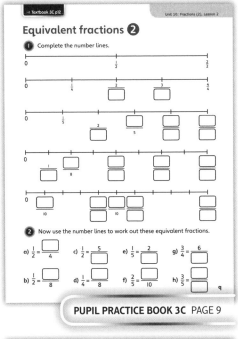

PUPIL PRACTICE BOOK 3C PAGE 9

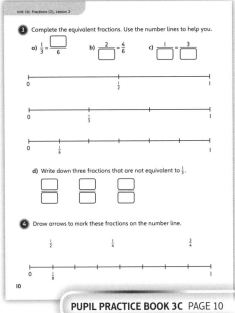

PUPIL PRACTICE BOOK 3C PAGE 10

Reflect

WAYS OF WORKING Pair work

IN FOCUS Start by giving children time to discuss with a partner how to use number lines to find equivalent fractions. Once children have discussed their methods, give them time to write their explanations. Challenge them to make a missing number question for their partner.

ASSESSMENT CHECKPOINT Look for clarity in children's explanations. They should make reference to the fact that equivalent fractions are the same size, but can be split into a different number of equal parts.

ANSWERS Answers for the **Reflect** part of the lesson appear in the separate **Practice and Reflect answer guide**.

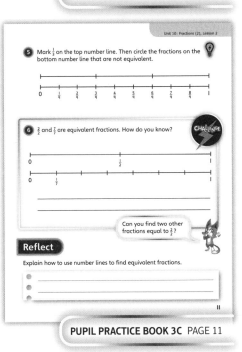

PUPIL PRACTICE BOOK 3C PAGE 11

After the lesson

- Can children show equivalent fractions using number lines and use number lines to help them find equivalent fractions?
- Were children able to use diagrams to support their findings?
- Were children able to explain their reasoning?

Equivalent fractions ③

Learning focus

In this lesson, children will continue to develop their ability to find equivalent fractions using proportional reasoning. Diagrams are used to build children's understanding of pattern and numerical reasoning.

Small steps

→ Previous step: Equivalent fractions (2)
→ **This step: Equivalent fractions (3)**
→ Next step: Comparing fractions

NATIONAL CURRICULUM LINKS

Year 3 Number – Fractions
- Recognise and show, using diagrams, equivalent fractions with small denominators.
- Solve problems that involve [equivalent fractions with small denominators].

ASSESSING MASTERY

Children can use proportional reasoning to understand equivalent fractions and pairs of fractions, through the relationship between the numerator and denominator of each fraction.

COMMON MISCONCEPTIONS

Some children will use methods that do not apply to all scenarios. For example, if you double the fraction to find families of equivalent fractions, this will work for $\frac{1}{3} = \frac{2}{6} = \frac{4}{12}$, but not for finding $\frac{5}{15}$ or $\frac{6}{18}$. Children need to understand the meaning of the digits in a fraction, rather than relying on rules they cannot explain. Ask:
- *What are the numerator and denominator in $\frac{2}{4}$ showing us? What is the relationship between them? Can you think of an equivalent fraction that uses different numbers, but shows the same thing?*

STRENGTHENING UNDERSTANDING

Show children concrete representations of $\frac{1}{3}$, such as $\frac{1}{3}$ of a chocolate bar. Split each third into 3 equal parts. Children establish that $\frac{1}{3} = \frac{3}{9}$. Move from concrete to pictorial representation, by asking children to find $\frac{1}{3}$ on a fraction wall or number line.

GOING DEEPER

Ask children to look at the relationship between the numerator and denominator of $\frac{1}{3}$. 1 is a third of 3, or 3 is three times greater than 1. Now ask children to look at $\frac{3}{9}$. Ask: *What relationship is there between the numerator and denominator of $\frac{3}{9}$?* Give children opportunities to develop their proportional reasoning when considering the relationship between the numerator and denominator in a fraction.

KEY LANGUAGE

In lesson: numerator, denominator, equivalent fraction, pattern, multiply by, divide by

Other language to be used by the teacher: proportional reasoning, missing fraction, relationship, unit fraction, whole

STRUCTURES AND REPRESENTATIONS

fraction strip model, number line, fraction wall

RESOURCES

Mandatory: fraction cards, number lines, fraction strips, paper strips

Optional: number cards

 In the eTextbook of this lesson, you will find interactive links to a selection of teaching tools.

Before you teach

- Are children confident in showing equivalent fractions?
- Are children confident using number lines and fraction strips?
- What resources will you provide beyond the number lines and fraction strips so that the lesson is as hands-on as possible?

Discover

WAYS OF WORKING Pair work

ASK

- Question ① a): *What are equivalent fractions? What fraction does Reena need to find an equivalent to? What is the relationship between the numerator and denominator in $\frac{1}{2}$?*
- Question ① b): *What fractions can you make with the numbers shown?*

IN FOCUS Use this task to encourage children to use the visual diagrams they have seen in previous lessons to find other fractions that are equal to $\frac{1}{2}$. This is an opportunity to recap and briefly assess children's current understanding of the numerator and denominator in a fraction. In question ① a), encourage children to realise that they can use any of the four available number cards, but only some combinations will make an equivalent for $\frac{1}{2}$. In question ① b) they have the numbers 1 to 6 available. Ask: *Can you think of a pair of equivalent fractions, or suggest a fraction to start with?*

PRACTICAL TIPS Make sure each pair or group has five paper strips folded into halves, thirds, quarters, fifths and sixths. Remind children that they are looking to make $\frac{1}{2}$. Children could test for themselves how many $\frac{1}{3}, \frac{1}{4}, \frac{1}{5}$ or $\frac{1}{6}$ they need to make $\frac{1}{2}$ (if any).

ANSWERS

Question ① a): $\frac{1}{2} = \frac{3}{6}$

Question ① b): Various possible answers: $\frac{1}{2} = \frac{3}{6}; \frac{2}{3} = \frac{4}{6}; \frac{1}{3} = \frac{2}{6};$
$\frac{4}{6} = \frac{2}{3}, \frac{3}{6} = \frac{1}{2}, \frac{2}{6} = \frac{1}{3}$

Share

WAYS OF WORKING Whole class teacher led

ASK

- Question ① a): *Tell me a fraction that is equivalent to $\frac{1}{2}$. What cards does Reena have? Can you make the equivalent of $\frac{1}{2}$ a different way, using the remaining cards? How do you know without checking the diagram?*
- Question ① b): *Can you make another fraction? Can you find an equivalent fraction to that? Are there any other pairs of equivalent fractions you could make?*

IN FOCUS Children can show their understanding of equivalent fractions in these activities. Ask: *Can you explain why these fractions are equal? Are there other fractions equal to them?* Watch for, and discuss, any potential misconceptions children may have.

STRENGTHEN This is a good opportunity to reinforce the relationship that may exist between the numerator and denominator. For example, children could be looking for fractions where the numerator is two times or three times less than the denominator (or where the denominator is two times, or three times greater).

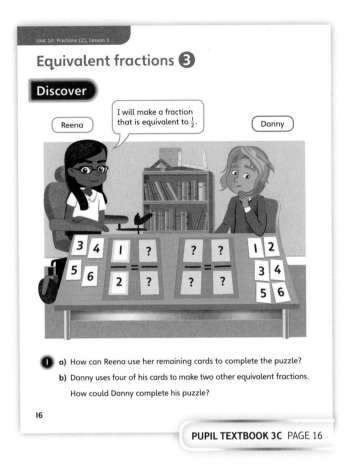

PUPIL TEXTBOOK 3C PAGE 16

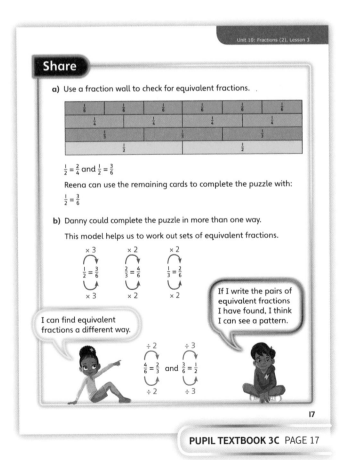

PUPIL TEXTBOOK 3C PAGE 17

Think together

WAYS OF WORKING **WAYS OF WORKING** Whole class teacher led (I do, We do, You do)

ASK

- Question ❶ a): *What are equivalent fractions? How can you use number lines to find equivalent fractions?*
- Question ❷ : *What does each numerator show? What does each denominator show? How can you use this information to find the missing numerators and denominators?*

IN FOCUS Questions ❶ and ❷ will help scaffold the children's use of diagrams. Ask children to match the number lines with the fractions they are making.

STRENGTHEN In question ❶, ask children to describe the pattern in each pair of fractions they make. Ask: *How many times bigger is the denominator than the numerator?* In question ❷, look for the pattern that exists between both fractions. Ask: *How many times bigger is one denominator than the other? Will you multiply or divide to find the missing number?*

DEEPEN Challenge children in question ❸ by asking them to think about different ways in which the question can be answered. Not only will they practise finding equivalent fractions, but they will also have an opportunity to reason which method they prefer and why. To deepen their understanding even further, ask them to draw diagrams to support their answers.

ASSESSMENT CHECKPOINT At this point in the lesson, children should be more confident in finding equivalent fractions using proportional reasoning. Visual diagrams are used to build their understanding of pattern and numerical reasoning.

They are becoming increasingly fluent in keeping the same relationship between numerator and denominator in all equivalent fractions.

ANSWERS

Question ❶ a): $\frac{1}{2} = \frac{5}{10}$ or $\frac{1}{5} = \frac{2}{10}$

Question ❶ b): $\frac{1}{5} = \frac{2}{10}$ or $\frac{1}{2} = \frac{5}{10}$

Question ❷ a): $\frac{2}{5} = \frac{4}{10}$

Question ❷ b): $\frac{3}{10} = \frac{6}{20}$

Question ❷ c): $\frac{8}{10} = \frac{4}{5}$

Question ❷ d): $\frac{6}{8} = \frac{3}{4}$

Question ❸ a): $\frac{1}{5} = \frac{4}{20}$

Question ❸ b): $\frac{8}{20} = \frac{4}{10}$

Question ❸ c): $\frac{8}{16} = \frac{1}{2}$

Question ❸ d): $\frac{6}{9} = \frac{2}{3}$

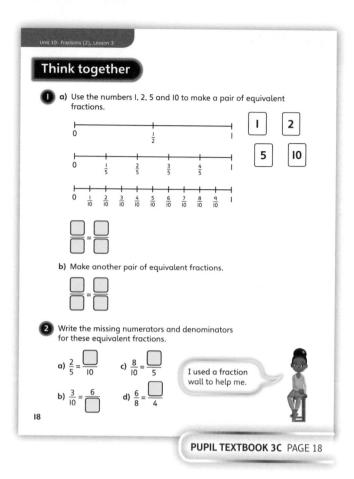

PUPIL TEXTBOOK 3C PAGE 18

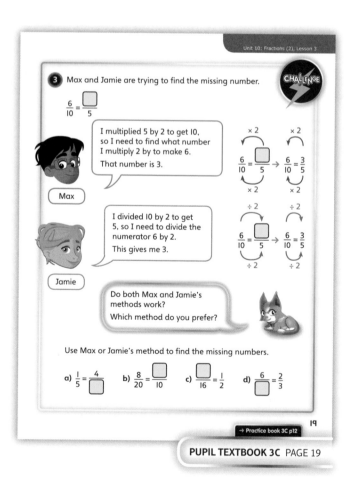

PUPIL TEXTBOOK 3C PAGE 19

Practice

Independent thinking

IN FOCUS Question ❶ scaffolds children's understanding of using diagrams to find equivalent fractions. Shading representations of the fractions is very beneficial in giving children an opportunity to develop their fluency in finding missing numerators.

STRENGTHEN If children need support with question ❷, it may be helpful to use number lines and fraction strips to make each of the fractions presented in the question. Ask: *How do you know you are right?* Once they have a clear visual representation in their heads, help them develop their proportional reasoning. Ask: *What can you divide 12 by to get 3? What can you multiply 2 by to get 8?*

DEEPEN Use question ❺ to deepen their explanation and reasoning skills. Ask: *What part of the lesson did Emma not understand? How will you explain the mistake? What should the answer have been? Can you draw a diagram to show your answer?*

THINK DIFFERENTLY Question ❹ offers children an opportunity to problem solve and think independently. Children have to work systematically to find the answer. Ask: *Can you find another answer? Can you explain your answer in two ways?* This is a good opportunity to clarify any misconceptions that children may have. Ask: *What clues did you use to find the answer? Can you use a number line to support your answer?*

ASSESSMENT CHECKPOINT At this point in the lesson, children should be able to confidently use their understanding of pattern and numerical reasoning to find equivalent fractions.

ANSWERS Answers for the **Practice** part of the lesson appear in the separate **Practice and Reflect answer guide**.

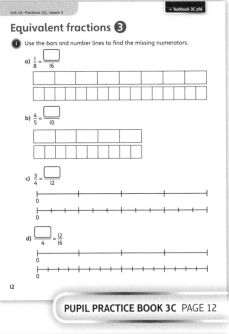

PUPIL PRACTICE BOOK 3C PAGE 12

PUPIL PRACTICE BOOK 3C PAGE 13

Reflect

Independent thinking

IN FOCUS This question offers a good opportunity to observe children's reasoning. Pay particular attention to their thinking about the relationship between the numerator and denominator of a single fraction, or the proportional relationship between the numerators and denominators in a pair of fractions.

ASSESSMENT CHECKPOINT Look for children who are able to clearly explain their reasoning. They can use a concrete representation or picture to justify their answer, rather than reverting to a preferred rule or shortcut to try to find the answer.

ANSWERS Answers for the **Reflect** part of the lesson appear in the separate **Practice and Reflect answer guide**.

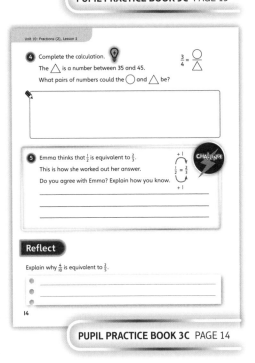

After the lesson

- Have children recognised the links between the concepts explored in the past three lessons?
- How will you reinforce these links?

PUPIL PRACTICE BOOK 3C PAGE 14

Comparing fractions

Learning focus

In this lesson, children will compare two fractions using a fraction wall and use the <, > or = signs.

Small steps

→ Previous step: Equivalent fractions (3)
→ **This step: Comparing fractions**
→ Next step: Comparing and ordering fractions

NATIONAL CURRICULUM LINKS

Year 3 Number – Fractions
- Recognise and show, using diagrams, equivalent fractions with small denominators.
- Compare and order unit fractions, and fractions with the same denominators.

ASSESSING MASTERY

Children can compare and order unit fractions and fractions with the same denominator. Children can use a fraction wall to help them compare and order fractions with different denominators.

COMMON MISCONCEPTIONS

Children may think that when comparing fractions they must compare both the numerator and the denominator, for example, that $\frac{2}{8} > \frac{1}{2}$ since 2 > 1 and 8 > 2. Provide fraction strips showing $\frac{1}{8}$s and $\frac{1}{2}$s. Use fraction strips to represent the fractions. Ask:
- *Which fraction is bigger? How do you know? What does the denominator of each fraction show? Does the number of parts matter when comparing fractions?*

STRENGTHENING UNDERSTANDING

Make sure children are familiar with how to use a fraction wall, and what each bar represents. Ask: *What is the biggest unit fraction you can see? What is the smallest?*

GOING DEEPER

Help children to create their own fraction wall using folded paper strips glued onto a piece of cardboard. This resource will help children to understand the parts of the fraction wall, and become fluent in using it to compare fractions..

KEY LANGUAGE

In lesson: inequality statement, fraction wall, numerator, denominator, inequality, compare, greater than (>), less than (<)

Other language to be used by the teacher: partition, unit fraction, whole

STRUCTURES AND REPRESENTATIONS

fraction strip, number line, fraction wall

RESOURCES

Mandatory: fraction wall

Optional: coloured paper to make fraction strips

 In the eTextbook of this lesson, you will find interactive links to a selection of teaching tools.

Before you teach

- Can children recognise and use unit and non-unit fractions?
- Is your classroom set up to allow children to compare fractions easily and regularly?
- Do children have access to different fraction representations to develop their fluency?

Discover

WAYS OF WORKING Pair work

ASK

- Question ❶ a): *Which turtle is closer to the sea, the top one or the bottom one? Can you estimate which turtle will arrive at the sea first? How do you know? What do the signs <, > and = mean?*
- Question ❶ b): *Look at the fraction wall in the picture. Can you find $\frac{2}{3}$? What does the denominator 4 mean? Which lines in the fraction wall do we need to find and compare?*

IN FOCUS Use the picture to recap and briefly assess children's current understanding of unit fractions. Begin by making sure they understand the meaning of the digits in a fraction. Children may need to be reminded of what the comparison signs <, > and = mean.

For question ❶ a), ask children to focus on finding $\frac{1}{3}$ and $\frac{1}{4}$ on the fraction wall. Ask: *Which fraction is greater?*

PRACTICAL TIPS Ask children to use the fraction wall they have made or the one in the **Discover** picture. Encourage children to identify a fraction that is less than $\frac{1}{2}$ and another one greater than $\frac{1}{2}$. Repeat for $\frac{2}{3}$ and so on.

ANSWERS

Question ❶ a): $\frac{1}{4} < \frac{1}{3}$ so Bella is correct.

Question ❶ b): $\frac{2}{3} < \frac{3}{4}$ or $\frac{2}{3} < \frac{4}{4}$

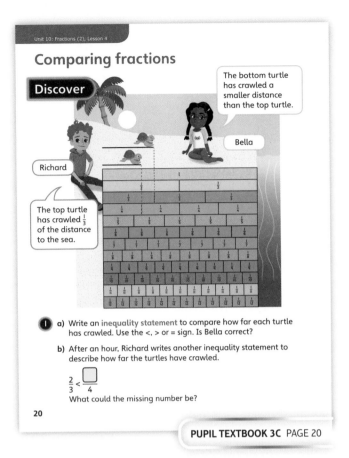

Comparing fractions

Discover

The bottom turtle has crawled a smaller distance than the top turtle.

Bella

Richard

The top turtle has crawled $\frac{1}{3}$ of the distance to the sea.

❶ a) Write an inequality statement to compare how far each turtle has crawled. Use the <, > or = sign. Is Bella correct?

b) After an hour, Richard writes another inequality statement to describe how far the turtles have crawled.

$$\frac{2}{3} < \frac{\square}{4}$$

What could the missing number be?

20

Share

WAYS OF WORKING Whole class teacher led

ASK

- Question ❶ a): *Look at the fraction each bar represents. Which one is longer? Which one is shorter? Do you agree with Astrid? How could you help her learn from her mistake?*
- Question ❶ b): *What fraction strip will you compare $\frac{2}{3}$ with? What does the denominator of 4 in the second fraction show? Where in the line will $\frac{2}{3}$ be? Will the other fraction be placed on the left or on the right of $\frac{2}{3}$ on the line? How do you know?*

IN FOCUS Use this opportunity to make sure children are confident comparing fractions. Use question ❶ b) to make sure children know that they are comparing the total length of the bar, rather than the number of bars each fraction represents.

STRENGTHEN It is important to make sure that children are confident in writing their own comparison statements. Ask: *Is $\frac{2}{3}$ greater or less than $\frac{1}{4}$? How do you know? Is $\frac{2}{3}$ greater or less than $\frac{2}{4}$?* Children can use the fraction strips to compare fractions and explain their answers.

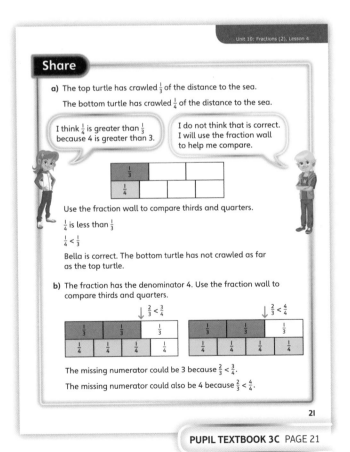

Share

a) The top turtle has crawled $\frac{1}{3}$ of the distance to the sea.

The bottom turtle has crawled $\frac{1}{4}$ of the distance to the sea.

I think $\frac{1}{4}$ is greater than $\frac{1}{3}$ because 4 is greater than 3.

I do not think that is correct. I will use the fraction wall to help me compare.

Use the fraction wall to compare thirds and quarters.

$\frac{1}{4}$ is less than $\frac{1}{3}$

$\frac{1}{4} < \frac{1}{3}$

Bella is correct. The bottom turtle has not crawled as far as the top turtle.

b) The fraction has the denominator 4. Use the fraction wall to compare thirds and quarters.

$\frac{2}{3} < \frac{3}{4}$ $\frac{2}{3} < \frac{4}{4}$

The missing numerator could be 3 because $\frac{2}{3} < \frac{3}{4}$.

The missing numerator could also be 4 because $\frac{2}{3} < \frac{4}{4}$.

21

Think together

Think together

WAYS OF WORKING Whole class teacher led (I do, We do, You do)

ASK

- Question ❶ a): *What fraction does the first strip represent?*
- Question ❶ b): *Find $\frac{1}{2}$ on the relevant number line. Find $\frac{3}{4}$. Is $\frac{3}{4}$ more or less than $\frac{1}{2}$?*
- Question ❷ a): *What does a denominator of 3 show? What does a denominator of 9 show?*
- Question ❷ b): *Which fraction strips are you comparing? How can you record your findings?*

IN FOCUS Questions ❶ and ❷ give an opportunity to compare unit fractions, and fractions with small denominators. Children use their knowledge of locating fractions on a number line, and compare the fractions based on their location. Ask: *How far is each fraction from 0? Which fraction is further from 0?*

STRENGTHEN For all the questions in this section of the lesson, ask children to use the fraction wall to compare fractions. Children can use their knowledge of equivalent fractions when justifying their answers, for instance $\frac{3}{4} = \frac{9}{12}$ and $\frac{9}{12} > \frac{7}{12}$, hence $\frac{3}{4} > \frac{7}{12}$.

DEEPEN Deepen children's conceptual understanding of comparing fractions. Ask: *When comparing unit fractions, does a bigger denominator mean the fraction is bigger? Explain your answer. Would it make a difference if all the fractions had the same numerator of 2? What about 3?*

Listen for children who can generalise, and encourage them to use the correct mathematical vocabulary when explaining their findings.

ASSESSMENT CHECKPOINT Children should now be confident in using the fraction wall to discuss the position of fractions and compare them accordingly. Listen to their reasoning when working through question ❷. They should be able to record their findings using the signs <, > and =, and be able to justify their thinking.

ANSWERS

Question ❶ a): $\frac{1}{5} > \frac{1}{6}$

Question ❶ b): $\frac{1}{2} < \frac{3}{4}$

Question ❷ a): $\frac{1}{3} > \frac{1}{9}$

Question ❷ b): $\frac{1}{8} < \frac{2}{9}$

Question ❷ c): $\frac{3}{4} > \frac{7}{12}$

Question ❸ a): Various possible correct answers, including $\frac{1}{8} > \frac{1}{10} > \frac{1}{12}$

Question ❸ b): Various possible explanations. For example, the bars offer a visual representation of the size of the parts, so it can be seen that $\frac{1}{8}$ is a bigger bar than $\frac{1}{10}$.

Question ❹ a): No, Isla is not correct. $\frac{7}{10} < \frac{4}{5}$ because $\frac{4}{5}$ is equivalent to $\frac{8}{10}$ and $\frac{7}{10} < \frac{8}{10}$.

Question ❹ b): Various possible answers, such as $\frac{4}{5} > \frac{3}{6}$ and $\frac{4}{5} > \frac{6}{9}$

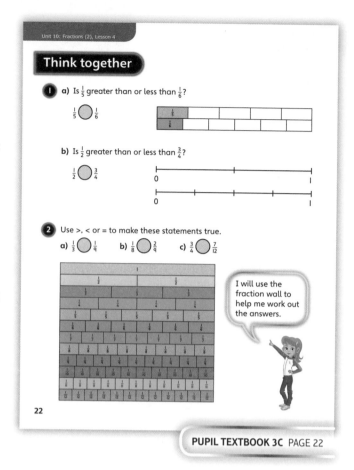

PUPIL TEXTBOOK 3C PAGE 22

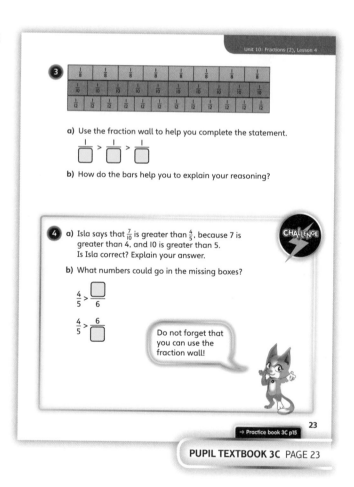

PUPIL TEXTBOOK 3C PAGE 23

Practice

WAYS OF WORKING Independent thinking

IN FOCUS In question **1**, fractions are illustrated in different ways. This will deepen children's conceptual understanding and help them to see the fractions in new, and sometimes non-linear, representations.

STRENGTHEN Children should continue to use the fraction wall to find the missing numbers in questions **3**, **4**, and **5**. For these questions, provide children with copies of the fraction wall, which they may colour in to help them with the comparisons. Add fraction scaffolds to encourage children to complete the questions independently.

DEEPEN Ask children to use the fraction wall to come up with their own questions similar to question **6**, to ask each other. For example, ask: *Which fraction might I be thinking of, if it is greater than $\frac{1}{3}$ but less than $\frac{3}{5}$? Are there any other possible answers?*

THINK DIFFERENTLY Question **5** provides a good opportunity for children to work systematically to compare fractions, while also identifying fractions that are equivalent. Encourage children to explain the reasoning behind their choices, using the appropriate vocabulary.

ASSESSMENT CHECKPOINT Children should be confident in comparing fractions. They should recognise equivalent fractions, and use their knowledge to compare unit fractions and fractions with small denominators.

ANSWERS Answers for the **Practice** part of the lesson appear in the separate **Practice and Reflect answer guide**.

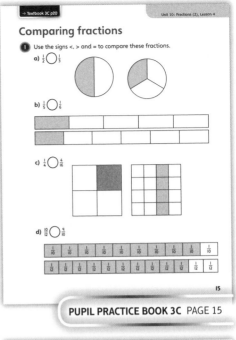

PUPIL PRACTICE BOOK 3C PAGE 15

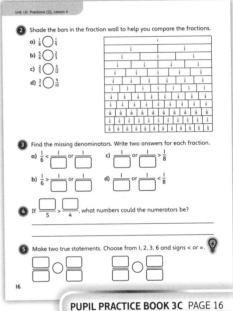

PUPIL PRACTICE BOOK 3C PAGE 16

Reflect

WAYS OF WORKING Pair work

IN FOCUS Give children the opportunity to share their ideas with their partner. If they have answered the question differently, can they explain each other's method?

ASSESSMENT CHECKPOINT Children should be comfortable using a variety of concrete and pictorial manipulatives, as well as appropriate vocabulary to explain their ideas.

ANSWERS Answers for the **Reflect** part of the lesson appear in the separate **Practice and Reflect answer guide**.

After the lesson

- Are children able to use a fraction wall to compare fractions?
- What are the main areas that children need more practice with before moving on to the next lesson?

PUPIL PRACTICE BOOK 3C PAGE 17

Comparing and ordering fractions

Learning focus

In this lesson, children will learn to compare two fractions using fraction strips and to order a set of fractions on a number line.

Small steps

→ Previous step: Comparing fractions
→ **This step: Comparing and ordering fractions**
→ Next step: Adding fractions

NATIONAL CURRICULUM LINKS

Year 3 Number – Fractions

Compare and order unit fractions, and fractions with the same denominators.

ASSESSING MASTERY

Children understand that fractions are numbers in their own right. They can compare and order fractions using a number line.

COMMON MISCONCEPTIONS

Some children will only put fractions with the same denominator on the same number line. Remind them that denominators locate a fraction on a number line. Ask:
- Is the fraction less than $\frac{1}{2}$? Is it bigger than $\frac{1}{2}$?

Use fraction strips to help secure children's understanding of how to compare different pairs of fractions.

STRENGTHENING UNDERSTANDING

Provide plenty of visual representations to compare fractions and help children to place them on the number line. Rather than just using the traditional 'pizza' representation, provide children with fraction strips, which they can place above one another when comparing fractions. Ask: *What do you notice about the fraction strips for thirds and sixths? How do these fractions compare with quarters?*

GOING DEEPER

Placing a number line above a fraction strip is helpful. This will help children to see where the fractions fit on the number line. Ask: *What do you notice? Which fraction comes first on the number line?*

KEY LANGUAGE

In lesson: equivalent fraction, numerator, denominator, fraction, order, less than (<), greater than (>)

Other language to be used by the teacher: unit fraction, fraction wall, compare, partition

STRUCTURES AND REPRESENTATIONS

bar model, number line, fraction wall

RESOURCES

Mandatory: fraction strips, number lines

Optional: fraction walls, paper strips

 In the eTextbook of this lesson, you will find interactive links to a selection of teaching tools.

Before you teach

- Are children confident using the denominator to determine the number of equal parts in the whole?
- Can children order fractions with the same denominator?

Discover

WAYS OF WORKING Pair work

ASK

- Question ❶ a): *Can you count in quarters? What comes before $\frac{3}{4}$? And after? Can you make $\frac{2}{4}$ or $\frac{1}{4}$ with the number cards you have available?*
- Question ❶ b): *Do the fractions have different denominators? How can you work out which is bigger?*

IN FOCUS Children can decide what resources or representations to use, and work out the answer methodically. They need to have a firm understanding of what the denominator and numerator represent. Watch for any misconceptions, such as: 'the larger the denominator, the larger the fraction'.

PRACTICAL TIPS Provide children with paper strips and number lines labelled from 0 to 1. The more opportunity children have to use fractions, the stronger their understanding will be. Ask them to fold the strips of paper into quarters, eighths, fifths, tenths and halves, to support them in finding solutions to the questions.

ANSWERS

Question ❶ a): $\frac{2}{4} < \frac{3}{4}$; $\frac{4}{8} > \frac{4}{10}$; $\frac{5}{10} = \frac{4}{8}$

Question ❶ b): $\frac{1}{8} < \frac{2}{10} < \frac{4}{5}$

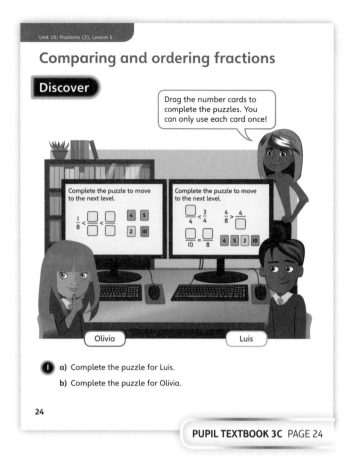

a) Complete the puzzle for Luis.

b) Complete the puzzle for Olivia.

24

PUPIL TEXTBOOK 3C PAGE 24

Share

WAYS OF WORKING Whole class teacher led

ASK

- Question ❶ a): *How can you use number lines to compare fractions?*
- Question ❶ a): *What do you notice about comparing fractions that have the same denominator? Is this different to comparing fractions with the same numerator?*
- Question ❶ a): *What do you notice about the equivalent fractions?*

IN FOCUS In question ❶ a), children need to pay attention to both the given and the missing numbers. The first two fractions have denominators of 4; hence both number lines are split into 4 equal parts. The second two fractions have equal numerators (both 4); hence the smaller the denominator, the bigger the fraction will be. The third two fractions are equal. Ask: *How do you know that the two fractions in this puzzle are equal? Did you notice the 'equal to' sign?* They should use number lines that go up in $\frac{1}{10}$s and $\frac{1}{8}$s to identify equal fractions.

STRENGTHEN In question ❶ b), encourage children to place the fractions they are comparing on a single number line labelled 0 to 1. Ask: *Would this fraction be closer to 0 or 1? How do you know? Has it passed the half-way line? What do you notice?*

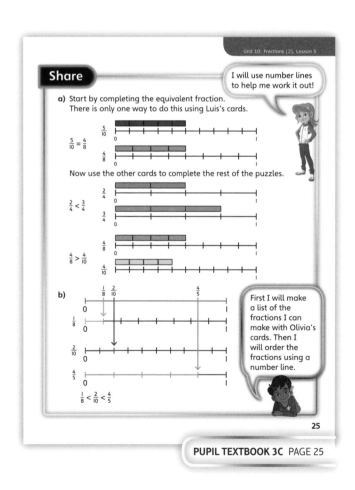

25

PUPIL TEXTBOOK 3C PAGE 25

Think together

WAYS OF WORKING Whole class teacher led (I do, We do, You do)

ASK

- Question ❶ b): *How does Ash know that $\frac{5}{6}$ is less than one whole? How can one whole be represented?*
- Question ❷ : *How many parts has each number line been split into? Which is the smallest of the fractions?*

IN FOCUS Question ❶ a) requires children to compare fractions with the same denominator, while question ❶ b) requires children to compare fractions with the same numerator. Ask: *Will your approach be different? What could the missing number be? What do you notice about the size of the fraction and the denominator? What do you notice about the size of the fraction and the numerator?*

For all questions in this section, encourage children to use number lines to check the missing number answers. Ask: *Can you think of another number that the numerator can be? Can the denominator be different?* Questions ❶, ❷ and ❸ all provide opportunities for children to order fractions on a number line.

DEEPEN Ask children to organise the fractions from the lesson so far into two groups: 'less than $\frac{1}{2}$' and 'greater than $\frac{1}{2}$'. Ask: *In which group will this fraction go? How do you know you have organised the fractions correctly?*

To extend this further, ask children to place all the fractions on a single number line. Ask children whether they could use the fraction wall to check each fraction is in the correct position.

ASSESSMENT CHECKPOINT Children should be able to compare fractions with the same denominator. They can place fractions with small denominators on a number line and compare them with each other.

ANSWERS

Question ❶ a): $\frac{3}{5} > \frac{2}{5}$ or $\frac{1}{5}$

Question ❶ b): $\frac{5}{6} < \frac{5}{5}$

Question ❷ a): $\frac{2}{8}, \frac{6}{8}, \frac{8}{8}$

Question ❷ b): $\frac{1}{4}, \frac{1}{3}, \frac{1}{2}$

Question ❷ c): $\frac{1}{3}, \frac{1}{2}, \frac{3}{4}$

Question ❸ a): $\frac{1}{10}, \frac{1}{8}, \frac{3}{8}, \frac{7}{8}$

Question ❸ b): $\frac{7}{8} > \frac{3}{8} > \frac{1}{8} > \frac{1}{10}$

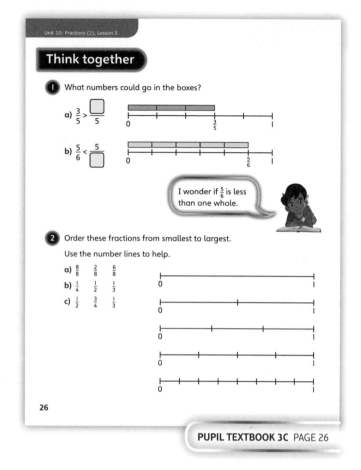

PUPIL TEXTBOOK 3C PAGE 26

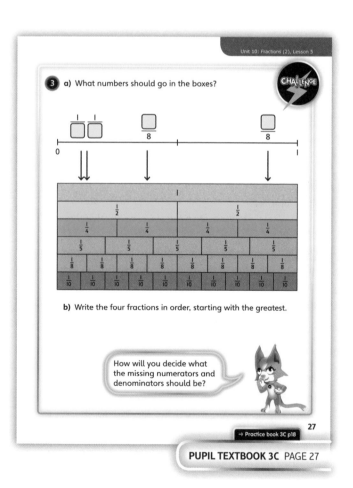

PUPIL TEXTBOOK 3C PAGE 27

Practice

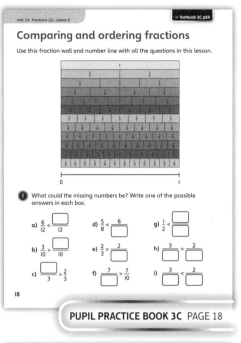

PUPIL PRACTICE BOOK 3C PAGE 18

WAYS OF WORKING Independent thinking

IN FOCUS Questions ❶ and ❷ help children to develop fluency with fractions, identifying them using a fraction wall and a number line. To find the missing numbers, children build on their knowledge of unit fractions, equivalent fractions and using fractions as numbers.

In question ❺, children first need to work out what the numerator and denominator of each fraction could be, and then check that the numbers add up to 10. They can then place their fractions on the number line. Encourage children to justify their reasoning clearly.

STRENGTHEN If children are having trouble finding the mistake in question ❸, provide a number line labelled from 0 to 1. Ask children to position the fractions $\frac{1}{10}$, $\frac{1}{2}$, $\frac{1}{5}$ and $\frac{9}{10}$ on the number line. Can they establish which fraction is in the wrong place?

DEEPEN Use question ❹ to deepen children's reasoning and explanation skills. Ask: *What resource will you use to explain your findings? How many different answers can you find?*

ASSESSMENT CHECKPOINT At this point in the lesson, children should be able to confidently recognise and order fractions on a number line. Their answers to question ❸ should demonstrate their ability to do this. They can record their findings using the signs <, >, = and fluently describe their findings. Question ❹ should offer a good indication of their current level of understanding.

ANSWERS Answers for the **Practice** part of the lesson appear in the separate **Practice and Reflect answer guide**.

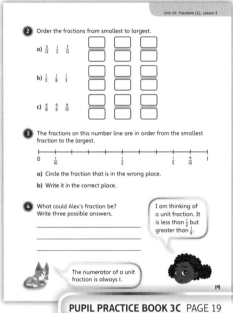

PUPIL PRACTICE BOOK 3C PAGE 19

Reflect

WAYS OF WORKING Independent thinking

IN FOCUS Give children an opportunity to develop their own line of thinking. They should be able to link vocabulary they have learnt in past lessons to justify their thinking in this lesson.

ASSESSMENT CHECKPOINT Children should be comfortable using different methods to compare fractions. They should be able to explain confidently the importance of using different resources.

ANSWERS Answers for the **Reflect** part of the lesson appear in the separate **Practice and Reflect answer guide**.

After the lesson

- Are children able to compare fractions confidently?
- Are children able to order fractions on a number line?
- How will you build in more opportunities to practise these skills?

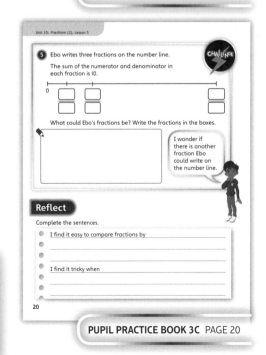

PUPIL PRACTICE BOOK 3C PAGE 20

Adding fractions

Learning focus

In this lesson, children will add two or more fractions with the same denominator.

Small steps

→ Previous step: Comparing and ordering fractions
→ **This step: Adding fractions**
→ Next step: Subtracting fractions

NATIONAL CURRICULUM LINKS

Year 3 Number – Fractions

Add and subtract fractions with the same denominator within one whole [for example, $\frac{5}{7} + \frac{1}{7} = \frac{6}{7}$].

ASSESSING MASTERY

Children will count fraction steps of a constant size, using their understanding of fractions as numbers. This will help them to make sense of adding fractions with the same denominator. They can find pairs of fractions that total one.

COMMON MISCONCEPTIONS

Children may try to add fractions by adding both the numerators and the denominators (for example, $\frac{2}{5} + \frac{1}{5} = \frac{3}{10}$). Ask:
• *How many parts has the whole been split into? If we start with $\frac{2}{5}$ and count on another $\frac{1}{5}$, how many do we have now? Has the denominator stayed the same size?*

Children may be confused by a whole being made of different fractions. Show them a 'whole', and then split it into fractions. Ask:
• *What does the whole look like? How many equal pieces has it been split into? If the whole has been split into 6 equal pieces, it is represented as $\frac{6}{6}$ – what if it is split into 5 pieces instead?*

STRENGTHENING UNDERSTANDING

Show fifths on a number line or fraction wall. Practise counting in fifths up to one whole. Provide children with a fraction strip split into 5 equal parts. Ask them to count along in fifths. Practise addition calculations, such as: 'start at $\frac{2}{5}$ and count on one more fifth'. Explain that this is written as $\frac{2}{5} + \frac{1}{5} = \frac{3}{5}$.

GOING DEEPER

Ask questions that require children to count fractions within the whole. Ask: *I started at $\frac{3}{8}$ and counted on $\frac{2}{8}$. Where did I land? I started at $\frac{1}{8}$ and landed at $\frac{6}{8}$. How many eighths have I counted? I counted on $\frac{5}{8}$ and landed at $\frac{6}{8}$. Where did I start?* Show how this is adding fractions, by recording as $\frac{3}{8} + \frac{2}{8} = \frac{5}{8}$ or $\frac{1}{8} + \frac{5}{8} = \frac{6}{8}$.

Provide different images of a 'whole'. For instance, when the denominator is 2, a whole can be represented as $\frac{2}{2}$. When the denominator is 5, a whole can be represented as $\frac{5}{5}$.

KEY LANGUAGE

In lesson: fraction, add, fraction strip, number line, calculation

Other language to be used by the teacher: numerator, denominator, unit fraction, non-unit fraction, whole, subtract

STRUCTURES AND REPRESENTATIONS

bar model, number line, fraction 'pizza'

RESOURCES

Mandatory: fraction strips, number lines

Optional: paper circles (paper plates), interlocking cubes

 In the eTextbook of this lesson, you will find interactive links to a selection of teaching tools.

Before you teach

• Are children confident about what the numerator and denominator in a fraction show?
• Are children confident in describing one whole as a fraction?
• Are children confident with counting in different fraction steps?

Discover

WAYS OF WORKING Pair work

ASK

- Question ① a): *How many parts has each pizza been cut into? How many parts of each pizza are left?*
- Question ① a): *What fraction of the pizza is left in the first box? And in the second box?*
- Question ① a): *What does 'altogether' mean? How can you show this on a number line?*

IN FOCUS This picture shows fractions in a real-life context. Recap the misconception of adding the denominators, by asking children: *How many parts has each pizza been cut into? Does that number change if you eat a slice of the pizza?*

PRACTICAL TIPS On each table, provide a fraction strip split into 10 equal parts. This will help children to visualise one whole made up of 10 parts. It will also provide them with an opportunity to count along the strip in tenths.

Alternatively, offer a practical example. Make 'pizzas' out of paper plates divided into 10 equal pieces. Put 4 slices of pizza out. Discuss what fraction is being represented. Add 3 more slices of pizza and ask: *How many pieces do we have now? What fraction is this?*

ANSWERS

Question ① a): $\frac{4}{10} + \frac{3}{10} = \frac{7}{10}$ There is $\frac{7}{10}$ left over altogether.

Question ① b): Check children's number lines.

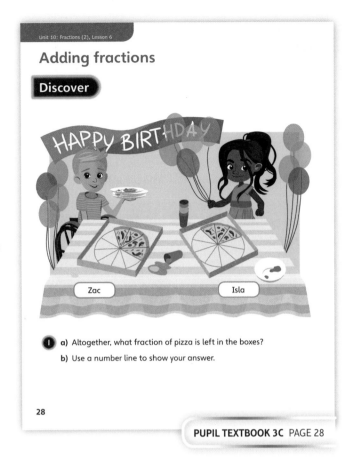

Share

WAYS OF WORKING Whole class teacher led

ASK

- Question ① a): *What fraction of the pizza is left in each box?*
- Question ① a): *Why did you decide to add the two fractions?*
- Question ① a): *Why has the numerator changed? Why is the denominator still 10?*
- Question ① b): *Look at Astrid and Flo's methods of adding using a number line. Which do you prefer? Why?*

IN FOCUS It is important to give children opportunities to add different fractions with the same numerator. Establish that we can show calculations with fractions on a number line, just as we can show calculations with whole numbers. You could also use fraction strips to show counting on, before helping children to transition to using a number line. Ask: *What mistakes might happen when adding fractions?* Clarify any misconceptions.

STRENGTHEN To support children with question ① b), ask them to look at the fraction strip or the number line. Ask: *How many more tenths must we count to complete the whole? How can you show this as a fraction?*

Ask children to investigate Ash's comment. Ask: *Would your answer be different if you added $\frac{3}{10} + \frac{4}{10}$? Can you explain your answer using a diagram?*

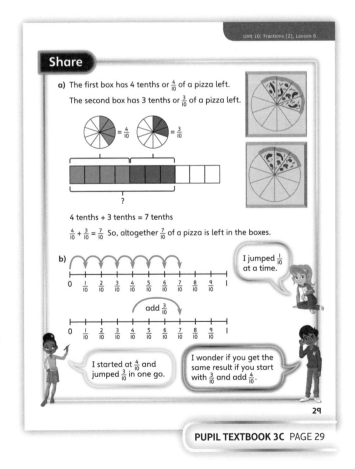

Think together

WAYS OF WORKING Whole class teacher led (I do, We do, You do)

ASK

- Question ❶ : *What fractions are shown in each diagram?*
- Question ❶ : *Will the numerator change? Will the denominator stay the same? How do you know?*
- Question ❷ : *What diagrams can you use to check your answers?*

IN FOCUS Questions ❶ and ❷ provide children with practice in adding fractions with the same denominator. Ask them to explain what they are doing as they progress through the questions. Ensure children really understand what happens to the fractions when they are added. Ask: *Why does the denominator not change? What happens if you add the denominators? In your diagram, where are the fractions you are adding? Where is the answer?*

STRENGTHEN In question ❸ b), strengthen the link between fractions being numbers, and adding fractions with the same denominator. Encourage children to use number bonds to think of different ways to make a fraction that is less than $\frac{11}{11}$. Ask: *Does the order in which we add the fractions matter?*

DEEPEN Encourage children to find different solutions to question ❸ b). Ask: *What two numbers make less than 1?* Being confident with number bonds will help children to think of all the possible solutions. Ask children to investigate Ash's question. Ask: *How many answers can you find? How will you record your answers?* Encourage children to work systematically.

ASSESSMENT CHECKPOINT At this point in the lesson, children should be more confident adding fractions with the same denominator. They understand that fractions are numbers and are exploring their properties.

ANSWERS

Question ❶ a): $\frac{5}{8}$

Question ❶ b): $\frac{6}{9}$

Question ❶ c): $\frac{6}{6}$

Question ❷ a): $\frac{4}{5}$

Question ❷ b): $\frac{5}{5}$

Question ❷ c): $\frac{4}{6}$

Question ❷ d): $\frac{6}{12}$

Question ❸ a): $\frac{2}{11} + \frac{6}{11} = \frac{8}{11}$

Question ❸ b): Various possible answers that should total less than $\frac{11}{11}$. For example, $\frac{1}{11} + \frac{9}{11} = \frac{10}{11}$, $\frac{2}{11} + \frac{8}{11} = \frac{10}{11}$, $\frac{3}{11} + \frac{7}{11} = \frac{10}{11}$ etc. Three fractions could also offer various answers; for example,
$\frac{1}{11} + \frac{2}{11} + \frac{3}{11} = \frac{6}{11}$, $\frac{2}{11} + \frac{3}{11} + \frac{4}{11} = \frac{9}{11}$ and so on.

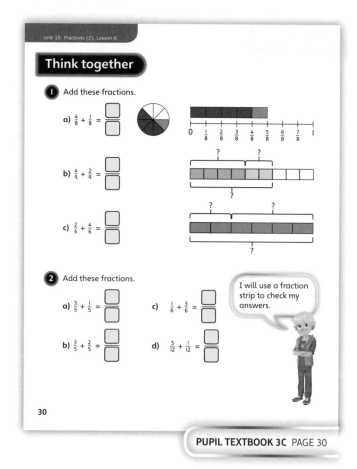

PUPIL TEXTBOOK 3C PAGE 30

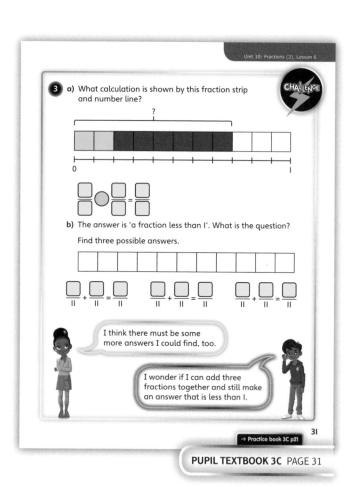

PUPIL TEXTBOOK 3C PAGE 31

Practice

WAYS OF WORKING Independent thinking

IN FOCUS Questions ❶ and ❷ provide children with visual images of fractions and require them to complete the additions. Do children understand how they can colour the shapes to help them find the answers?

Question ❻ requires children to have a secure understanding of what a 'whole' is. Children use number bonds and visual representations to explore pairs of fractions that total 1. If the children know that $5 + 3 = 8$, this will help them to recognise that $\frac{5}{8} + \frac{3}{8} = \frac{8}{8}$.

STRENGTHEN Question ❹ requires children to add fractions with the same denominator, without the support of a visual representation. Encourage them to explain their answers. Ask: *What can you do to check your answer?* Allow children to use fraction strips or number lines as support, if needed.

DEEPEN You could deepen question ❺ by asking children to prove their ideas using diagrams. Ask: *How many ways can you demonstrate the answer? Explain how you know you have found them all.*

ASSESSMENT CHECKPOINT Children should be confident in understanding how to add fractions. They should understand that they can show calculations with fractions on a number line, in the same way they do with whole numbers.

ANSWERS Answers for the **Practice** part of the lesson appear in the separate **Practice and Reflect answer guide**.

Reflect

WAYS OF WORKING Independent thinking

IN FOCUS Give children time to explain who they think is correct and why. Once they have recorded their thinking, ask them to share their ideas with their partner. Encourage them to use diagrams to support their thinking. Ask: *Can they explain to Richard how to add fractions with the same denominator?*

ASSESSMENT CHECKPOINT Look for clarity in children's explanations. Rather than learning a rule or short-cut to find the answers, children must know what is happening to the fractions when they are added and why.

ANSWERS Answers for the **Reflect** part of the lesson appear in the separate **Practice and Reflect answer guide**.

After the lesson ⏸

- Are children able to confidently explain how to add fractions with the same denominator within one whole?
- Do they fully understand what they are doing and why, or are they relying on a rule to answer questions?
- Can children confidently explain how to use number lines and fraction strips to support their answers?
- How will you build in more opportunities to practise adding fractions throughout the school day?

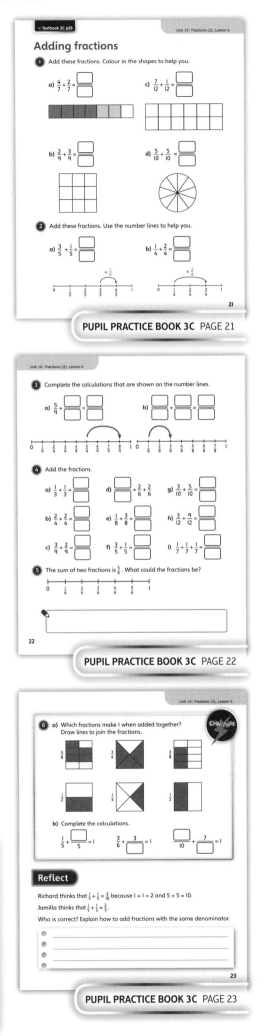

PUPIL PRACTICE BOOK 3C PAGE 21

PUPIL PRACTICE BOOK 3C PAGE 22

PUPIL PRACTICE BOOK 3C PAGE 23

Subtracting fractions

Learning focus

In this lesson, children will learn to subtract fractions with the same denominator.

Small steps

→ Previous step: Adding fractions
→ **This step: Subtracting fractions**
→ Next step: Problem solving – adding and subtracting fractions

NATIONAL CURRICULUM LINKS

Year 3 Number – Fractions

Add and subtract fractions with the same denominator within one whole [for example, $\frac{5}{7} + \frac{1}{7} = \frac{6}{7}$].

ASSESSING MASTERY

Children will draw on their understanding of fractions as numbers and of counting in fraction steps of a constant size. This will help them make sense of subtracting fractions with the same denominator. They can find the difference between two fractions with the same denominator.

COMMON MISCONCEPTIONS

When subtracting fractions, children may subtract the numerators and the denominators separately. For example, they may think that $\frac{3}{5} - \frac{2}{5} = 1$, because $3 - 2 = 1$ and $5 - 5 = 0$. Ask:

- *If you do $\frac{3}{5} - \frac{2}{5}$, how many parts are in the whole? How many of these parts do you have to start with? How many of them are you subtracting? What do you have left?*

Children may think that whole numbers have the same denominator as the fraction subtracted, for example $1 - \frac{3}{8} = \frac{1}{8} - \frac{3}{8} = \frac{2}{8}$. With this misconception, children will often move the numerators around before subtracting. Ask:

- *If you are working in eighths and you do $1 - \frac{3}{8}$, how many eighths make up the 1 (the whole)? If you calculate $\frac{8}{8} - \frac{3}{8}$ what answer do you get?*

STRENGTHENING UNDERSTANDING

Present children with a real-life problem. Show them an orange and say: *If you have $\frac{3}{5}$ of this orange left and you give your friend 2 of the parts, what fraction of the original orange will you have left? If you had a whole orange and split it into 8 equal parts, what fraction of the orange would be left if you ate 3 of the parts?*

GOING DEEPER

When subtracting with fractions on a number line, children should work in the same way as with whole numbers. Encourage them to use a fraction strip and number line, and practise counting on and back in different fraction steps. Ask questions that require counting fractions within the whole, for instance: *I started at $\frac{7}{12}$ and counted back $\frac{2}{12}$. Where did I land? I started on $\frac{7}{12}$ and landed on $\frac{2}{12}$. How many twelfths have I counted?* Relate the counting to subtracting fractions and record it as $\frac{7}{12} - \frac{2}{12} = \frac{5}{12}$.

KEY LANGUAGE

In lesson: subtract, difference, fraction, whole, calculate

Other language to be used by the teacher: numerator, denominator, unit fraction, non-unit fraction, add, fraction strips

STRUCTURES AND REPRESENTATIONS

bar model, number line

RESOURCES

Mandatory: fraction strips, number lines

Optional: paper circles, interlocking cubes

 In the eTextbook of this lesson, you will find interactive links to a selection of teaching tools.

Before you teach

- Do children understand what the numerator and denominator show in a fraction?
- Are they confident describing a whole as a fraction?
- Are they comfortable counting back in different fraction steps?

Discover

WAYS OF WORKING Pair work

ASK

- Question ❶ a): *What fraction of the fuel is there to start with? How do you know?*
- Question ❶ a): *What fraction of the fuel will be used on the journey? How much will there be left?*
- Question ❶ b): *What is the question asking? Can you use a fraction strip to show the question?*

IN FOCUS Using a concrete pictorial approach, children will see how a real-life situation can be translated on paper using fraction strips and number lines. In order to calculate the fraction of fuel left, it is important they think of the fractions as numbers. Ask: *What would you do if the question said: 'There are 5 litres of fuel, 3 litres are used. How many litres are left?'*

PRACTICAL TIPS A fraction strip split into 8 equal parts will help children to visualise a whole made up of 8 parts. It will also allow children to count along the strip if needed. Provide a fraction bar for each table.

ANSWERS

Question ❶ a): There will be $\frac{2}{8}$ left after the journey.

Question ❶ b): If the fuel was full at the start, there would be $\frac{5}{8}$ left after the journey.

Subtracting fractions

Discover

I a) How much fuel will be left after the journey home?

b) If the fuel was full before the journey home, what would the answer be?

32

Share

WAYS OF WORKING Whole class teacher led

ASK

- Question ❶ a): *What does the coloured area on the fraction strip show?*
- Question ❶ a): *Why has the numerator changed?*
- Question ❶ b): *Why is the denominator still 8? Can you explain your answer using the diagrams?*

IN FOCUS It is important to give children opportunities to subtract different fractions with the same denominator. Establish that we can show calculations with fractions on a number line in the same way as we do with whole numbers. Fraction strips can be used to support counting back and the transition to using a number line. Some children may try to simplify $\frac{2}{8}$ to $\frac{1}{4}$. Avoid deliberately simplifying at this stage, as equivalent fractions should be encountered (with the support of a representation such as a fraction wall).

STRENGTHEN Relate the counting they have been doing with the subtraction of fractions, for example, record $\frac{5}{8} - \frac{3}{8} = \frac{2}{8}$. Ask children to quickly practise $\frac{3}{8} - \frac{2}{8}, \frac{7}{8} - \frac{2}{8}$ and so on. Clarify any misconceptions. To strengthen the idea of 'whole', ask children to calculate what fraction of the whole tank is empty.

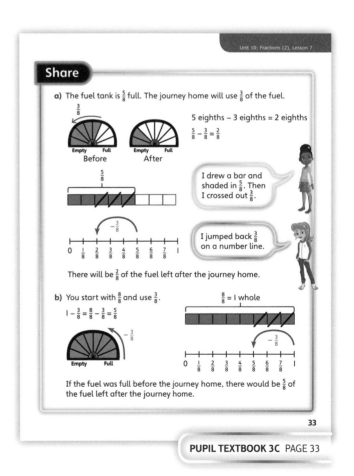

Share

a) The fuel tank is $\frac{5}{8}$ full. The journey home will use $\frac{3}{8}$ of the fuel.

$\frac{3}{8}$

5 eighths − 3 eighths = 2 eighths

$\frac{5}{8} - \frac{3}{8} = \frac{2}{8}$

Empty   Full   Empty   Full
Before   After

$\frac{5}{8}$

I drew a bar and shaded in $\frac{5}{8}$. Then I crossed out $\frac{3}{8}$.

$-\frac{3}{8}$

0 $\frac{1}{8}$ $\frac{2}{8}$ $\frac{3}{8}$ $\frac{4}{8}$ $\frac{5}{8}$ $\frac{6}{8}$ $\frac{7}{8}$ I

I jumped back $\frac{3}{8}$ on a number line.

There will be $\frac{2}{8}$ of the fuel left after the journey home.

b) You start with $\frac{8}{8}$ and use $\frac{3}{8}$.

$1 - \frac{3}{8} = \frac{8}{8} - \frac{3}{8} = \frac{5}{8}$

$\frac{8}{8}$ = I whole

$-\frac{3}{8}$

Empty   Full

$-\frac{3}{8}$

0 $\frac{1}{8}$ $\frac{2}{8}$ $\frac{3}{8}$ $\frac{4}{8}$ $\frac{5}{8}$ $\frac{6}{8}$ $\frac{7}{8}$ I

If the fuel was full before the journey home, there would be $\frac{5}{8}$ of the fuel left after the journey home.

33

Think together

WAYS OF WORKING   Whole class teacher led (I do, We do, You do)

ASK

- Question ❶ : *What fractions are shown in each diagram?*
- Question ❶ : *Will the numerators change? Will the denominators stay the same? How do you know?*
- Question ❷ b): *What fraction can be used to represent 1 in this question? Why?*

IN FOCUS   Questions ❶ and ❷ provide children with different visual representations of subtracting fractions with the same denominator. Ask children to explain their working to ensure they really understand what happens to the fractions when they are subtracted. Ask: *Why is the denominator not changing? What happens if you subtract the denominators? Would the answer be different?*

STRENGTHEN   For question ❸, strengthen the link between fractions being numbers and subtracting fractions with the same denominator. Use simple calculations, such as $7 - 4 = 3$, to show that finding the difference is another model of subtraction.

DEEPEN   For question ❸ b), draw two fraction strips or number lines, one above the other. Ask: *If the difference between the fractions is $\frac{3}{10}$, what will the fractions be? How can you show a difference of $\frac{3}{10}$ in the diagram?* Ask children to investigate Sparks' question. *How will you find all the answers? How can you record your answer?*

ASSESSMENT CHECKPOINT   At this point in the lesson, children should be more confident in subtracting fractions with the same denominator. They are able to use a number line to count back.

ANSWERS

Question ❶ a): $\frac{2}{8}$

Question ❶ b): $\frac{7}{10}$

Question ❷ a): $\frac{4}{11}$

Question ❷ b): $\frac{3}{4}$

Question ❸ a): $\frac{7}{7} - \frac{5}{7} = \frac{2}{7}; \frac{6}{7} - \frac{4}{7} = \frac{2}{7}; \frac{5}{7} - \frac{3}{7} = \frac{2}{7}; \frac{4}{7} - \frac{2}{7} = \frac{2}{7}; \frac{3}{7} - \frac{1}{7} = \frac{2}{7}$

Question ❸ b): $\frac{4}{10}$ and $\frac{1}{10}$; $\frac{5}{10}$ and $\frac{2}{10}$; $\frac{6}{10}$ and $\frac{3}{10}$; $\frac{7}{10}$ and $\frac{4}{10}$; $\frac{8}{10}$ and $\frac{5}{10}$; $\frac{9}{10}$ and $\frac{6}{10}$; $\frac{10}{10}$ and $\frac{7}{10}$

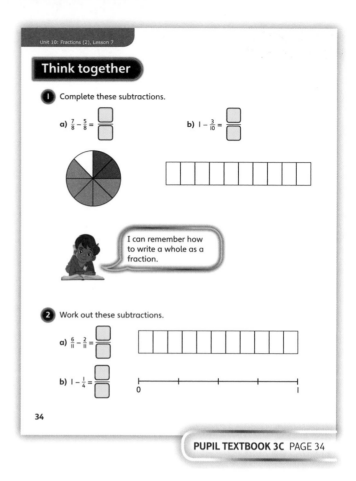

PUPIL TEXTBOOK 3C PAGE 34

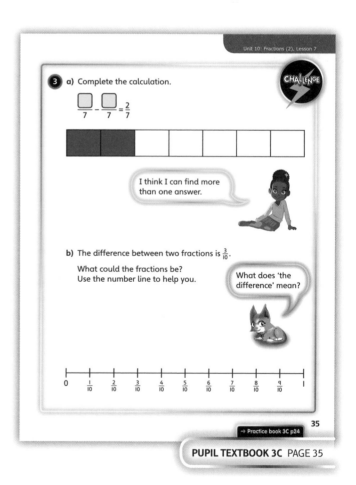

PUPIL TEXTBOOK 3C PAGE 35

Practice

WAYS OF WORKING Independent thinking

IN FOCUS Questions **1** and **2** provide children with visual images of fractions and require them to complete the subtractions.

STRENGTHEN Question **4** requires children to subtract fractions with the same denominator, without a visual representation. Encourage children to explain their answers. Ask: *How can you be sure you are correct? What can you do to check your answer?* Address any misconceptions around working with whole numbers. Discuss how number lines might be useful.

Question **6** requires children to have a secure understanding of using number lines to subtract. Encourage children to use number lines in question **7** to check their answers.

DEEPEN You could extend question **6** by asking children to check their answer to the subtraction by using addition. Ask: *What happens if you add $\frac{2}{10} + \frac{7}{10}$?* Encourage them to write alternative subtractions using the same number line. In question **7**, explore what happens when adding and subtracting fractions at the same time. Ask: *Would the answer be different if you changed the order of calculations?*

ASSESSMENT CHECKPOINT Children should have a good understanding of how to subtract fractions. They can show calculations with fractions on a number line in the same way as they do with whole numbers.

ANSWERS Answers for the **Practice** part of the lesson appear in the separate **Practice and Reflect answer guide**.

Reflect

WAYS OF WORKING Pair work

IN FOCUS Once they have recorded their thinking, give children an opportunity to share their ideas with their partner. Encourage them to use diagrams to support their thinking. Can they explain how Reena could find the difference between the fractions?

ASSESSMENT CHECKPOINT Look for clarity in children's explanations. Children should know that when finding the difference between two fractions they need to subtract them, as they would with two whole numbers. They can use fraction strips or number lines to support their answers.

ANSWERS Answers for the **Reflect** part of the lesson appear in the separate **Practice and Reflect answer guide**.

After the lesson ⏸

- Can children confidently explain how to subtract fractions with the same denominator within one whole?
- Can they explain how to use number lines and fraction strips to support their answers?
- Are children confident that they need to subtract to find the difference between two fractions?

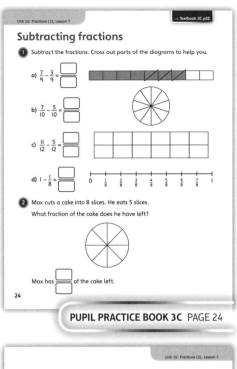

PUPIL PRACTICE BOOK 3C PAGE 24

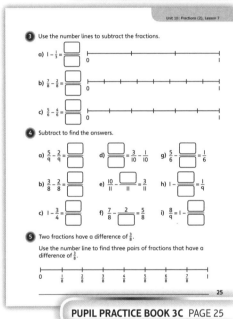

PUPIL PRACTICE BOOK 3C PAGE 25

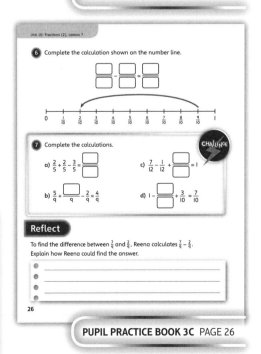

PUPIL PRACTICE BOOK 3C PAGE 26

Problem solving – adding and subtracting fractions

Learning focus

In this lesson, children will learn to reason mathematically and solve problems by adding and subtracting fractions.

Small steps

→ Previous step: Subtracting fractions
→ **This step: Problem solving – adding and subtracting fractions**
→ Next step: Problem solving – fractions of measures

NATIONAL CURRICULUM LINKS

Year 3 Number – Fractions
- Solve problems that involve addition and subtraction of fractions.
- Add and subtract fractions with the same denominator, within one whole [for example, $\frac{5}{7} + \frac{1}{7} = \frac{6}{7}$].

ASSESSING MASTERY

Children can recognise the operation needed to answer a word problem. They can write the necessary calculation to answer the problem and successfully find and write the correct answer.

COMMON MISCONCEPTIONS

In previous units, children have added and subtracted fractions, using images such as a number line, following explicit instructions. In this unit, they decide which operation to use. Children may find it difficult to identify exactly what the question is asking. Instead of applying their knowledge of fractions, this uncertainty can lead them to guess at the answer. Ask:
- *Can you draw a picture or a diagram that describes the problem?*

STRENGTHENING UNDERSTANDING

Resources such as fraction strips should be available. Encourage children to make sense of any problem before attempting to solve it, and show them how to organise their thinking. Ask: *What is it about? Can you describe it?* If they are unsure, ask them to read the question again. Ask: *Have you used all the information given?*

GOING DEEPER

Challenge children to find different ways to find the answer to the same question. Sometimes, children who work out the answer more quickly, are less inclined to look for different ways to answer the question, moving on as soon as they have found an answer. Remind them that the route to finding the answer can be more important than the answer itself.

KEY LANGUAGE

In lesson: fraction, more, add, subtract

Other language to be used by the teacher: calculate, word problem, less, greatest, addition, subtraction

STRUCTURES AND REPRESENTATIONS

bar model, number line

RESOURCES

Optional: bar models, counters, coloured rods, part-whole models

 In the eTextbook of this lesson, you will find interactive links to a selection of teaching tools.

Before you teach

- Which resources will children find the most useful to represent the given information?
- How will you ensure that children are able to interpret the different types of question they will encounter?

Discover

ASK

- Question ❶ a): *What fraction of the food was used on Monday? And on Tuesday? How can you work out how much food was used in total?*
- Question ❶ b): *If $\frac{4}{10}$ of the food has been used, how much is left? Has more been used or is there more left?*

IN FOCUS Use these pictures to discuss the food that children use at home. Ask: *If you know how much food is used each day of the week, how can you work out how much food is used in the whole week?*

PRACTICAL TIPS Use fraction strips with 10 equal parts to help children visualise the question. It might be useful to revisit how the number line can be used to add and subtract fractions within one whole.

ANSWERS

Question ❶ a): $\frac{6}{10}$ of the food is left in the box.

Question ❶ b): More of the food is left than has been used. $\frac{2}{10}$ more of the food is left than has been used.

Problem solving – adding and subtracting fractions

Discover

> We used $\frac{1}{10}$ of the food on Monday and $\frac{3}{10}$ of the food on Tuesday.

❶ a) What fraction of the food is left in the box?

b) Has more food been used or left in the box? How much more?

36

PUPIL TEXTBOOK 3C PAGE 36

Share

ASK

Question ❶ a): *To work out the fraction of food left, what information do you need to know? What fraction of food was there to start with? What fraction of food has been used in total?*

Question ❶ b): *Is there more food left than has been used? How can you work out how much more food is left?*

IN FOCUS In this section, children must interpret the questions accurately in order to solve the problems. They also need to be confident in adding and subtracting fractions within a whole.

STRENGTHEN Set up two fraction strips at the front of the class or on the whiteboard. Next to the first fraction strip write: Monday $1 - \frac{1}{10} = \frac{9}{10}$. Next to the second fraction strip write: Tuesday $\frac{9}{10} - \frac{3}{10} = \frac{6}{10}$. Ask: *Is this answer correct? How can you explain it? What does each step represent?*

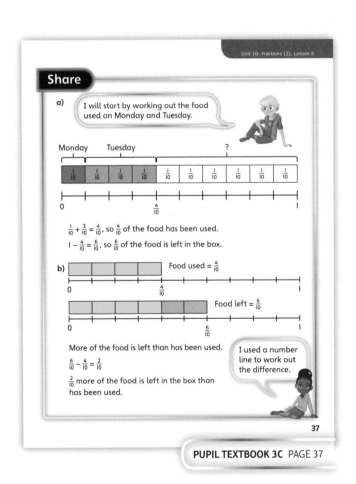

Share

a)
> I will start by working out the food used on Monday and Tuesday.

Monday   Tuesday   ?

$\frac{1}{10} + \frac{3}{10} = \frac{4}{10}$, so $\frac{4}{10}$ of the food has been used.

$1 - \frac{4}{10} = \frac{6}{10}$, so $\frac{6}{10}$ of the food is left in the box.

b)   Food used = $\frac{4}{10}$

Food left = $\frac{6}{10}$

More of the food is left than has been used.

$\frac{6}{10} - \frac{4}{10} = \frac{2}{2}$

$\frac{2}{10}$ more of the food is left in the box than has been used.

> I used a number line to work out the difference.

37

PUPIL TEXTBOOK 3C PAGE 37

Think together

ASK

- Question **1** : *What fraction of the journey did Sofia and Amal walk? What fraction of the journey did they ski?*
- Question **2** a): *What fraction of the tents are blue? And red? How can you find the fraction that are yellow?*
- Question **2** b): *What is the question asking? What clues are given? Can you solve it a different way?*

IN FOCUS Questions **1** and **2** are two-step problems. First, children need to find the total amount; then they need to subtract the answer from 1. Questions **2** b) and **3** progress from comparing fractions, to finding the difference between two fractions.

STRENGTHEN Some children may find it difficult to answer question **3**. Discuss Astrid's suggestion that children find the fraction Max ate first. Some children may misinterpret this information and assume that Max ate $\frac{1}{5}$ of the packet. Ask them to read the question carefully. Discuss how they can check if their answer is correct.

DEEPEN In question **3**, use a fraction strip split into 5 equal parts. The fraction strips should be accessible for all children. Concrete visual resources are a powerful tool to help deepen children's understanding of fractions. Challenge children to think of fraction word problems, swap them with a partner and draw or use representations to model the answers.

ASSESSMENT CHECKPOINT At this point in the lesson, children should be able to understand and interpret the questions and identify the operations required to solve the question. They should also be able to explain any manipulatives they have chosen to use.

ANSWERS

Question **1** : There are $\frac{2}{8}$ of the journey left.

Question **2** a): $\frac{5}{9}$ of the tents are yellow.

Question **2** b): There are $\frac{2}{9}$ more yellow tents than blue tents.

Question **3** a): Max and Alex ate $\frac{3}{5}$ of the packet of raisins altogether.

Question **3** b): $\frac{2}{5}$ of the packet of raisins was left.

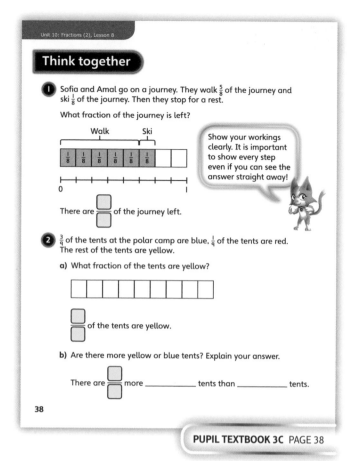

PUPIL TEXTBOOK 3C PAGE 38

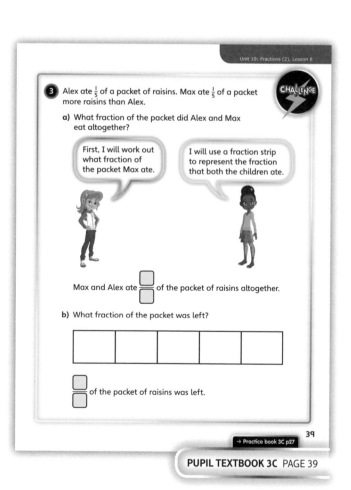

PUPIL TEXTBOOK 3C PAGE 39

Practice

WAYS OF WORKING Independent thinking

IN FOCUS Question **3** challenges children to create six different questions that all have the same answer. Children need to use a systematic approach when solving this problem in order to organise their thinking and results.

STRENGTHEN Encourage any children who are finding question **4** difficult to use a fraction strip, number line or both. Remind them to read the question slowly and record their findings step-by-step. Encourage children to label their findings for each step, so they can share their thinking through the stages, and check their answer at the end.

DEEPEN Question **5** will challenge children's ability to solve problems. The question replicates a common mistake – rushing through the question and answering what they think is being asked, rather than the actual question. Ask them to consider: *What information is given? What is the answer to this calculation?*

ASSESSMENT CHECKPOINT By this point in the lesson, children should be showing confidence in solving problems. They should be able to use representations to demonstrate a question visually, and use a systematic approach to solve it.

ANSWERS Answers for the **Practice** part of the lesson appear in the separate **Practice and Reflect answer guide**.

Reflect

WAYS OF WORKING Independent thinking

IN FOCUS Give children an opportunity to develop their own fraction problems independently. Can they answer the questions themselves? What method do they prefer to use to answer their own questions? Ask them to swap problems with a partner. They should compare the methods they used. Ask: *Whose method is more efficient?*

ASSESSMENT CHECKPOINT Children should be using different representations fluently to solve fraction problems. Assess their written explanation of what they think they should pay attention to when solving fraction problems. Look and listen for children's reasoning, clarify any misconceptions and ensure children are learning to anticipate these.

ANSWERS Answers for the **Reflect** part of the lesson appear in the separate **Practice and Reflect answer guide**.

After the lesson

- Can children confidently work in different ways to solve a problem?
- Are they confident in choosing different types of representation to solve problems independently?
- What opportunities will you provide for them to practise solving multi-step problems outside the lesson?

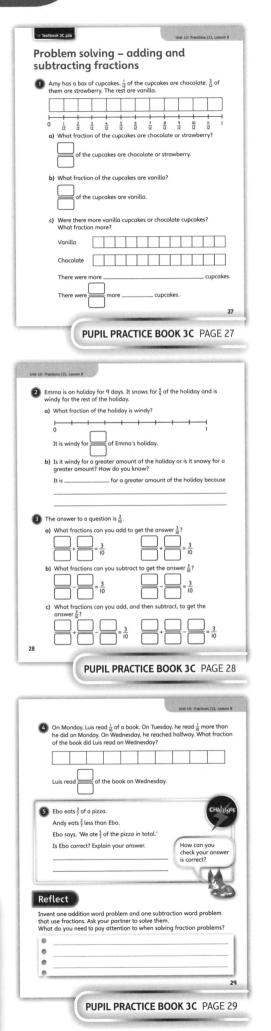

PUPIL PRACTICE BOOK 3C PAGE 27

PUPIL PRACTICE BOOK 3C PAGE 28

PUPIL PRACTICE BOOK 3C PAGE 29

71

Problem solving – fractions of measures

Learning focus

In this lesson, children will learn to reason mathematically, and solve problems involving fractions and money by adding and subtracting fractions.

Small steps

→ Previous step: Problem solving – adding and subtracting fractions
→ **This step: Problem solving – fractions of measures**
→ Next step: Months and years

NATIONAL CURRICULUM LINKS

Year 3 Number – Fractions
- Recognise, find and write fractions of a discrete set of objects: unit fractions and non-unit fractions with small denominators.
- Recognise and use fractions as numbers: unit fractions and non-unit fractions with small denominators.
- Solve problems that involve all of the above.

ASSESSING MASTERY

Children can recognise the operation needed to answer a word problem. They write the necessary calculation to answer the problem and find the correct solution.

COMMON MISCONCEPTIONS

Some children will overgeneralise and assume that, for example 'all quarters' are the same. They do not understand that the size of the whole determines the size of the fractional part. Ask:
- Which is bigger, $\frac{1}{4}$ of a 2 litre bottle or $\frac{1}{4}$ of a 500 ml bottle?

Some children misunderstand the idea that 'the bigger the denominator the smaller the part' and ignore the numerators when comparing fractions. For instance, they may think that $\frac{1}{4} > \frac{3}{5}$ because quarters are bigger than fifths. Ask:
- Which is greater, $\frac{1}{4}$ or $\frac{3}{5}$? How do you know? What information have you looked at to decide?

STRENGTHENING UNDERSTANDING

Provide containers that differ in shape, but still hold the same amount, such as 1 litre. Appearances can be misleading, so ask children to estimate amounts held by containers in a range of shapes and heights. Recall that 1 litre = 1,000 ml. Give two children one measuring jug each. One of the jugs holds 1 litre, the other 2 litres. Ask each child to $\frac{1}{2}$ fill their jug with water. Ask: Who has more water? How do you know? Repeat for different fractions, for instance $\frac{1}{4}$ or $\frac{1}{3}$. Encourage children to make sense of each problem before they start to solve it. Ask: What is it about? Can you describe it? What resources can you use to check your answer?

GOING DEEPER

The more hands-on experience children gain, the deeper their understanding will be. Provide real-life examples of fractions of measurements, for instance a cake recipe which includes fractions of different amounts. Give children time to discuss and compare the different amounts and encourage them to refer to a fraction wall to check their answers.

KEY LANGUAGE

In lesson: fraction, amount, subtract, method

Other language to be used by the teacher: word problem, mass, capacity, scales, litre (l), add, calculate, measure, greater

STRUCTURES AND REPRESENTATIONS

bar model

RESOURCES

Optional: bar models, capacity measuring equipment, coloured rods, part-whole models

 In the eTextbook of this lesson, you will find interactive links to a selection of teaching tools.

Before you teach

- What resources will you be using in the lesson? Which resources will children find most useful?
- Can children use division to find fractions of an amount and consider what is left?
- What previous opportunities have children had to find measurements?

Discover

Unit 10: Fractions (2), Lesson 9

WAYS OF WORKING Pair work

ASK

- Question ❶ a): *How much money do the children have? What fraction of the money have they allocated for juice? And for fruit? How can you work out the total fraction of money they have allocated for juice and fruit?*
- Question ❶ a): *Would the fraction change if the children had £15 to spend in total?*

IN FOCUS In this section, children must interpret the question correctly in order to understand how to solve it. They will use skills from previous lessons to establish how to use the information and interpret what the question requires.

PRACTICAL TIPS Ask children to imagine they have £10 to £20 to spend on a picnic with friends. Ask: *How would you spend the money? What fraction would you spend on drinks? What about on different food items?* Do not give children an exact amount; this will keep the focus on making sense of the fractions rather than calculating actual values.

ANSWERS

Question ❶ a): Lee and Amelia spend $\frac{4}{10}$ of £20 on sandwiches.

Question ❶ b): They will have £8 left to spend on sandwiches.

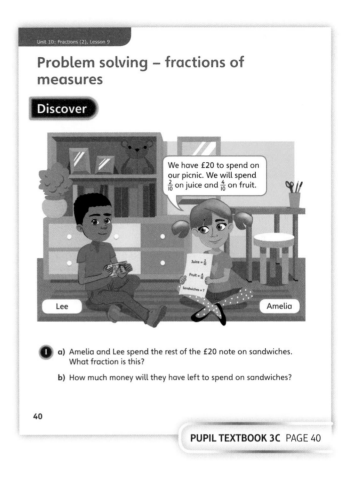

PUPIL TEXTBOOK 3C PAGE 40

Share

WAYS OF WORKING Whole class teacher led

ASK

- Question ❶ b): *To work out the fraction of the money that is left, what information do we need to know?*
- Question ❶ b): *Each $\frac{1}{10}$ of £20 is £2. If $\frac{4}{10}$ is left for sandwiches, how much money is this? How much has been spent on juice and fruit? How do you know? How can you check your answer?*

IN FOCUS To solve the question, children need to be confident in adding and subtracting fractions within a whole. For question ❶ a), discuss Astrid's suggestion. Explore how they can use a fraction strip to find the answer.

STRENGTHEN Set up two fraction strips at the front of the class. Divide both strips into ten equal parts. Cross out two of the bars on the first fraction strip and write: 'Juice: $1 - \frac{2}{10} = \frac{8}{10}$'. Cross out four of the bars on the second fraction strip and write: 'Fruit: $\frac{8}{10} - \frac{4}{10} = \frac{4}{10}$'. Answer: $\frac{4}{10}$ of the money is left to spend on sandwiches.' Ask: *Is this answer correct? How can you explain it? What does each step represent?*

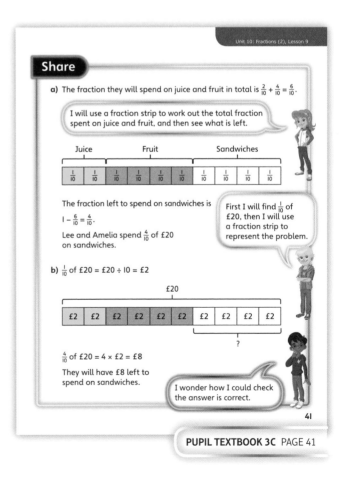

PUPIL TEXTBOOK 3C PAGE 41

Think together

Whole class teacher led (I do, We do, You do)

ASK

- Question **1** a): *How can you find the fraction of the oranges left?*
- Question **2** : *What is the question asking? What clues will help you to solve the question? Have you used all the information given? How can you check your answer?*
- Question **2** : *Do you have to find the actual amounts to be able to compare them?*

IN FOCUS Question **3** a) is a two-step question. First, children need to find the total amount, and then they need to subtract the answer from 1. Question **3** b) encourages children to consider alternative ways of solving the same problem, and to assess which method they prefer.

STRENGTHEN Discuss Astrid and Flo's suggestions in question **3** . Ask: *Can you recognise a difference between the methods? What answer does each method give? Can you give the answer in a different way?* For support, children may wish to use a bar model and colour in the fractions already walked, to give a visual indication of the distance left to go.

DEEPEN Encourage children to model question **3** by drawing their own representations, such as a number line, bar model or other appropriate image. Ask: *Which method do you prefer?* Listen for clear explanations and a systematic approach to solving the task.

ASSESSMENT CHECKPOINT Children should understand the questions and explain what is required. They should be able to explain the operations used to solve the question and demonstrate using manipulatives.

ANSWERS

Question **1** a): $\frac{1}{6}$ of the oranges are left.

Question **1** b): 2 kg of oranges are left.

Question **2** A, C and F on the large table; B, D and E on the small table.

Question **3** a): They have $\frac{2}{8}$ of the journey left to walk. They have 4 km left to walk.

Question **3** b): Children's answers will vary.

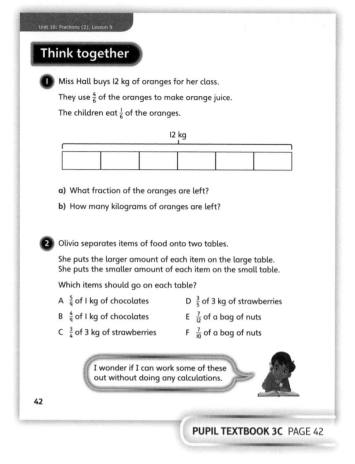

PUPIL TEXTBOOK 3C PAGE 42

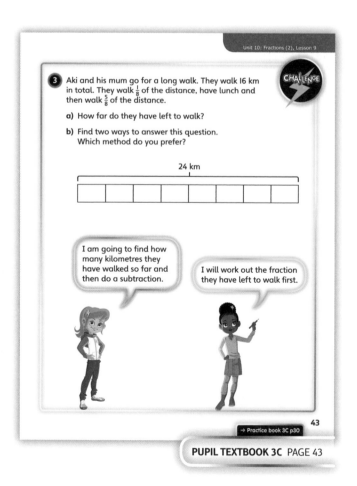

PUPIL TEXTBOOK 3C PAGE 43

Practice

WAYS OF WORKING Independent thinking

IN FOCUS Question **2** offers the opportunity to work with fractions of measurements, without finding the actual amounts. The amounts stay the same, so children need to pay attention to the fractions compared in each case.

STRENGTHEN For questions **3** and **4**, encourage children to use a fraction strip, number line, or both, to work through the steps of the problem. Remind them to read the question carefully and record their findings. Encourage children to label their findings, so they can follow their work and check the answer at the end.

DEEPEN Question **5** challenges children's ability to solve problems. They will need to be systematic, and organise their thinking and results. Deepen their understanding by asking them to represent the problem pictorially. Draw the original sunflower and label its height as 12 cm. Repeat for week 1 and week 2, labelling each flower with both its height in cm, and the fractional amount it has grown.

ASSESSMENT CHECKPOINT At this point, children should be confident in problem solving with fractions of measurements. They should be able to use multiple representations for a question and follow a systematic approach to solve problems.

ANSWERS Answers for the **Practice** part of the lesson appear in the separate **Practice and Reflect answer guide**.

Reflect

WAYS OF WORKING Independent thinking

IN FOCUS Give children an opportunity to independently develop their reasoning. Ask: *What advice can you give Olivia? What method would you use? Why?* Encourage children to compare their method with their partner. Whose method is the more efficient?

ASSESSMENT CHECKPOINT Children should be increasingly confident in solving different types of problem independently. They first make sense of the problem, and then use the information given to identify what is required. Children are confident using different types of representation to solve fraction problems.

ANSWERS Answers for the **Reflect** part of the lesson appear in the separate **Practice and Reflect answer guide**.

After the lesson ⏸

- What opportunities will children have to compare fractions of measures outside this lesson?
- What opportunities will children have to problem-solve independently?
- Are they confident in choosing different types of representation to solve problems?

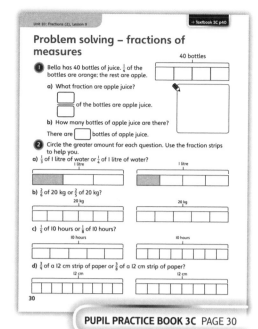

PUPIL PRACTICE BOOK 3C PAGE 30

PUPIL PRACTICE BOOK 3C PAGE 31

PUPIL PRACTICE BOOK 3C PAGE 32

75

End of unit check

Don't forget the *Power Maths* unit assessment grid on p26.

WAYS OF WORKING Group work adult led

IN FOCUS

- Question ❶ assesses children's ability to recognise equivalent fractions to $\frac{2}{3}$. Ask: *How can you use the number line to check your answer?*
- Question ❷ assesses children's ability to find the missing numerator or denominator of equivalent fractions. Ask: *What representations can you use to help you with this question?*
- Question ❸ assesses children's ability to compare unit fractions. Ask: *Can you explain how you found the answer? How do you compare unit fractions?*
- Question ❹ assesses children's ability to add and subtract fractions to make 1. Ask: *For each of these calculations, how can 1 be represented as a fraction? Why?*
- Question ❺ assesses children's ability to solve a problem by adding and subtracting fractions. Ask: *Can you solve the question in two ways?*
- Question ❻ assesses children's ability to find fractions of measures. Ask: *Can you find two answers?*
- Question ❼ is a SATS-style question and assesses children's ability to order non-unit fractions based on their size. Ask: *Which is the smallest fraction? How do you know?*

ANSWERS AND COMMENTARY

Children will demonstrate mastery by finding equivalent fractions and comparing fractions. They can use bar models and number lines to support their answers. Children can add and subtract fractions with confidence and can solve fraction problems including solving problems of fractions of measures.

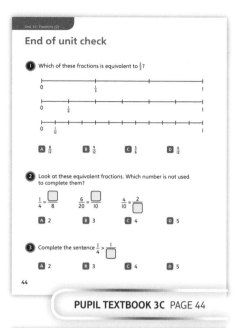

PUPIL TEXTBOOK 3C PAGE 44

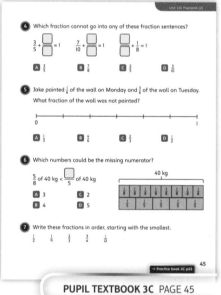

PUPIL TEXTBOOK 3C PAGE 45

Q	A	WRONG ANSWERS AND MISCONCEPTIONS	STRENGTHENING UNDERSTANDING
1	A	Choosing B or D may indicate a lack of understanding about using number lines.	To help children gain fluency in their understanding of fractions: • Make sure they have access to a fraction wall throughout the day. • Ensure all the representations of number lines are labelled clearly. • Give children access to fraction rods throughout the day. • Ensure children have access to unit fractions made of different numbers of equal parts.
2	C	Choosing A, B or D may indicate a lack of understanding about identifying equivalent fractions.	
3	D	Choosing A or B may indicate a lack of understanding about how to compare unit fractions. Choosing C may indicate that children misread the question.	
4	A	Choosing B, C or D may indicate that children lack experience in adding and subtracting fractions to make one whole.	
5	A	Choosing B may indicate children misread the question. Choosing C or D may indicate a lack of understanding of how to subtract fractions and identify equivalent fractions.	
6	B, D	Choosing A or C may indicate that children lack an understanding of comparing fractions of measures.	
7	$\frac{1}{12}, \frac{1}{9}, \frac{1}{2}, \frac{2}{3}, \frac{3}{4}$	Check children have looked at both the numerator and denominator.	

My journal

WAYS OF WORKING Independent thinking

ANSWERS AND COMMENTARY

Children may record answers such as those shown below.

When comparing the circle to the square:
- They are unit fractions and the first fraction is smaller than the second.
- The more parts a unit is divided into, the smaller the size of each part.
- Looking at a fraction wall, the bigger the denominator, the smaller the size of the bar. Some children may prove this using real examples and show that, for example $\frac{1}{3} < \frac{1}{2}$ or $\frac{1}{10} < \frac{1}{8}$.

When comparing the triangle with the pentagon:
- The denominators are the same so the greater the numerator, the greater the fraction.
- If I look at a fraction strip split into 5 equal parts, the more parts I have, the bigger the fraction is.
- Some children may prove this by using real examples and show that, for example, $\frac{4}{5} > \frac{2}{5}$.

If children are finding it difficult to give reasons for their answers, ask: *What does the numerator show? What does the denominator show? Show me the fractions in the number line. Which one is bigger?*

Power check

WAYS OF WORKING Independent thinking

ASK
- *What did you know about adding and subtracting fractions before you started this unit? What new things have you learnt?*
- *How confident do you feel about adding and subtracting fractions? How does it differ from adding and subtracting with whole numbers?*
- *What do you feel you could improve on in this unit? What do you need more help or practice with?*

Power puzzle

WAYS OF WORKING Pair work

IN FOCUS This game will assess children's ability to add and subtract fractions with the same denominator. Children can use a bar model or number line to support their answers and show their calculations clearly.

ANSWERS AND COMMENTARY When using three cards, some children are not sure whether to add or subtract first. Provide more opportunities to practise counting on and back on a number line using fraction steps. Encourage children to pay attention to the result. Does it change depending on which calculation they do first?

After the unit

- Is your classroom a 'fraction-rich' environment? How many opportunities are there for children to engage with fractions around the school environment? Are the fraction representatives visible and available for all children to use?

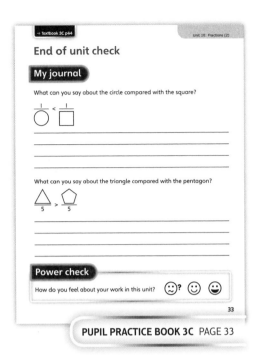

PUPIL PRACTICE BOOK 3C PAGE 33

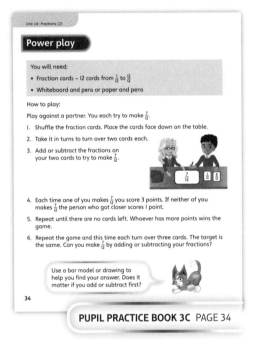

PUPIL PRACTICE BOOK 3C PAGE 34

Strengthen and **Deepen** activities for this unit can be found in the *Power Maths* online subscription.

Unit II
Time

Don't forget to watch the Unit 11 video!

Mastery Expert tip! "Look for real-life learning opportunities. Ask children to write the timetable of all Year 3 classes using 12- and 24-hour time, and to ask the teachers which they prefer and why. They can then discuss why they think one is more popular than the other."

WHY THIS UNIT IS IMPORTANT

This unit is important because it will help to develop children's understanding of the length of a day, and their awareness of times of day of which they may have little real-life experience. These concepts will be used for reading, estimating and measuring time, and in problem-solving contexts.

WHERE THIS UNIT FITS

→ Unit 10: Fractions

→ **Unit 11: Time**

→ Unit 12: Angles and properties of shape

In this unit, children will begin by recapping their understanding of time from Year 2. They will develop a deeper understanding of the length of a year, a month, a day, an hour, a minute and a second, and will use this to solve problems involving reading and measuring time.

Before they start this unit, it is expected that children:
- know the number of minutes in an hour, and read and write time on a clock to five minutes
- know the months of the year and key dates (including everyday usage)
- have some prior knowledge of everyday usage of time and o'clock times that occur throughout the day
- are familiar with moving from a start time through a duration to an end time.

ASSESSING MASTERY

Children who have mastered this unit know the number of days and months in a year, and the number of days in each month. They can explain what a leap year is and apply this in different contexts. They understand that there are 24 hours in a day, 60 minutes in an hour and 60 seconds in a minute, and can use this to estimate times. Children can tell time on analogue clocks to 5 minutes and to the nearest minute. They use am and pm appropriately and can read 12-hour and 24-hour analogue and digital clocks, including Roman numerals.

COMMON MISCONCEPTIONS	STRENGTHENING UNDERSTANDING	GOING DEEPER
Children think that one day begins when they wake up and ends when they go to bed.	Discuss how sunrise and sunset differ between countries. When is it light/ dark in the evenings? Does it change in the summer holidays?	Ask children to discuss if they notice the sunset and sunrise times changing during the different seasons.
Children may think that the hour hand always points directly to a number.	Show four school activities. Children draw minute and hour hands on clocks to match and put the activities in order.	Give children four clocks with just the hour hand showing four different times within an hour. Children should put the clocks in order. Ask: *Where could the minute hand be?*
Children try to find end time by adding duration to start time minutes to the next hour; for example, start: 12 minutes to 4, duration: 10 minutes, end: 22 minutes to 4.	Provide real examples of duration (such as cooking instructions). Ask children what the end time might be, given a specific start time.	Look at a local bus timetable. Ask: *Where can you travel to if you leave now and need to arrive at another stop before X am?*

Unit II: Time

WAYS OF WORKING

Go through the unit starter pages of the **Textbook** and introduce the unit focus. Use the characters to explore different ways of working.

STRUCTURES AND REPRESENTATIONS

Analogue and digital clock: These models are used regularly to represent 12-hour times; some analogue clocks use Roman numerals and digital clocks can also show 24-hour times. Children will also complete analogue clock faces with no hands, to demonstrate their understanding.

Number line: This model helps children to visualise the order of numbers. It can help them to count on and back in minutes from a given start time, and to identify patterns within the count. In this unit, the number line will be used to represent minutes within an hour, so will go from 0 to 60.

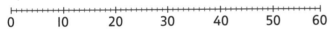

Bar model: This model helps children to find the time left in problem-solving questions.

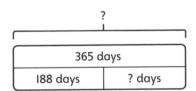

KEY LANGUAGE

There is some key language that children will need to know as part of the learning in this unit.

→ month, year, leap year
→ January, February, March, April, May, June, July, August, September, October, November, December
→ day, hour, minute, second
→ midnight, midday/noon
→ hour hand, minute hand, past, to, half past, o'clock, quarter past, quarter to, Roman numerals
→ longer, shorter, the same, units, last, convert, how long, left, passed, fastest, slowest
→ 12-hour clock, 24-hour clock
→ start time, end time, duration, time taken, finish, forwards, backwards, twice
→ daytime, night time, around the clock, am, pm
→ morning, afternoon, evening, night.

PUPIL TEXTBOOK 3C PAGE 46

PUPIL TEXTBOOK 3C PAGE 47

79

Months and years

Learning focus

In this lesson, children will learn what a year is and explain what a leap year is. They will learn the number of days in each month.

Small steps

→ Previous step: Problem solving – fractions of measures
→ **This step: Months and years**
→ Next step: Hours in a day

NATIONAL CURRICULUM LINKS

Year 3 Measurement

Know the number of seconds in a minute and the number of days in each month, year and leap year.

ASSESSING MASTERY

Children know the number of days and months in a year and can say the number of days in each month. Children can explain what a leap year is and apply the concept in different contexts.

COMMON MISCONCEPTIONS

Children may not see the difference between calendar facts that are fixed each year (months in the year, days in each month – apart from February) and those that change (the days of the week that individual dates fall on). Ask:
• *True or false? 1. All years have 365 days. 2. All years have 12 months.*

STRENGTHENING UNDERSTANDING

If children cannot remember how many days are in each month, ask them to make fists of both hands. From the left, point to knuckles and dips between knuckles as we say the months (ignore the thumbs). Any month we say when we point to a knuckle has 31 days; other months have 30 days, apart from February (28, or 29 if it is a leap year).

GOING DEEPER

Ask children to find if a year is a leap year. If it can be divided by 4 but not 100, it is a leap year. If it can be divided by 4 and by 100, it is also a leap year. If it can be divided by 100, but not 400, it is not a leap year.

KEY LANGUAGE

In lesson: month, year, day, week, calendar, January, February, March, April, May, June, July, August, September, October, November, December, leap year, adjust

Other language to be used by the teacher: common year

STRUCTURES AND REPRESENTATIONS

bar model

RESOURCES

Mandatory: calendars

 In the eTextbook of this lesson, you will find interactive links to a selection of teaching tools.

Before you teach

• Can children name the months of the year?
• Can children name the days of the week?

Discover

WAYS OF WORKING Pair work

ASK

- Question **1** a): *What does the picture show? How many months are shown in the picture?*

IN FOCUS Question **1** a) brings attention to the number of days in each month. The picture should encourage children to look for the date of the last day in each month, as this will show how many days are in that month. For example, January's last day is Wednesday the 31st. January has 31 days.

PRACTICAL TIPS Make sure each pair or group has a copy of the same calendar, so they can discuss the number of days in each month.

ANSWERS

Question **1** a): There are 12 months in a year. January, March, May, July, August, October and December have 31 days. April, June, September and November have 30 days. February has 28 days.

Question **1** b): There are 365 days in a year.

Months and years

Discover

1 a) How many months are in a year?
   How many days are in each month?

   b) How many days are in a year?

48

PUPIL TEXTBOOK 3C PAGE 48

Share

WAYS OF WORKING Whole class teacher led

ASK

- Question **1** a): *Do you know any of the months of the year? What order do they come in? Try counting the months along your knuckles. Do you notice a pattern? How can you check how many days there are in one year?*

IN FOCUS This may be a good opportunity to clarify any misconceptions that children have.

Ensure children are confident that every year has 12 months, and every week has 7 days. Some children may think they need to count the number of days in each of the 12 months individually. Remind them that the calendar makes it clear how many days are in each month. Ensure children understand that leap years have 366 days, as February has an extra day (29 days) in these years.

STRENGTHEN Discuss special days. Ask: *What dates of the year are special to you?* Talk to children about dates they look forward to every year. Ask: *Can you find these dates in the calendar?* Provide a printout of a calendar for children to explore. Ask them to circle the last day of each month in the calendar. Then ask them to write how many days each month has, next to the name of the month. Ask: *What do you notice?*

Provide children with calendars for different years. Include a calendar for a leap year, for example 2016 or 2020. Ask: *If the years are different, what do you notice? Is this year a leap year?*

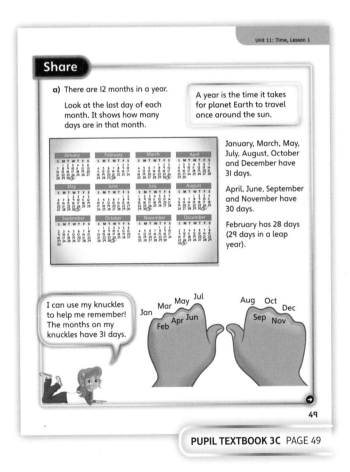

Share

a) There are 12 months in a year.

Look at the last day of each month. It shows how many days are in that month.

A year is the time it takes for planet Earth to travel once around the sun.

January, March, May, July, August, October and December have 31 days.

April, June, September and November have 30 days.

February has 28 days (29 days in a leap year).

I can use my knuckles to help me remember! The months on my knuckles have 31 days.

49

PUPIL TEXTBOOK 3C PAGE 49

Think together

WAYS OF WORKING Whole class teacher led (I do, We do, You do)

ASK

- Question **1**: *How many days are there in a week? If today is Monday 1st, what date will the next Monday be? If today is the 20th, what date is it tomorrow? What date was it yesterday?*
- Question **2**: *How many days are there in a common year? How can you use the bar model to work out how many days are left?*

IN FOCUS In question **2**, highlight the link between the number of days in the year and the bar model.

Question **3** asks children to use their knowledge of fractions to explain why leap years usually occur every 4 years. The bar model provides a visual connection between four $\frac{1}{4}$s and one whole.

STRENGTHEN For questions **2** and **3**, strengthen children's understanding of what a year is by showing a picture of Earth travelling around the Sun, so that children can visualise the journey.

$365\frac{1}{4}$ days is not exact, so some adjustments are made in deciding when there is a leap year and when there is not. If a year does not end in '00' and is a multiple of 4, then it is a leap year (for example 2212).

If a year ends in '00', to be a leap year the first 2 digits must be a multiple of 4. For example, 2400 is a leap year because 24 is a multiple of 4. However, 2100 is not a leap year because 21 is not a multiple of 4.

DEEPEN When children have solved question **3**, deepen their understanding by asking them to predict years that are leap years, and years that are not. Encourage them to explain their reasoning clearly.

ASSESSMENT CHECKPOINT Children know the number of days in a year. They can identify which months have 30 days and which have 31 days. They can differentiate between a leap year and a common year.

ANSWERS

Question **1** a): 15 April, 16 April, 17 April, 18 April, 19 April, 20 April, 21 April

Question **1** b): 23 July, 16 July, 9 July, 2 July

Question **2**: There are 177 days left in the year.

Question **3**: Four $\frac{1}{4}$ days make 1 whole day. So one extra day is added to the year in every leap year (29 February).

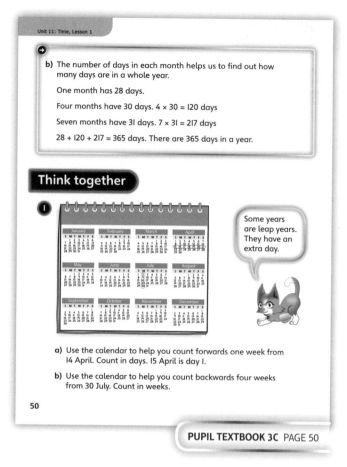

PUPIL TEXTBOOK 3C PAGE 50

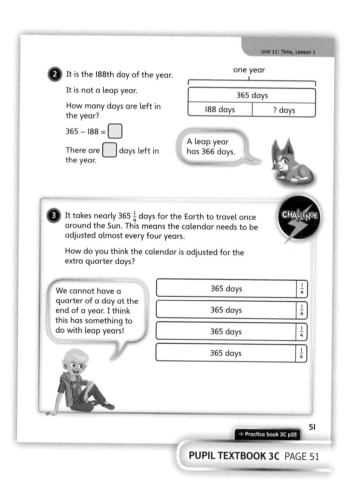

PUPIL TEXTBOOK 3C PAGE 51

Practice

WAYS OF WORKING Independent thinking

IN FOCUS When working independently on the questions in this section, children should continue to secure their understanding of how many days there are in a week, month and year. In question ❶, encourage children to circle the starting date. Some children may find it helpful to have access to a number line to help them count backwards and forwards to find the date in 1 week, 10 days and 14 days from a given date.

STRENGTHEN If children are finding it difficult to calculate how many days are left in question ❷, ask them to use a bar model similar to the one used in the lesson. Ask: *How many days are there in a leap year? Where in the bar model will you write that number?*

DEEPEN When children are working on question ❺, ask them to find two different solutions depending on the year. Ask: *Will the answer be the same in a leap year and in a common year? Can you predict what the difference will be?*

ASSESSMENT CHECKPOINT Children's knowledge of the number of days in each month should be secure. Children can relate the number of days in a year to the journey of the Earth orbiting the Sun, and understand why leap years exist.

ANSWERS Answers for the **Practice** part of the lesson appear in the separate **Practice and Reflect answer guide**.

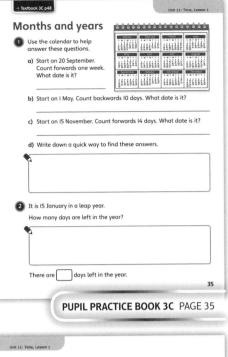

PUPIL PRACTICE BOOK 3C PAGE 35

PUPIL PRACTICE BOOK 3C PAGE 36

Reflect

WAYS OF WORKING Pair work

IN FOCUS Give children time to discuss with their partner whether the statement is true or not. Ask: *How can you be certain that the statement is true or false? Is there a way to check?* Once children have discussed their methods, give them time to write their explanations.

ASSESSMENT CHECKPOINT Look for clarity in children's explanations. They should make reference to the fact that leap years have an extra day, as February has 29 days in a leap year. Additionally, they may give examples of years that are leap years, and years that are not leap years.

ANSWERS Answers for the **Reflect** part of the lesson appear in the separate **Practice and Reflect answer guide**.

After the lesson

- Do children know how many days there are in each month?
- Do children know how many days there are in a leap year?
- Can children explain why there are leap years and common years?

Hours in a day

Learning focus

Children will be introduced to 24 hours in a day including noon and midnight. They will learn how many days in a week, as part of a month.

Small steps

→ Previous step: Months and years
→ **This step: Hours in a day**
→ Next step: Estimating time

NATIONAL CURRICULUM LINKS

Year 3 Measurement
- Estimate and read time with increasing accuracy to the nearest minute; record and compare time in terms of seconds, minutes and hours; use vocabulary such as o'clock, am/pm, morning, afternoon, noon and midnight.
- Tell and write the time from an analogue clock, including using Roman numerals from I to XII, and 12-hour and 24-hour clocks.

ASSESSING MASTERY

Children understand that there are 24 hours in a day and that a day runs from midnight until midnight. Children are able to apply this in different contexts.

COMMON MISCONCEPTIONS

Some children think one day is only during daytime, or begins when they wake up and ends when they go to bed. Ask:
- *How many hours in a day? How many hours have you counted? Do these two amounts match up?*

Some children think that the hour hand goes around the clock once a day. Ask:
- *When does your birthday start? How many hours are you asleep? How many hours are you at school?*

STRENGTHENING UNDERSTANDING

Give opportunities to discuss how sunrise and sunset differ from winter to summer, and in other countries. Ask: *When is it light/dark in the evenings? Do your school days change? Does it change in the summer holidays?*

Encourage discussion about how 'one day' is not linked with sunlight or daytime.

GOING DEEPER

Ask children to investigate how many hours are between sunrise and sunset today. Draw a timeline from midnight to midnight labelling each hour. Emphasise that there are 24 hours in a day including noon and midnight. Ask children to think of 24 activities, one that could happen each hour in one day, and place them on their timeline.

KEY LANGUAGE

In lesson: day, hour, midnight, midday/noon, morning, night, hour hand, minute hand

Other language to be used by the teacher: sunset, sunrise, afternoon, evening, twice, night time, duration

STRUCTURES AND REPRESENTATIONS

bar model, number line

RESOURCES

Optional: analogue clock manipulatives, pictures of sunset and sunrise, laminated pictures of clock faces, 24 pictures of activities linked with each hour in the day, soft toys for role play

 In the eTextbook of this lesson, you will find interactive links to a selection of teaching tools.

Before you teach

- Do children use o'clock times to describe events?
- How can you give real-life experiences of time?

Discover

WAYS OF WORKING Pair work

ASK

• Question ❶ a): *What does the picture show? Which of the children is correct?*

IN FOCUS The answers the children give offer an opportunity to discuss when the day starts and ends, and how many hours there are in a day. Emphasise that one of the children says the day ends at midnight the next day, to encourage children to realise that 24 hours have passed.

PRACTICAL TIPS Try to give each pair or group access to an analogue clock. Provide pictures of motorway workers, street cleaners, nurses and doctors. Ask: *What time are their working hours?* Include examples of working hours throughout a 24-hour day.

ANSWERS

Question ❶ a): The start of the day is 12 o'clock at night. This is called midnight. The end of the day is the next midnight. This is when a new day begins.

Question ❶ b): There are 24 hours in one day.

PUPIL TEXTBOOK 3C PAGE 52

Share

WAYS OF WORKING Whole class teacher led

ASK

• *Where have you come across the idea of 24 hours before?*
• *Can you think of an example from real-life concerned with a new day beginning at midnight? (For example, New Year's Eve, the fairy tale Cinderella)*

IN FOCUS Use this opportunity to correct potential misconceptions and give children the opportunity to show their understanding of the hours in a day. Ask them to explain where each child has gone wrong with their reasoning. What real-life examples can children give to justify their answers?

STRENGTHEN Challenge children to explore hints from everyday life that show there are 24 hours in a day. For example, a 24-hour petrol station, a 24-hour emergency care vet.

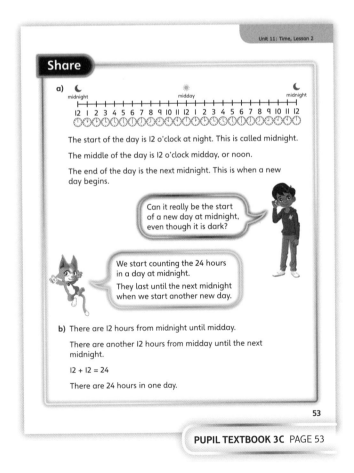

PUPIL TEXTBOOK 3C PAGE 53

Think together

WAYS OF WORKING Whole class teacher led (I do, We do, You do)

ASK

- Question **1**: *How do you know when to start counting in hours? How do you know when to stop counting in hours?*
- Question **2**: *To move through 24 hours, how many times will the hour hand travel around the clock?*

IN FOCUS Questions **1** and **2** offer a good opportunity to reinforce the understanding that a day is made up of 24 hours, which is twice round the clock. Use a model to show how the hands move around a clock face. Encourage children to use analogue clocks to move through 24 hours, counting the hours as they do so. Ask children to think about the number of minutes in an hour. Ask: *How many times does the minute hand go around the clock in one day? What about the hour hand?*

STRENGTHEN In question **3**, if children are finding it difficult to work out the number of hours, ask them to use the information from the previous two questions. Provide them with three clock faces. The first clock represents Tuesday at 1 o'clock, the second clock represents Wednesday at 1 o'clock and the third clock represents Wednesday at 3 o'clock. Ask: *How can you make it easier to compare the times? How many hours are there from Tuesday at 1 o'clock to Wednesday at 1 o'clock? Which of the clocks represents Wednesday at 1 o'clock?*

DEEPEN Ask children to think about the number of days in one week and the number of hours in one day. They could use a bar model to show how to work out the number of hours in one week and why. Ask: *How many hours from 1 o'clock in the morning on Tuesday, to 3 o'clock in the morning next week on Wednesday? How did you come to that solution?*

ASSESSMENT CHECKPOINT Children should be confident that there are 24 hours in a day and 7 days in a week. They should use their knowledge of hours and time to recognise and explain how they can find 24 hours from a given time. Children are confident that the day starts at 12 o'clock midnight and ends at 12 o'clock midnight the day after.

ANSWERS

Question **1**: One day lasts for 24 hours. It starts at 12 o'clock midnight and ends at 12 o'clock midnight the following day.

Question **2** a): 24 times

Question **2** b): 2 times

Question **3** a): 26 hours

Question **3** b): 168 hours

PUPIL TEXTBOOK 3C PAGE 54

PUPIL TEXTBOOK 3C PAGE 55

Practice

WAYS OF WORKING Independent thinking

IN FOCUS Question ❶ gives children a pictorial representation of the time to scaffold their independent learning. Provide plastic clocks or laminated clock pictures to support children's work.

Question ❷ revisits the potential misconception that the day lasts from 12 midnight until 12 noon.

STRENGTHEN Some children may find the amount of information in question ❷ challenging, and identifying what they need to do. Discuss the question prior to the task. If any children are still unsure, offer them a timeline with the hours of the day recorded on it. Ask children to explain each other's answers and clarify any misconceptions. Encourage children to use the correct vocabulary.

DEEPEN When solving question ❻, deepen children's reasoning. After colouring the first activity, ask: How many hours are left? What fraction of the day have you spent in total?

THINK DIFFERENTLY Question ❹ links fractions and time by using grids of 24. Children are used to linking time with a clock face. This question offers the opportunity for children to think of the day as a unit made of 24 equal parts. Ask children to think of different ways to represent a 24-hour day. Choose different representations and show them to the whole class. Ask: How do they differ? What do they have in common?

ASSESSMENT CHECKPOINT Children should be able to confidently explain that there are 24 hours in a day. They should be able to find the time 24 hours in the future and explain how the time stays the same and the day changes. Children should be able to solve simple problems confidently using their knowledge of hours in a day and days in a week.

ANSWERS Answers for the **Practice** part of the lesson appear in the separate **Practice and Reflect answer guide**.

Reflect

WAYS OF WORKING Pair work

IN FOCUS Once children have discussed the mistake that Olivia has made, ask them: What advice would you give Olivia to correct her mistake? How would you prove that Olivia is wrong? How would you prove to her that the day begins at 12 o'clock midnight, and ends at 12 o'clock midnight the day after?

ASSESSMENT CHECKPOINT Children should recognise that there can be confusion over when the day starts and ends. Children should be able to explain to Olivia that different people get up and go to bed at different times. Even she may go to bed and wake up at different times throughout the year. Children may use different representations to show that there are 24 hours in a day, and that the length of a day does not depend on our sleeping patterns.

ANSWERS Answers for the **Reflect** part of the lesson appear in the separate **Practice and Reflect answer guide**.

After the lesson

- Are children confident that there are 24 hours in a day?
- How did you challenge children's assumptions about times they were not familiar with?
- Are children confident that the day starts at 12 o'clock midnight and ends at 12 o'clock midnight the day after?

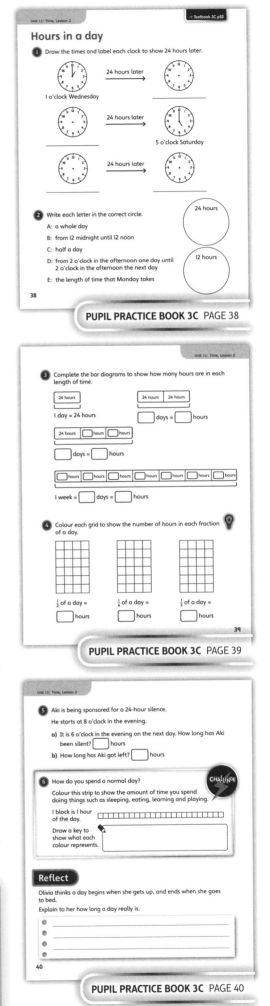

PUPIL PRACTICE BOOK 3C PAGE 38

PUPIL PRACTICE BOOK 3C PAGE 39

PUPIL PRACTICE BOOK 3C PAGE 40

Estimating time

Learning focus

In this lesson, children estimate the time just by looking at the hour hand.

Small steps

→ Previous step: Hours in a day
→ **This step: Estimating time**
→ Next step: Telling time to 5 minutes

NATIONAL CURRICULUM LINKS

Year 3 Measurement

Tell and write the time from an analogue clock, including using Roman numerals from I to XII, and 12-hour and 24-hour clocks.

ASSESSING MASTERY

Children know that there are 60 minutes in 1 hour. They can use this information to estimate times where only the hour hand is shown.

COMMON MISCONCEPTIONS

Children may think they need both clock hands to tell the time, not recognising that they can use just the hour hand. Ask:
• *Is the hour hand pointing right at the number? Where is it pointing?*

Children may think that the hour hand points directly to a number (for example, at quarter past 8, it points directly at the 8). Ask:
• *Compare some times. What number is the hour hand pointing to? What is the minute hand pointing to?*

STRENGTHENING UNDERSTANDING

Provide pictures of four different clocks, each showing the time of an activity in the school day (such as registration, lesson, break, lunch). Ask children to draw the minute and hour hands on blank clock-faces and put the activities in order. By drawing the hands themselves, children will notice that they do not always point directly at the numbers.

GOING DEEPER

Provide four different clocks with just the hour hand, showing times within an hour (such as quarter past 9, half past 9, quarter to 10 and 10 o'clock). Ask children to put the clocks in order. Ask: *Where could the minute hand be?* This will develop their ability to recognise times. It also links time with fractions, and awareness of quarter or half or three quarters of the journey that the hour and minute hands travel in an hour.

KEY LANGUAGE

In lesson: time, estimate, hour hand, minute hand, o'clock, half past, half-way, quarter to

Other language to be used by the teacher: quarter past, analogue

RESOURCES

Mandatory: analogue clock manipulatives, flash cards ('o'clock', 'half past', 'quarter past', 'quarter to')

 In the eTextbook of this lesson, you will find interactive links to a selection of teaching tools.

Before you teach

• Can children easily see the time in the classroom?
• Can they access a variety of analogue clocks?

Discover

Pair work

ASK

- Question ❶: *How many minutes are there in an hour?*
- Question ❶ a): *How many minutes does it take for the hour hand to move between two numbers?*
- Question ❶ b): *Where is the hour hand pointing? What number has the hour hand passed? What number is it trying to reach?*
- Question ❶ b): *Can you estimate what the time may be?*

IN FOCUS Use the picture to recap and briefly assess children's current understanding. Begin by reinforcing that the hour hand does not jump from hour to hour, but travels between the numbers gradually.

PRACTICAL TIPS Unscrew the minute hand from the classroom clock if possible, or use a clock that has only the hour hand. Challenge children to estimate the time throughout the day, just by looking at the hour hand.

ANSWERS

Question ❶ a): We can use the position of the hour hand to help estimate the time. At an o'clock time, the hour hand points directly at a number. At a half-past time, it points half-way between two numbers.

Question ❶ b): We can estimate that the time is about half past 10.

Unit 11: Time, Lesson 3

Estimating time

Discover

❶ a) How can we estimate the time, even though the minute hand has fallen off?

b) What time do you estimate it is?

56

PUPIL TEXTBOOK 3C PAGE 56

Share

Whole class teacher led

ASK

- Question ❶ a): *How many minutes are there in half an hour? Quarter of an hour?*
- Question ❶ a): *How many minutes does it take for the hour hand to move half-way between two numbers? To move a quarter of the way between two numbers?*
- Question ❶ a): *Does the hour hand move quickly or slowly?*
- Question ❶ b): *What time do you think the clock face shows? Is this the actual time or an estimate? Why?*

IN FOCUS Children need to be confident with estimating. Clarify the misconception that both hands are needed to tell the time. Get children to estimate times on clocks. Ask them to draw times onto blank clock faces.

STRENGTHEN Children need to be confident with the concept that 1 hour is 60 minutes, 15 minutes is a quarter of an hour and 30 minutes is half an hour. They need to know that at quarter past 2, the hour hand has moved $\frac{1}{4}$ of the way from number 2 to number 3; and that at quarter to 4, the hour hand is $\frac{3}{4}$ of the way past the number 3, and $\frac{1}{4}$ away from the number 4. Ask: *If we can estimate the time without the minute hand, why do we even need a minute hand?* Discuss where estimating can be used in real life and where using the exact time is necessary.

Unit 11: Time, Lesson 3

Share

a) The hour hand takes one hour to move between two numbers.

We can use its position to estimate what the time is.

At an o'clock time, the hour hand points directly at a number.

At a half-past time, it has moved to half-way between two numbers.

The hour hand has now passed the half-way point. I will use this to help me estimate!

b) The hour hand is pointing half-way between the 10 and the 11.

We can estimate that the time is about half past 10.

57

PUPIL TEXTBOOK 3C PAGE 57

Think together

Whole class teacher led (I do, We do, You do)

ASK

- Question ❶: *If you continue the line the hour hand makes, where will it point? Has it reached half-way between 6 and 7? What is the time if it points half-way? What could the time be if it points less than half-way? More than half-way?*
- Question ❷: *Why do we say a quarter to 4? What does this mean? Where would the minute hand have been? Has the hour hand passed the number 4? How do you know? How can you find a quarter of something?*

IN FOCUS Questions ❶ and ❷ give children the opportunity to practise their recognition of 'half past', 'quarter past' and 'quarter to' times. Discuss the clues they can use to recognise what the time could be. Children have the opportunity to scaffold their knowledge of fractions in estimating the time accurately.

STRENGTHEN For all the questions in this section, ask children to make the times shown. Some children find it difficult to find 'a quarter to 4' using a clock that has 60 minutes marks. They think they need to find a quarter of the 5 notches between the numbers 3 and 4. Provide clocks without minute marks to begin with. Once children are confident in estimating, and to extend, provide clocks with different type of face to develop fluency.

DEEPEN Deepen question ❸, by allowing children to explore that 1 hour is made of 60 minutes. Give each child a circle and ask them to turn it into a clock. Ask: *Imagine you will be teaching younger children what a clock looks like. You need to be very clear when describing it. How can you show that the clock is made of 60 minutes? How can you show that all the minutes are the same? How many minutes are there from one number to the next?* Children may use the part-whole model (where the whole is made of 12 equal parts and each of the parts has 5 minutes) to explain that 1 hour has 60 minutes.

ASSESSMENT CHECKPOINT Children should be confident in their understanding that there are 60 minutes in one hour. They should know that the numbers around the clock do not link directly with the number of minutes in an hour.

ANSWERS

Question ❶: The time is about quarter past 6.

Question ❷: The hour hand should be $\frac{3}{4}$ of the way past the number 3 and $\frac{1}{4}$ away from the number 4.

Question ❸ a): There are 60 minutes in one hour.

Question ❸ b): Each small mark is worth 12 minutes.

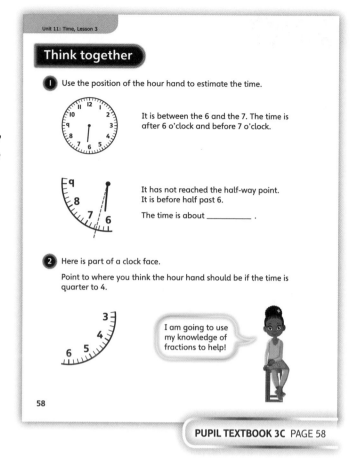

PUPIL TEXTBOOK 3C PAGE 58

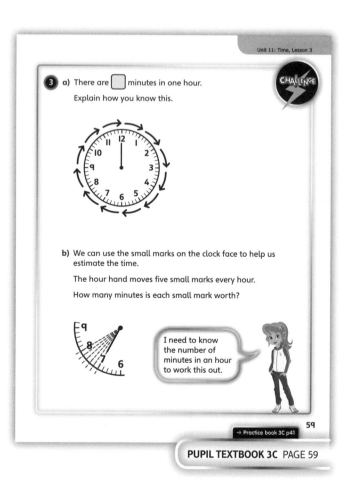

PUPIL TEXTBOOK 3C PAGE 59

Practice

Independent thinking

IN FOCUS Questions **1**, **2** and **3** practise vocabulary relating to times children know. Children can visualise the position of the hour and minute hands (use flash cards). Ask: *What is different between 'o'clock', 'half past', 'quarter past' and 'quarter to'. Can you describe the position of the minute hand? What about the hour hand?*

STRENGTHEN Question **5** strengthens 'half past', 'quarter past' and 'quarter to'. Time is linked with fractions. Ask: *How many minutes in an hour? How can you use this to work out the number of minutes in $\frac{1}{2}$ an hour? How many minutes in $\frac{1}{4}$ of an hour?*

DEEPEN Question **4** revisits a misconception that both clock hands are needed to estimate the time. If children recognise that Emma is wrong, they can write some advice using pictures and appropriate vocabulary.

ASSESSMENT CHECKPOINT Children understand the role of the hour hand in an analogue clock. They explain clearly how the hour hand looks for an o'clock time, half past, quarter past and quarter to. Children should confidently estimate these times. They can draw times on blank clocks themselves or make them using manipulatives.

ANSWERS Answers for the **Practice** part of the lesson appear in the separate **Practice and Reflect answer guide**.

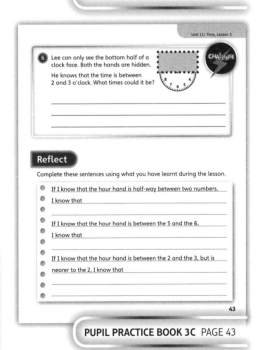

PUPIL PRACTICE BOOK 3C PAGE 41

PUPIL PRACTICE BOOK 3C PAGE 42

Reflect

Pair work

IN FOCUS This question allows children to reason and justify how they can estimate the time by looking at the position of the hour hand.

ASSESSMENT CHECKPOINT Children can estimate the time by thinking about the position of the hour hand only. Listen to their discussion and reasoning as they describe differences between an o'clock time, a half-past time, minutes past and minutes to.

ANSWERS Answers for the **Reflect** part of the lesson appear in the separate **Practice and Reflect answer guide**.

After the lesson

- Are children able to estimate time?
- How will you build in more opportunities for them to practise the skills they have learnt throughout the school day?
- What advice can you give them to practise time outside school?

PUPIL PRACTICE BOOK 3C PAGE 43

Telling time to 5 minutes

Learning focus

Children will continue to develop their ability to tell the time to 5 minutes and link this to prior knowledge of reading analogue clocks by reading the 5-minute intervals.

Small steps

→ Previous step: Estimating time
→ **This step: Telling time to 5 minutes**
→ Next step: Telling time to the minute (1)

NATIONAL CURRICULUM LINKS

Year 3 Measurement

Tell and write the time from an analogue clock, including using Roman numerals from I to XII, and 12-hour and 24-hour clocks.

ASSESSING MASTERY

Children can tell times displayed on analogue clocks to 5 minutes (including all 5 minutes past and to the hour). Children will be able to transfer this knowledge when using clocks with Roman numerals.

COMMON MISCONCEPTIONS

Some will mix up the roles of the hour and minute hands. They think '10 to' means the hour hand points to the number 10. Ask:

• *It is 10 o'clock. Where is the hour hand? Where is the minute hand? What do they show us?*

STRENGTHENING UNDERSTANDING

Show children an analogue clock and ask them to read around the clock in steps of 5 minutes, for example, *5 past, 10 past,* etc. Change the time on the clock. Repeat with a mixture of 'past' and 'to' times.

GOING DEEPER

Ask: *What different activities can you do within an hour?* For example, wake up, brush teeth, get ready for school, have breakfast. Show these as multiples of 5-minute times on the analogue clock. Begin with times past the hour, then times to the hour. Ask: *Can you make a timetable of the activities you chose?*

KEY LANGUAGE

In lesson: hour hand, minute hand, minutes to, o'clock, Roman numerals

Other language to be used by the teacher: minutes past, quarter past, quarter to, half past

RESOURCES

Mandatory: analogue clock manipulatives, flash cards ('o'clock', 'half past', 'quarter past', 'quarter to'), analogue clock and written time flash cards

 In the eTextbook of this lesson, you will find interactive links to a selection of teaching tools.

Before you teach

• Are children confident in counting in 5s?
• What other practical resources will you provide?

Discover

Telling time to 5 minutes

WAYS OF WORKING Pair work

ASK

- Question ❶ a): *What time does the clock show? What time is 1 hour before the time shown? What time is 1 hour later than the time shown?*
- Question ❶ b): *What time would the train have arrived if it had got there five minutes later? What time would the train have arrived if it got there five minutes earlier?*

IN FOCUS Use the picture to recap and briefly assess children's current understanding. Make sure they know that the numbers on the clock are for the hours, and not the minutes shown by the minute hand.

PRACTICAL TIPS Show examples of simple bus or train timetables. Ask: *Why is it important for trains and buses to leave at the same time each weekday? Why is it useful to know that they leave at the same time?*

ANSWERS

Question ❶ a): It has been 55 minutes since the last train left.

Question ❶ b): It will be 5 minutes until the next train leaves.

Discover

❶ a) How long has it been since the last train left?

b) How long will it be until the next train leaves?

60

PUPIL TEXTBOOK 3C PAGE 60

Share

WAYS OF WORKING Whole class teacher led

ASK

- Question ❶ a): *Do you know what 'on the hour' means? Why do you think we say this to mean 'at each o'clock time'?*
- Question ❶ a): *I think 45 minutes past 8, quarter to 9, and 15 minutes to 9 are all the same time. Is this true or false? How would you choose to say this time?*

IN FOCUS Use this opportunity to correct potential misconceptions. Point out times to five minutes during the lesson. Allow children to show the times on clock manipulatives, or get them to draw times onto blank clock faces, or call out times when shown different clocks. Ask: *What was the last five-minute time? What will be the next five-minute time? What will it look like?*

STRENGTHEN Point at each number around a clock face, starting at 1. First, ask children to say each number as you point to it. Repeat, this time asking children to count up in 5s as you go around the clock face, from 5 to 60. Repeat again, but now ask children to say *five past, ten past, quarter past, ... , half past, twenty-five to, ... , quarter to, ten to, ... o'clock.* Continue until they can get all the way round the clock with no mistakes.

Share

61

PUPIL TEXTBOOK 3C PAGE 61

Think together

Whole class teacher led (I do, We do, You do)

ASK

- Question ❶: *Compare a clock face with Roman numerals, with a clock face with standard numbers. How do they differ?*
- Question ❶: *If X = 10, V = 5 and I = 1, why do you think VIII = 8 and IX = 9?*
- Question ❶: *Is the time closer to 3 or 4 o'clock?*
- Question ❶: *How can you count backwards from 4 o'clock?*
- Question ❷: *What could you count to make it easier to read the minutes?*

IN FOCUS Questions ❶ and ❷ will help scaffold children's counting in 5-minutes intervals. Children are counting backwards from a number. Ask children to match the picture with an analogue clock face (with standard numbers and showing all the minute divisions).

STRENGTHEN You could draw out a large clock in the playground and ask children to walk around it, counting the 5-minute intervals. Make sure to reinforce the 'past' and 'to' elements of the clock face. In question ❸, children's understanding will be strengthened if they draw all the times they can think of. Ask: *Where would the minute hand be? Where would the hour hand be? How do you know you are correct?*

DEEPEN Challenge children in question ❸ by asking them to find as many answers as they can within 5 minutes. This will help them practise reading the time. It will also give them an opportunity to estimate and get a sense of what 5 minutes could be. To deepen their understanding even further, ask them to draw the times on a clock that uses Roman numerals.

ASSESSMENT CHECKPOINT At this point in the lesson, children should be more confident in telling the time to 5 minutes, by counting forwards and backwards in 5-minute intervals. They should be increasingly fluent in using 'minutes past' and 'minutes to' and reading the time using analogue clocks (including those with Roman numerals).

ANSWERS

Question ❶: There are 20 minutes until 4 o'clock. So, the time is twenty to 4.

Question ❷: 25 minutes past 1, 10 minutes to 9

Question ❸ a): Answers will vary, but should refer to the minute hand being in the first half of the clock, and the hour hand pointing between the 6 and the 7.

Question ❸ b): Answers will vary, but should refer to the minute hand being in the second half of the clock, and the hour hand pointing between the 9 and the 10.

Question ❸ c): Answers will vary, but should refer to the minute hand pointing to the '8' on the clock, and the hour hand pointing more than half-way between any two numbers.

PUPIL TEXTBOOK 3C PAGE 62

PUPIL TEXTBOOK 3C PAGE 63

Practice

WAYS OF WORKING Independent thinking

IN FOCUS Questions ❶ and ❷ scaffold children's understanding of reading an analogue clock in 5-minute intervals. It will help children to develop their fluency if you also use shaded representations of time, and clocks with Roman numerals and standard numbers.

STRENGTHEN For children finding question ❹ challenging, it may help to use a clock with moving hands. Children could make 6 o'clock, then move the minute hand a full turn. Ask: *What happens to the hour hand? Does it move? Is the time more than 6 o'clock? How do you know?*

DEEPEN Use question ❸ to deepen children's explanation and reasoning skills. Ask: *What part of the lesson did Lexi not understand? What would you say to explain her mistake? What should the answer have been? Can you shade the clock to show the journey of the minute hand?*

ASSESSMENT CHECKPOINT Children should be able to tell the time confidently, and not just by reading the numbers the minute and hour hands point to. They should be able to recognise and record different times on an analogue clock, including clocks with Roman numerals.

ANSWERS Answers for the **Practice** part of the lesson appear in the separate **Practice and Reflect answer guide**.

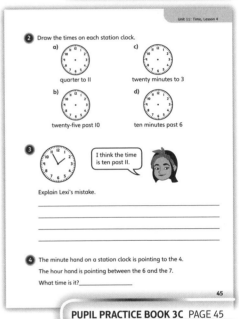

PUPIL PRACTICE BOOK 3C PAGE 44

PUPIL PRACTICE BOOK 3C PAGE 45

Reflect

WAYS OF WORKING Pair work

IN FOCUS Pay particular attention to children's reasoning when it comes to 'twenty-five past' and 'twenty-five to'. Ask: *Does a clock showing twenty-five minutes to 4 also show twenty-five minutes past 4? Can you draw both times? Can you explain how these times differ?*

ASSESSMENT CHECKPOINT Children should recognise that at 'twenty-five to', the minute hand points to the 7. Children should be able to explain their reasoning clearly. They may use a concrete representation or picture to justify their answer.

ANSWERS Answers for the **Reflect** part of the lesson appear in the separate **Practice and Reflect answer guide**.

After the lesson ⏸

- Have children recognised how the concepts they have learnt in the past four lessons link together?
- How will you reinforce this link?

PUPIL PRACTICE BOOK 3C PAGE 46

Telling time to the minute ❶

Learning focus

In this lesson, children will tell the time using 'minutes past' and 'minutes to' and using the 12-hour analogue clock. They will read and describe times to the nearest minute.

Small steps

→ Previous step: Telling time to 5 minutes
→ **This step: Telling time to the minute (1)**
→ Next step: Telling time to the minute (2)

NATIONAL CURRICULUM LINKS

Year 3 Measurement

Estimate and read time with increasing accuracy to the nearest minute; record and compare time in terms of seconds, minutes and hours; use vocabulary such as o'clock, am/pm, morning, afternoon, noon and midnight.

ASSESSING MASTERY

Children can tell times displayed on analogue clocks to the minute. Children recognise that there are 60 minutes in an hour, and are able to use this information when giving times past and to the hour.

COMMON MISCONCEPTIONS

Children may think that the minute hand moves straight from number to number. Ask:
• *How many minutes in an hour? How does the minute hand show this?*

Children may read 'five to 3' as' five to 2' because the hour hand is between the 2 and the 3. Ask:
• *What o'clock time has just happened? What o'clock time will come next?*

STRENGTHENING UNDERSTANDING

Show '50 minutes past 3' on an analogue clock. Ask: *What time is it? Show me the time 10 minutes later. Has the hour hand moved?*

GOING DEEPER

Compare two clocks showing 'five to' times, with one hour difference. Ask: *What times do they show? Which is later? How do they differ?* Repeat for 6 o'clock, half past 12, quarter past 9 and quarter to 3. Encourage children to use 'minutes past' and 'minutes to', and to describe the position of the hour hand and minute hand.

KEY LANGUAGE

In lesson: time, past, to, o'clock

Other language to be used by the teacher: hour hand, minute hand, analogue

STRUCTURES AND REPRESENTATIONS

number line

RESOURCES

Mandatory: analogue clock manipulatives

Optional: analogue clock flash cards, written time and hoops, number cards from 1 to 12, large pieces of paper

 In the eTextbook of this lesson, you will find interactive links to a selection of teaching tools.

Before you teach

• Can children see the time easily in the classroom?
• Can you provide a variety of analogue clocks?

Discover

WAYS OF WORKING Pair work

ASK

- Question ❶ a): *What does the picture show? What do the hands mean on the clock? How many minutes are there in an hour?*
- Question ❶ b): *If the minute hand was at number 6, what would the time have been? How many minutes past number 6 is the minute hand showing?*

IN FOCUS Use the picture to recap and briefly assess children's understanding. Begin by reinforcing the idea that the minute hand does not jump from one number to the next, but travels gradually around the clock.

PRACTICAL TIPS Place a large hoop on the floor, on a large piece of paper. Ask children to place number cards from 1 to 12 inside the hoop to make a clock. Using a pen, divide the gap between each pair of numbers into five, so that there are 60 divisions altogether on the clock. Children can make their own clocks. Encourage them to put the numbers in the correct places. They can set their own clock-based problems, telling the time to the nearest minute.

ANSWERS

Question ❶ a): The photo was taken at 33 minutes past 10.

Question ❶ b): Another way to say this time is 27 minutes to 11.

Share

WAYS OF WORKING Whole class teacher led

ASK

- Question ❶ a): *Can you use a clock face to prove that there are 60 minutes in an hour? How?*
- Question ❶ a): *There are 60 minutes in an hour. If 35 minutes have gone by since the last o'clock time, how many minutes until the next hour? How many minutes have gone by if it is ten minutes to the hour?*
- Question ❶ b): *How can we say the time in two different ways? Which is the more common way?*

IN FOCUS Use this opportunity to address the misconception that the hands jump from one number to the next. Allow children to show their understanding of times – for example, by using clock manipulatives, drawing times on blank clock faces or calling out times when shown different clocks.

STRENGTHEN Provide two large classroom clocks that children can see clearly during the day; one clock should show the individual minutes, while the other does not. Ask children to read the time from each clock. Ask one group to read the time approximately (*It's about …*). Ask another group to read it exactly to the nearest minute (*It's exactly …*). Ask: *Do all clocks show each individual minute on their clock face? What do you notice? Is it easier to read the time to the minute with or without the minute marks?*

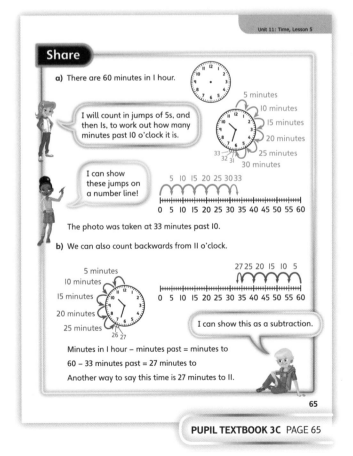

Think together

ASK

- Question **1**: *Why are we counting in 5s and 1s? How can you tell what hour it is? Which hand should you look at?*
- Question **2**: *What is different about the clocks in a) and b)? What would you be doing at these times in the afternoon?*

IN FOCUS Questions **1** and **2** give children an opportunity to practise their recognition of 'minutes past' and 'minutes to'. Discuss with children the clues they use to identify whether the clock is showing 'minutes past' or 'minutes to'. Ask: *Has the minute hand gone past the number 6 (half-way through an hour)? Has the hour hand gone past the number 4 or is it travelling towards the number 4?* Encourage discussion and share ideas.

STRENGTHEN For these questions, encourage children to make and to write in words all the times shown. Ask: *Can you think of two ways to say this time?* Questions **1**, **2** and **3** provide opportunities for children to estimate time. Ask and discuss: *Why is estimating time important in everyday life? Do you think you are more likely to hear 'about twenty to 3' or '21 minutes to 3' in real life? Does that mean reading the time exactly is not important?*

DEEPEN Ask children to organise the times they have seen in this lesson into two groups: 'minutes to' and 'minutes past'. Ask: *In which group will this time go? How do you know you have organised the times correctly? Can you draw a clock showing this time?*

ASSESSMENT CHECKPOINT Children should be able to identify clocks that show 'minutes to' and clocks that show 'minutes past'. Assess if children can recognise and explain how the position of the hour hand changes as the time moves from one hour to the next.

ANSWERS

Question **1** a): 18 minutes past 5

Question **1** b): 21 minutes to 12

Question **2** a): 9 minutes past 4

Question **2** b): 12 minutes to 5

Question **2** c): 3 minutes to 9

Question **2** d): 28 minutes past 1

Question **3**: 41 minutes past 9 or 19 minutes to 10

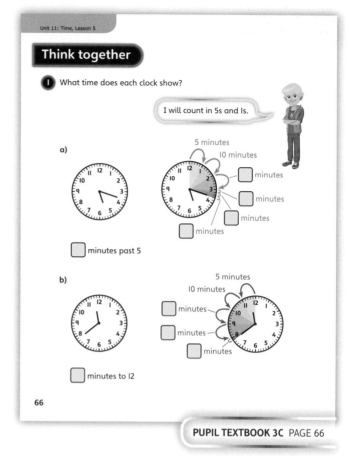

PUPIL TEXTBOOK 3C PAGE 66

PUPIL TEXTBOOK 3C PAGE 67

Practice

WAYS OF WORKING Independent thinking

IN FOCUS Question ❶ links the concepts from this lesson with children's real life experiences. It may be beneficial to provide blank clock faces and the statements written on slips of paper so children can draw the right time on each clock and match it with the corresponding activity. Question ❷ gives children the opportunity to develop fluency in recognising and recording different times.

STRENGTHEN For children struggling to match the 'minutes past' with the 'minutes to' in question ❸, it may be beneficial to use a number line. Ask: *How many minutes have gone by? How many minutes are there until the next hour?*

DEEPEN Use question ❹ to deepen children's reasoning and explanation skills. Ask children what part of the lesson they think Kate did not understand. Ask: *What would you say to help her understand? Can you explain where she went wrong? Can you use a resource or picture to help explain the mistake to her?*

ASSESSMENT CHECKPOINT At this point in the lesson, children should be able to confidently recognise and record times to the nearest minute. They should be able to use 'minutes past' and 'minutes to' and fluently describe the times they read.

ANSWERS Answers for the **Practice** part of the lesson appear in the separate **Practice and Reflect answer guide**.

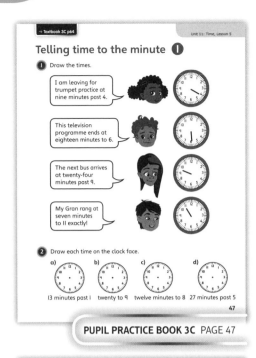

PUPIL PRACTICE BOOK 3C PAGE 47

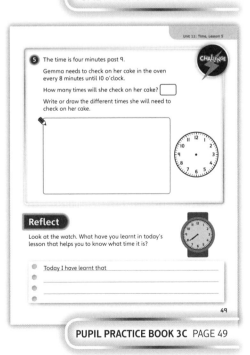

PUPIL PRACTICE BOOK 3C PAGE 48

Reflect

WAYS OF WORKING Independent thinking

IN FOCUS Give children an opportunity to develop their own line of thinking. They should be able to link the vocabulary they have learnt in the past with the vocabulary in this lesson to justify their reasoning.

ASSESSMENT CHECKPOINT Children should show a confident understanding of estimating and reading time to the nearest minute. They should be able to confidently and accurately explain the importance of being able to estimate time, and of being able to read the time to the nearest minute.

ANSWERS Answers for the **Reflect** part of the lesson appear in the separate **Practice and Reflect answer guide**.

After the lesson

- Are children able to confidently estimate time?
- Are children able to read the time accurately?
- How will you build in more opportunities to practise these skills throughout the school day?

PUPIL PRACTICE BOOK 3C PAGE 49

Telling time to the minute ❷

Learning focus

Children will read times using analogue and digital clocks. They will recap their learning about measuring time and describe time using am and pm, or morning and afternoon/evening.

Small steps

→ Previous step: Telling time to the minute (1)
→ **This step: Telling time to the minute (2)**
→ Next step: Telling time to the minute (3)

NATIONAL CURRICULUM LINKS

Year 3 Measurement

Estimate and read time with increasing accuracy to the nearest minute; record and compare time in terms of seconds, minutes, hours; use vocabulary such as o'clock, am/pm, morning, afternoon, noon and midnight.

ASSESSING MASTERY

Children can read times displayed on analogue clocks to the minute and use the terms am and pm appropriately. Children can read 12-hour digital times and make links between digital and analogue times.

COMMON MISCONCEPTIONS

Children may think that digital clock numbers are the same as analogue clock numbers – for instance, that 3:10 means the hour hand points to the 3, and the minute hand points to the 10. Ask:
• *What does the analogue clock show? What does this mean? How many hours? How many minutes?*

Children may think that am means daylight and pm means night time. Ask:
• *Is it sometimes dark at 7 am? Is it ever dark at 1 pm?*

STRENGTHENING UNDERSTANDING

Offer children opportunities to look at pictures of the same clock at different times in one hour (for example, 9 o'clock, 9:15, 9:20, 9:30, 9:40, 9:45, 9:55 and 10 o'clock). Ask them to describe the journey of the minute hand within this one hour, and then to describe the journey of the hour hand within this one hour.

GOING DEEPER

Challenge children to look at one channel in an online TV guide. Ask them to record each programme in a table with two columns: am and pm. Give children a set amount of time to do this, for example, 15 minutes. This will develop their ability to recognise the times, and will also help to develop their awareness of how long a certain number of minutes is.

KEY LANGUAGE

In lesson: past, to, **digital**, digit, **am**, **pm**, midday, midnight, morning, evening, time, minute, hour

Other language to be used by the teacher: hour hand, minute hand, o'clock, consecutive, analogue

RESOURCES

Mandatory: analogue clock manipulatives, digital clock

Optional: analogue clock and written time and written time flash cards

 In the eTextbook of this lesson, you will find interactive links to a selection of teaching tools.

Before you teach

• Are children confident using am and pm?
• Can children easily see the time in the classroom?

Discover

WAYS OF WORKING Pair work

ASK

- Question ❶ a): *What clocks can you see in this picture? How many minutes are there in an hour? Is the time shown closer to 8 o'clock or 9 o'clock?*
- Question ❶ b): *What information can we use to decide whether it is morning or afternoon/evening?*

IN FOCUS This picture provides children with experience of using different representations of time. Use this picture as an opportunity to discuss similarities and differences between digital and analogue time. Address the potential misconception that the hour and minute hand point to the numbers shown on a digital clock, to ensure children do not think this later.

PRACTICAL TIPS If possible, provide a digital and an analogue clock on each table, so children can observe how the time changes throughout the day. At regular intervals, ask children to tell the time on both clocks. Ask: *How do they differ?*

ANSWERS

Question ❶ a): The clock on the wall should show 54 minutes past 8, or 6 minutes to 9

Question ❶ b): It is morning because the digital clock says 'am'.

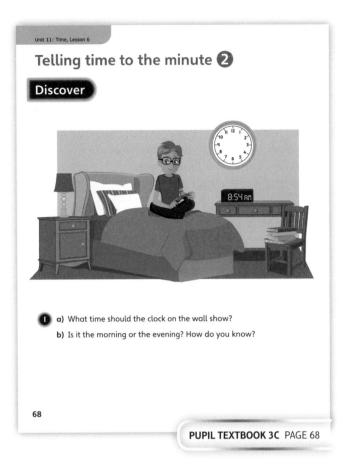

Telling time to the minute ❷

Discover

❶ a) What time should the clock on the wall show?

b) Is it the morning or the evening? How do you know?

68

PUPIL TEXTBOOK 3C PAGE 68

Share

WAYS OF WORKING Whole class teacher led

ASK

Revisit different times throughout the day.
- *Where would the minute hand point at 35 minutes past 2? What about the hour hand?*
- *The whole hour is 60 minutes. Can you use this to find out how many minutes until the hour is complete?*
- *Can you count around the clock face and show where the minute hand should be? How would this time look on a digital clock?*
- *How do you decide whether it is going to be am or pm?*

IN FOCUS Give children different times in the day, and ask them to think of activities they might be doing at these times. Reinforce what am and pm mean. Ask children to think of mistakes that they think might happen when using am and pm, such as linking them to daylight and night time. Clarify any misconceptions.

STRENGTHEN Have a class 'Clock day' where children can bring a clock from home. Also have different types of watches and clocks in the classroom. Ask: *Which one do you prefer? Why? How do they differ?* Ask children throughout the day to find what the time is.

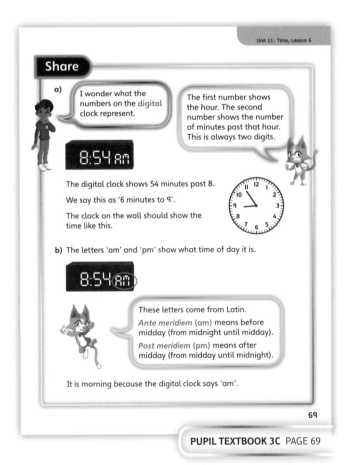

Share

a) I wonder what the numbers on the digital clock represent.

The first number shows the hour. The second number shows the number of minutes past that hour. This is always two digits.

The digital clock shows 54 minutes past 8.

We say this as '6 minutes to 9'.

The clock on the wall should show the time like this.

b) The letters 'am' and 'pm' show what time of day it is.

These letters come from Latin.

Ante meridiem (am) means before midday (from midnight until midday).

Post meridiem (pm) means after midday (from midday until midnight).

It is morning because the digital clock says 'am'.

69

PUPIL TEXTBOOK 3C PAGE 69

Think together

Whole class teacher led (I do, We do, You do)

ASK

- Question ❶: *How will you read the analogue clocks? How will you read the digital clocks? What clues can you look for when reading the time on each clock?*
- Question ❷: *Is it am or pm in the evening? Where is the hour hand pointing on the analogue clock?*

IN FOCUS Questions ❶ and ❷ make the link between analogue and digital times. Make sure children are confident when reading a digital time and are able to decide whether the time shown is morning or afternoon/evening.

STRENGTHEN In question ❸, strengthen the link between the times shown on the page; and the correct use of the mathematical vocabulary 'am', 'pm', 'minutes past' and 'minutes to' when reading the time. Ask children to explain how they will use the fact that there are '60 minutes in one hour' to help solve the problem.

DEEPEN Encourage children to use previous learning and the number line to help solve question ❸. Ask: *Can you think of a way to prove that your answer is right?*

ASSESSMENT CHECKPOINT At this point in the lesson, children should be more confident in reading analogue and digital times and explaining when to use 'minutes past' and 'minutes to'. Look for a confident and fluent understanding and use of 'am' and 'pm'.

ANSWERS

Question ❶: Clock A shows the same time as clock 2.
Clock B shows the same time as clock 3.
Clock C shows the same time as clock 4.
Clock D shows the same time as clock 1.

Question ❷: The clock face shows 7 minutes past 8. Evening is shown by the letters 'pm'. Digital clock D shows the same time as the clock face.

Question ❸: The time is 11 minutes to 1.

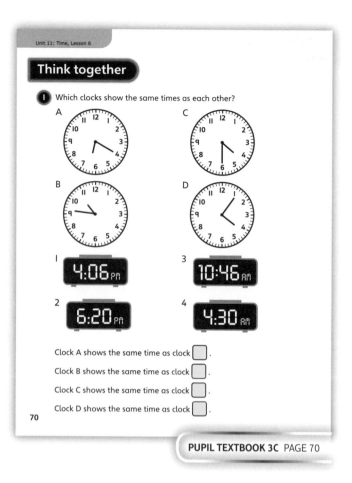

PUPIL TEXTBOOK 3C PAGE 70

PUPIL TEXTBOOK 3C PAGE 71

Practice

WAYS OF WORKING Independent thinking

IN FOCUS In questions ❶ and ❷, children need to draw digital times on analogue clock faces and vice-versa. Check that they understand what each number in a digital clock time represents and how this will be shown on an analogue clock. Ask: *Does this time show 'minutes past' or 'minutes to'? How will you write/draw that? Which half of the clock will the minute hand be in?* Explain that we do not show 'am' or 'pm' on analogue clocks.

STRENGTHEN Question ❸ requires children to practise recording the vocabulary of time. Remind them to draw on what they have learnt in previous lessons.

DEEPEN In question ❼, ask children to prove their ideas using evidence. Ask children to draw digital and analogue clocks and show the different times that it could be.

THINK DIFFERENTLY In question ❻, children have to think of consecutive digits in digital clock times. Ask them to show you how they have worked systematically to find all possible answers. Can they order their answers throughout the day?

ASSESSMENT CHECKPOINT Children should be showing a confident understanding of what 'am' and 'pm' mean. They should be able to read the time clearly using a digital or analogue clock. They should be able to clearly explain how to read the time using 'minutes past', and how to calculate 'minutes to' if the time shown is more than half past the hour.

ANSWERS Answers for the **Practice** part of the lesson appear in the separate **Practice and Reflect answer guide**.

Reflect

WAYS OF WORKING Pair work

IN FOCUS Children can think of their own ideas about when to use 'am' and 'pm', and share their ideas with their partner. Ask: *If you have different ideas, can you explain each other's ideas? Why did your partner think that?*

ASSESSMENT CHECKPOINT Children should clearly refer to the fact that 'am' and 'pm' are not related to whether it is dark or light outside. They should draw on previous knowledge that the day starts at 12 o'clock midnight and is 24 hours long.

ANSWERS Answers for the **Reflect** part of the lesson appear in the separate **Practice and Reflect answer guide**.

After the lesson

- Are children able to confidently explain the differences between 'am' and 'pm'?
- Are children able to confidently explain how analogue and digital clocks differ?
- How will you build in more opportunities to practise reading the time throughout the school day?

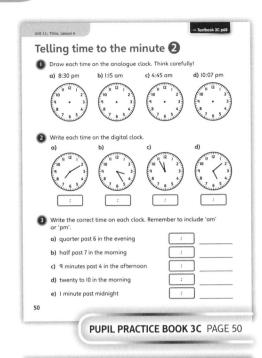

PUPIL PRACTICE BOOK 3C PAGE 50

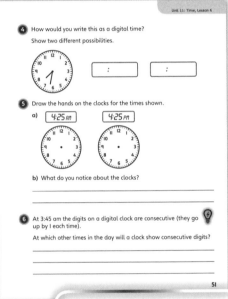

PUPIL PRACTICE BOOK 3C PAGE 51

PUPIL PRACTICE BOOK 3C PAGE 52

103

Telling time to the minute 3

Learning focus

In this lesson, children will tell the time using the 24-hour clock. They will learn how to convert the time from 12-hour clock to 24-hour clock.

Small steps

→ Previous step: Telling time to the minute (2)
→ **This step: Telling time to the minute (3)**
→ Next step: Finding the duration

NATIONAL CURRICULUM LINKS

Year 3 Measurement

- Tell and write the time from an analogue clock, including using Roman numerals from I to XII, and 12-hour and 24-hour clocks.
- Estimate and read time with increasing accuracy to the nearest minute; record and compare time in terms of seconds, minutes and hours; use vocabulary such as o'clock, am/pm, morning, afternoon, noon and midnight.

ASSESSING MASTERY

Children can read times on analogue clocks using the 24-hour clock. Children can fluently estimate and read the time to the nearest minute.

COMMON MISCONCEPTIONS

Children may add 12 to all 12-hour clock times to get 24-hour clock times. Ask:
- *How does the 24-hour clock help us to tell the difference between 'am' and 'pm'?*

Children may 12:5 for 5 minutes past 12, or 9:23 instead of 09:23. Ask:
- *How many digits must a 24-hour clock time have?*

Children may think that 12:00 and 00:00 show the same time, rather than noon and midnight. Ask:
- *Is this an 'am' time or a 'pm' time? How can you tell?*

STRENGTHENING UNDERSTANDING

Show 10:00 on a 24-hour digital clock. Change the display as children count up in hours, and then minutes. Explain that we read 13:45 as 'thirteen forty-five'. Ask: *Why do we use 24-hour clocks? Can you describe the way the time is recorded? Does this look like anything you have seen before? How is it similar to what you have seen? How is it different?*

GOING DEEPER

Challenge children to look at a train timetable which uses the 24-hour clock. Ask them to divide the train times into two groups: 'before midday' and 'after midday'. Ask children to discuss how they know that their answers are correct.

KEY LANGUAGE

In lesson: morning, afternoon, evening, 12-hour clock, 24-hour clock, digital clock, midday, time, hour, minute

Other language to be used by the teacher: analogue

RESOURCES

Mandatory: 24-hour clocks, digital clock

Optional: analogue clock manipulatives, analogue clock flash cards

 In the eTextbook of this lesson, you will find interactive links to a selection of teaching tools.

Before you teach

- Are children confident in using 'am' and 'pm'?
- Do children have access to 24-hour digital clocks?

Discover

Pair work

ASK

- Question **1**: *What clocks can you see in the picture?*
- Question **1**: *Are there any new ways of showing the time? How are they different to ones you have seen before?*
- Question **1**: *How many hours are there in the day?*
- Question **1** a): *What information can we use to decide whether it is morning or afternoon/evening?*
- Question **1** b): *What time does the analogue clock show?*

IN FOCUS This picture will give children their first experience of the 24-hour clock in this unit. Use this opportunity to discuss how this representation of time is different to what children have seen before. Question **1** a) draws attention to the way time is recorded using an analogue clock and a 24-hour digital clock. Show the time on the analogue clock and point out the equivalent time on the 24-hour digital clock. Ask: *What is different?* Look out for children who say that 12 is added to the number of hours to give the 24-hour clock time.

PRACTICAL TIPS Use two digital clocks, one with the 24-hour setting, the other with the 12-hour setting. Use the clocks to show the times that are included in the activity. Set both clocks to 12:00, then move the hour forward. Ask children to compare the two representations. Ask: *How can you tell the time is after midday on each of the clocks?*

ANSWERS

Question **1** a): The woodpecker was seen in the morning.
The fox was seen in the afternoon.

Question **1** b): The digital clock should show 22:30.

Share

Whole class teacher led

ASK

- *What do you notice about the times the animals were spotted? Can you see anything unusual about them?*
- *When do you think the time 07:32 is? When do you think the time 13:24 is? When might 13 hours be? If 1pm is 13:00, what is 2pm/3pm/4pm, etc? Can you spot a quick way to remember times in 24-hour clock notation?*

IN FOCUS At this point in the lesson, it is important to make sure children are confident with 24-hour clock notation and understand that the hours can be counted beyond 12 o'clock, noon. Be very clear about the link between 'am' and 'pm' and 24-hour clock times before or after midday.

Ask: *Why do you think we have 24-hour clock times?* Revisit concepts and listen to children's reasoning. Discuss the characteristics of the 24-hour clock. Clarify any misconceptions. Allow children to compare the different ways that time can be represented and discuss the characteristics of each method.

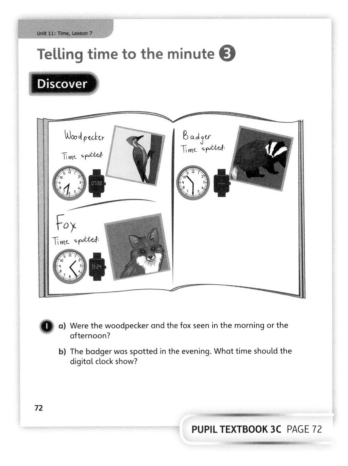

PUPIL TEXTBOOK 3C PAGE 72

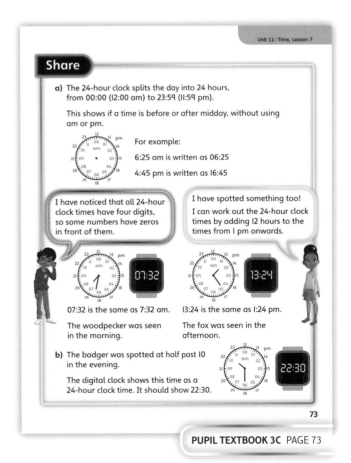

PUPIL TEXTBOOK 3C PAGE 73

Think together

Whole class teacher led (I do, We do, You do)

ASK

- Question **1**: *Did Mo spot the robin in the morning or the afternoon? How do you know? How can you change the 12-hour clock to 24-hour clock?*
- Question **2**: *What does am mean? What about pm? How many digits do all 24-hour clock times have? When do you use a zero as the first digit?*

IN FOCUS Questions **1** and **2** give children the opportunity to practise changing 12-hour times to 24-hour times. Discuss with children the clues they can use to identify whether the time is before midday or after midday.

STRENGTHEN For all questions in this section, encourage children to show the times by drawing the minute and hour hands on blank analogue clock faces.

DEEPEN Use question **3** to deepen children's reasoning and explanation skills. Revisit the potential misconceptions from the beginning of the lesson. Ask: *What would you say to Richard to help him understand his mistake? What would the answer be?* Listen for children who know that we use four digits to record the 24-hour time.

ASSESSMENT CHECKPOINT At this point in the lesson children should be confident in recognising and recording 24-hour clock times. They should be able to describe when and how to record the time before midday and after midday.

ANSWERS

Question **1**: 4 + 12 = 16. The robin was spotted at 16:46.

Question **2**: 09:16

        21:50

        23:15

Question **3**: Ambika is right. 14:50 is the same as 2:50 pm.

        Richard is wrong as he is adding 12 to change it to 24-hour time, even though it is not yet 1 pm.

        Jamila is wrong as she has forgotten to put 0 at the start of the time. The time should be 08:25.

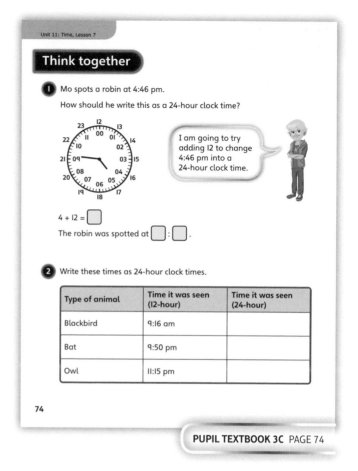

PUPIL TEXTBOOK 3C PAGE 74

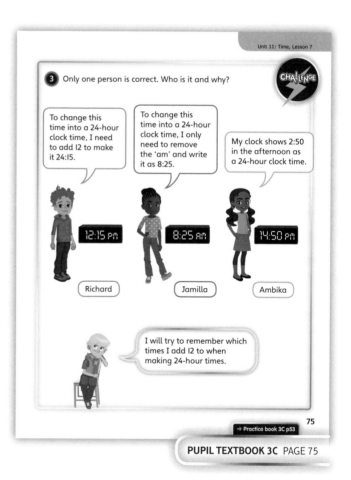

PUPIL TEXTBOOK 3C PAGE 75

Practice

WAYS OF WORKING Independent thinking

IN FOCUS Question ❶ offers the opportunity for children to recognise 24-hour times and represent them on analogue clocks. Question ❷ is more abstract and checks whether children know how to convert 12-hour times to 24-hour times. Ask: *What clues can you use to work out whether it is before midday or after midday?* Question ❸ requires children to summarise what they have learnt in the lesson.

STRENGTHEN If children struggle with question ❷, remind them that the time does not stop at 12 o'clock midday, but the hours continue as 13, 14 … up to 00. Draw a timeline from midday to midnight and mark 13:00 and 1 pm inat the correct point. Then ask children to complete the rest of the times.

DEEPEN When solving question ❻, deepen children's reasoning by discussing any potential misconceptions. Encourage children to explain Spark's comments. What else do they know about 24-hour time? Ask: *What is the latest time you can make using these digits? What is the earliest?*

THINK DIFFERENTLY Question ❺ asks children to problem solve. If they are unsure what to do, ask them to describe the information given in the question. Ask: *What is the smallest number you could use? What is the biggest? What does 'total' mean? What does 'multiple of 5' mean?* Ask children to draw [ ] [ ] : [ ] [ ] and fill in the blanks.

ASSESSMENT CHECKPOINT Children should be confident when converting 12-hour time to 24-hour time and vice versa.

ANSWERS Answers for the **Practice** part of the lesson appear in the separate **Practice and Reflect answer guide**.

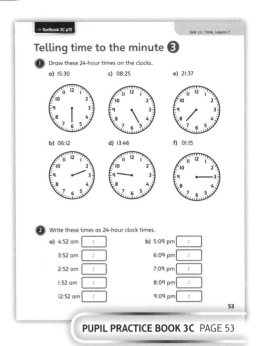

PUPIL PRACTICE BOOK 3C PAGE 53

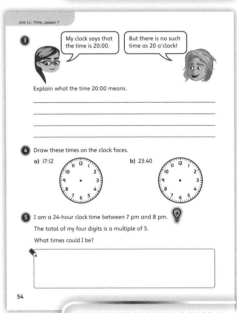

PUPIL PRACTICE BOOK 3C PAGE 54

Reflect

WAYS OF WORKING Independent thinking

IN FOCUS This question checks whether children can explain how 24-hour time is used instead of writing am or pm to tell us whether it is morning or evening.

ASSESSMENT CHECKPOINT Children should recognise that hours can be counted beyond 12:00 midday. They should be able to explain and show how they know that 18:58 is in the evening as it is after midday (12:00).

ANSWERS Answers for the **Reflect** part of the lesson appear in the separate **Practice and Reflect answer guide**.

After the lesson

- Are children confident when the 24-hour clock is being used?
- Are children secure when converting from the 12-hour clock to the 24-hour clock?

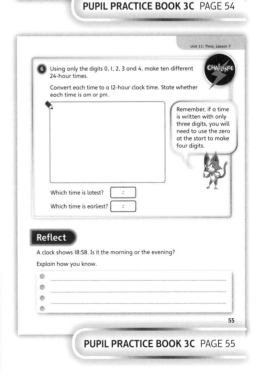

PUPIL PRACTICE BOOK 3C PAGE 55

Finding the duration

Learning focus

In this lesson, children will learn to find a duration between two times, including using the 24-hour clock.

Small steps

→ Previous step: Telling time to the minute (3)
→ **This step: Finding the duration**
→ Next step: Comparing duration

NATIONAL CURRICULUM LINKS

Year 3 Measurement

Estimate and read time with increasing accuracy to the nearest minute; record and compare time in terms of seconds, minutes and hours; use vocabulary such as o'clock, am/pm, morning, afternoon, noon and midnight.

ASSESSING MASTERY

Children are able to confidently find the duration between two times, either by counting forwards or backwards from one time to the other. Children should find durations to the nearest minute, including 24-hour times.

COMMON MISCONCEPTIONS

Children may add the number of minutes each time (for example, if the start time is '12 minutes to 4' and the duration is 10 minutes, they add 10 to 12 and get an end time of '22 minutes to 4'). Ask:
• *Will the end time be before or after the start time?*

Children may be unsure how to find durations when they cross the hour boundary. Ask:
• *How many minutes to the next hour? How many more minutes after that?*

STRENGTHENING UNDERSTANDING

Give children a clock with moving hands, and cards with numbers of minutes (such as 5 minutes, 10 minutes, 15 minutes, 20 minutes). Children work in pairs and take it in turns to pick a card. This is the number of minutes that the minute hand has to travel. They show the new time on the clock and draw it. Children score 3 points if they correctly say the original time, the new time and how many minutes the minute hand has travelled.

GOING DEEPER

Challenge children to look at a local bus timetable. Ask: *Where can you travel in less than 20 minutes? In less than one hour?*

KEY LANGUAGE

In lesson: start time, end time, **duration**, finish

Other language to be used by the teacher: amount, time taken

STRUCTURES AND REPRESENTATIONS

number line

RESOURCES

Mandatory: analogue clock manipulatives, digital clock

Optional: analogue clock and written time flash cards

 In the eTextbook of this lesson, you will find interactive links to a selection of teaching tools.

Before you teach

• Are children confident counting around the clock?
• Can children link a number line with a clock face?

Discover

WAYS OF WORKING Pair work

ASK

- Question ❶ a): *Where can you look to find how long the farmer takes to plough the field?*
- Question ❶ a): *What clocks are shown in the picture?*
- Question ❶ a): *What time did the farmer start? What time did he finish ploughing?*
- Question ❶ b): *How can you work out how long the farmer waits before he has a cup of tea?*

IN FOCUS Use the pictures to discuss the duration of some activities or clubs that children do. For example, ask: *When does choir practice start and finish? How long is it? What other things could we find the duration of time for?*

PRACTICAL TIPS A number line and clock faces will help children to calculate the length of time. It will be useful to revisit how the number line can be used and to remind children that 1 hour = 60 minutes, not 100 minutes.

ANSWERS

Question ❶ a): It takes the farmer 28 minutes to plough the field.

Question ❶ b): Another 28 minutes go by before the farmer has a cup of tea.

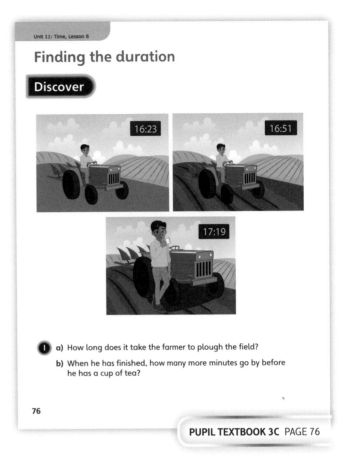

PUPIL TEXTBOOK 3C PAGE 76

Share

WAYS OF WORKING Whole class teacher led

ASK

- *What does 'duration' mean?*
- *To work out the duration of something, what information do we need to know?*

IN FOCUS Although children may have been introduced to duration in Year 2, this was non-statutory guidance, so do not assume they have done it or will remember it. It is important to scaffold children's use of the term 'duration' through your questioning and support. Providing concrete or pictorial representations of analogue and digital clocks will help children. Do not go into full conversion of minutes and hours, as this is covered in Year 4.

STRENGTHEN Set up two clocks at the front of the class. Ask one child to make any time on the first clock, and another to make any time on the second clock. The class works out the duration between the two times.

Show children a TV guide where the start and end times of programmes are given. Ask children to devise their own duration questions based on what they see.

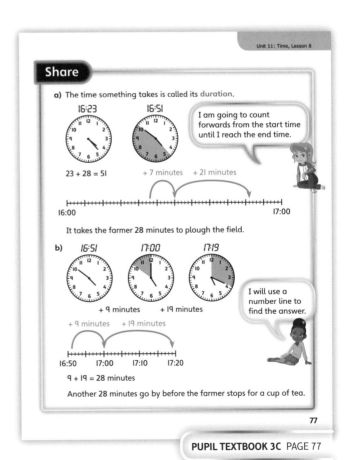

PUPIL TEXTBOOK 3C PAGE 77

Think together

WAYS OF WORKING Whole class teacher led (I do, We do, You do)

ASK

- *What is the start time? What is the end time? What does the shaded clock face show?*
- *How will you count the duration of time between the start and finish times?*
- *How can you show the duration using a number line?*
- *How will you record how many minutes the duration is? Could you record it in a different way?*

IN FOCUS Question ❶ scaffolds children's ability to find the duration within an hour. Question ❷ asks children to find a duration less than 60 minutes long, but crossing the hour boundary. Question ❸ progresses to finding a duration that is greater than 60 minutes and crosses the hour.

STRENGTHEN If children are unsure of how to complete questions ❶ and ❷, provide blank clock faces and ask children to mark the start and end times. They can then count the steps between the two times to measure the duration of time.

DEEPEN In question ❸, provide children with a number line showing two hours from 16:00 to 18:00, with each hour split into 60 minutes. Ask children to show how long the farmer took to collect the eggs on the number line.

ASSESSMENT CHECKPOINT At this point in the lesson, children should be able to calculate 'duration' by calculating the length of time between two points. Children should also recognise how and why a measurement of duration can be different to the number of minutes mentioned in the question or that the clock is showing.

ANSWERS

Question ❶: It takes the farmer 44 minutes to milk the cows.

Question ❷: 25 + 22 = 47

The lorry driver was at the farm for 47 minutes.

Question ❸: It takes the farmer 1 hour 23 minutes or 83 minutes.

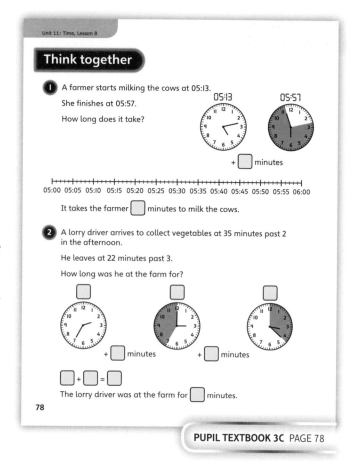

PUPIL TEXTBOOK 3C PAGE 78

PUPIL TEXTBOOK 3C PAGE 79

Practice

WAYS OF WORKING Independent thinking

IN FOCUS In question **1**, children work with pictorial representations of time to find a duration of time. Question **2** offers a procedural variation in finding the length of time. Encourage children to use shaded pictures in or a number line in question **2**, to calculate the duration of time. An analogue clock may also help them.

STRENGTHEN For question **4**, encourage children to use an analogue clock, number line, or both, to find the duration of time. Remind them to consider the number of hours and minutes, not only the minutes.

DEEPEN If children are confident in finding the length of time in question **5**, deepen their ability by asking them to find different ways to show their answer. In question **6**, children are provided with the opportunity to work on an open-ended investigative question. Children can choose the best representations to prove their ideas.

ASSESSMENT CHECKPOINT At this point in the lesson children should be confident in finding durations of time. They should be able to use multiple representations to find and visually demonstrate durations of time. Look for children explaining how they found durations that cross the hour boundary and using this understanding to solve real-life problems involving time independently.

ANSWERS Answers for the **Practice** part of the lesson appear in the separate **Practice and Reflect answer guide**.

Reflect

WAYS OF WORKING Pair work

IN FOCUS Give children an opportunity to develop their reasoning independently. Can they answer their own duration problem? What method do they prefer to use? Ask: *Why did you choose this method?* Encourage children to compare their method with a partner's. Ask: *Whose method is more efficient?*

ASSESSMENT CHECKPOINT Children should be able to identify a start and end time, and find the duration of time between them. Children should be using different types of representation fluently. Do they use different representations when the duration is within an hour, or when the duration crosses an hour boundary? Listen to children's reasoning as to why they have chosen a particular representation.

ANSWERS Answers for the **Reflect** part of the lesson appear in the separate **Practice and Reflect answer guide**.

After the lesson

- Are children confident in using the vocabulary they have learnt in the lesson?
- Can children confidently find a duration that crosses the hour?
- Can children choose different representations to independently solve problems?

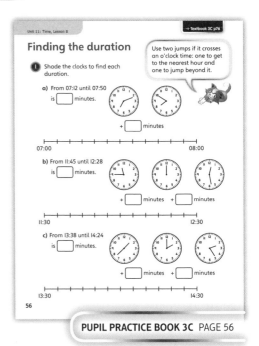

PUPIL PRACTICE BOOK 3C PAGE 56

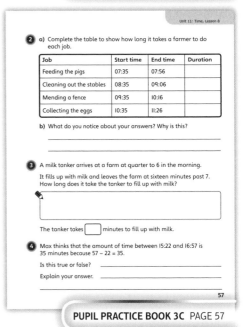

PUPIL PRACTICE BOOK 3C PAGE 57

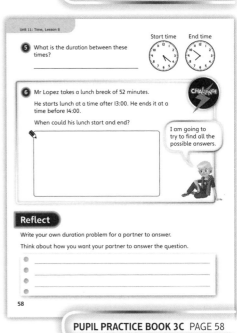

PUPIL PRACTICE BOOK 3C PAGE 58

Comparing duration

Learning focus

In this lesson, children will learn to compare durations of time.

Small steps

→ Previous step: Finding the duration
→ **This step: Comparing duration**
→ Next step: Finding start and end times

NATIONAL CURRICULUM LINKS

Year 3 Measurement

- Estimate and read time with increasing accuracy to the nearest minute; record and compare time in terms of seconds, minutes and hours; use vocabulary such as o'clock, am/pm, morning, afternoon, noon and midnight.
- Compare durations of events [for example to calculate the time taken by particular events or tasks].

ASSESSING MASTERY

Children confidently compare given durations, and can derive durations to compare. Children use their knowledge of place value and units of measurement to say whether a duration is a longer or shorter time. They can order durations, including working with digital times, 24-hour time and to the nearest minute.

COMMON MISCONCEPTIONS

Children may think that a duration that ends later, takes longer (when it may have started later and be shorter). Ask:
- *Would you rather play games between twenty-five to 4 and quarter past 4, or between five to 4 and twenty-five past 4? Why?*

STRENGTHENING UNDERSTANDING

Before the lesson, ask children to compare break time with lesson time. Ask: *Which is longer? Which is shorter?*

GOING DEEPER

Challenge children with a local bus timetable. Ask: *Where can you travel in less than 20 minutes? In one hour?*

KEY LANGUAGE

In lesson: duration, longer, longest, shortest, finish

Other language to be used by the teacher: amount, time taken, start time, end time, how long, shorter

STRUCTURES AND REPRESENTATIONS

number line

RESOURCES

Mandatory: analogue clock manipulatives, digital clock

Optional: analogue clock and written time flash cards

 In the eTextbook of this lesson, you will find interactive links to a selection of teaching tools.

Before you teach

- Are children confident in counting around a clock?
- Are children confident in using am and pm?
- Can children link a number line with a clock face?

Discover

WAYS OF WORKING Pair work

ASK

• Question ❶ a): *What word do we use to describe the length of time that something takes?*
• Question ❶ a): *What times are shown in the picture? How can we use the times to find the answer?*

IN FOCUS Use the picture to recap and briefly assess children's current understanding. Begin by discussing the duration of some of the activities in the school day. For example, does the morning assembly take more or less time than registration?

PRACTICAL TIPS Displaying the schedule of a normal school day will help children to visualise how their day is split and which activities take more time than the others. Using a number line may help children to see which number is larger or smaller and to compare durations of activities.

ANSWERS

Question ❶ a): The Poetry Workshop takes the longest.

Question ❶ b): The Arts and Crafts activity will end between 15:40 and 15:44.

PUPIL TEXTBOOK 3C PAGE 80

Share

WAYS OF WORKING Whole class teacher led

ASK

• *What information do we need to work out the duration of an event?*
• *How can you tell whether something takes a longer or shorter length of time?*

IN FOCUS Use this opportunity to recap the previous lesson and to scaffold what duration actually means. Providing concrete or pictorial representations of analogue and digital clocks will help children to find a duration. Encourage children to be systematic in their approach. To compare durations, they first need to find each one. Give children the opportunity to show their understanding of times and what duration means. Encourage them to justify which activity takes longest, rather than guessing or shouting out.

STRENGTHEN Address the misconception that a duration that ends later always takes longer (when in fact it may have started later and be shorter in duration). Set up two clocks at the front of the class. Ask one child to make the start time of the first library activity on the first clock, and the end time on the second clock. The class works out the duration between the two times. Repeat for all three activities. Set up a number line and ask children to place the duration of each activity on the number line. Ask: *Which number is largest? What does this mean?*

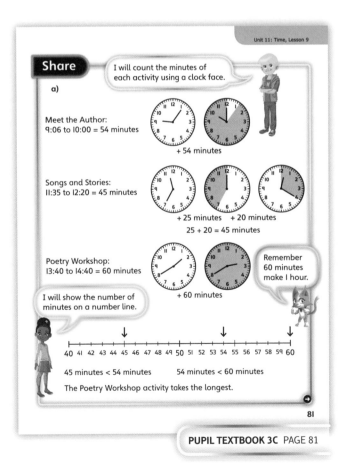

PUPIL TEXTBOOK 3C PAGE 81

Think together

WAYS OF WORKING Whole class teacher led (I do, We do, You do)

ASK

- Question **1**: *What is the start time? What is the end time? How will you count the duration of time between the start and end times?*
- Question **2**: *How can you tell whether something takes a longer or shorter length of time?*
- Question **2**: *How will you record how many minutes the duration is? Could you find and record the duration in a different way?*
- Question **3**: *Do you always have to work out each duration to be able to compare them? What resources could you use to help compare the durations?*

IN FOCUS It is important for children to make the distinction between question **1** and other questions that they have met so far. In question **1**, the times of both events are very similar but the second event starts 5 minutes later than the first one, and finishes 2 minutes later than the first. Ask children how they can use this information to work out which event is longer.

STRENGTHEN When working on question **2**, provide children with a number line that they can use to calculate the difference in duration between the times. In parts a) and b), children may subtract the end and start minutes from each other. In part c), remind children that there are 60 minutes in 1 hour (not 100). Provide laminated clock faces to draw on. Look for children who find the duration from 8:28 to 9:00, and 9:00 to 9:03 and add their answers.

DEEPEN Once children have demonstrated that they can solve question **3**, deepen their understanding of this kind of problem by challenging them to create a similar question for a partner. Ask: *What times would you use to make the question easier? How can you make the question harder? What resources could help to answer the question?*

ASSESSMENT CHECKPOINT At this point in the lesson, children should have demonstrated that they are able to confidently measure durations of time in minutes and hours. Children should be able to compare durations of time, explaining which is longer or shorter and giving their reasoning.

ANSWERS

Question **1**: Story Time = 29 minutes, Make a Book = 26 minutes. Story Time takes longer.

Question **2**: 8:12 am until 8:48 am = 36 minutes

8:43 am until 8:57 am = 14 minutes

8:28 am until 9:03 am = 35 minutes

a) 36 minutes is the longest.

Question **3**: D (63 minutes), B (64 minutes), C (65 minutes), A (67 minutes)

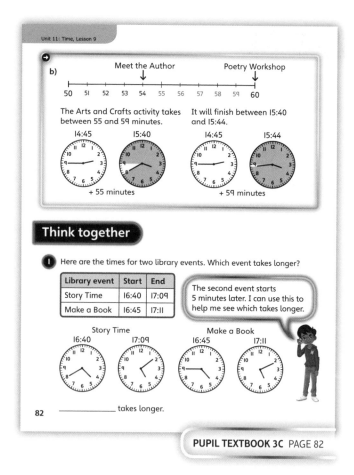

PUPIL TEXTBOOK 3C PAGE 82

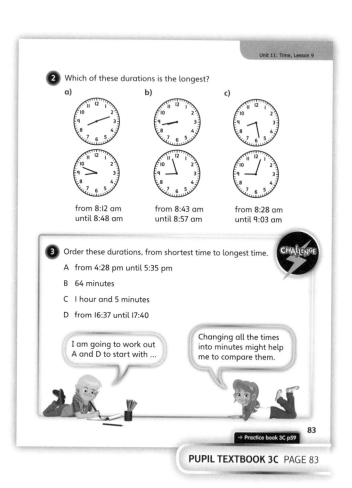

PUPIL TEXTBOOK 3C PAGE 83

Practice

WAYS OF WORKING Independent thinking

IN FOCUS Children colour the segments of time in question **1** to cement the process of counting a duration of time. Questions **2** and **3** encourage children to use their understanding of duration of time to solve problems. In question **4**, children should notice that to compare the times, they either need to convert both times to minutes, or convert them both to hours and minutes.

STRENGTHEN If children are struggling with question **2**, encourage them to re-read the question. Ask: *Can you describe it? What is it about?* The time is represented in an abstract way. Ask: *How could you represent the times?* It is important for children to notice that the fee of £1 is for 65 minutes rather than 1 hour. Ask: *Think of car park fees that you may have seen. How much would it cost to leave the car there for 2 hours? 3 hours?*

DEEPEN When working on question **5**, encourage children to explain their reasoning. Ask children to prove that they have found all possible solutions. To deepen their understanding, ask: *Does the order of the chosen activities matter? When answering the question, is it easier to use minutes, or hours and minutes?*

ASSESSMENT CHECKPOINT Children should be able to fluently measure durations of time in minutes and hours. They should be confident in comparing durations of time and using their understanding to solve mathematical problems.

ANSWERS Answers for the **Practice** part of the lesson appear in the separate **Practice and Reflect answer guide**.

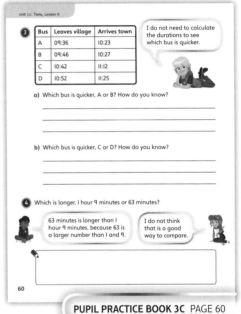

PUPIL PRACTICE BOOK 3C PAGE 59

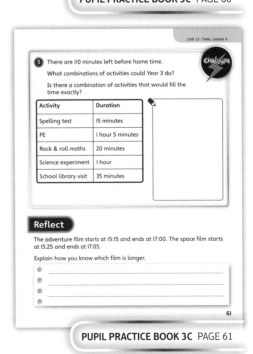

PUPIL PRACTICE BOOK 3C PAGE 60

Reflect

WAYS OF WORKING Independent thinking

IN FOCUS Give children the opportunity to record their methods. Ask: *What method do you prefer to use? Why?* Encourage children to compare their method with a partner's. Ask: *Whose method is more efficient?*

ASSESSMENT CHECKPOINT Look for clarity in children's explanations. They should be systematic in their approach and compare the lengths of time accurately. They should be able to use the appropriate vocabulary to explain how to compare durations of time.

ANSWERS Answers for the **Reflect** part of the lesson appear in the separate **Practice and Reflect answer guide**.

After the lesson

- Are children confident in using the vocabulary learnt in this lesson?
- Can children confidently find a duration that crosses an hour?
- Are they confident in choosing different representations to solve problems independently?

PUPIL PRACTICE BOOK 3C PAGE 61

Finding start and end times

Learning focus

In this lesson, children will learn to find start and end times to the minute for different events.

Small steps

→ Previous step: Comparing duration
→ **This step: Finding start and end times**
→ Next step: Measuring time in seconds

NATIONAL CURRICULUM LINKS

Year 3 Measurement
- Estimate and read time with increasing accuracy to the nearest minute; record and compare time in terms of seconds, minutes and hours; use vocabulary such as o'clock, am/pm, morning, afternoon, noon and midnight.
- Compare durations of events [for example to calculate the time taken by particular events or tasks].

ASSESSING MASTERY

Children can find the start or end time to the nearest minute, when given an end or start time and a duration, including using digital notation.

COMMON MISCONCEPTIONS

Children may add the number of minutes each time, for example, if the start time is '12 minutes to 4' and the duration is 10 minutes, they add 10 to 12 and get the end time of '22 minutes to 4'. Ask:
- *Will the end time be before or after the start time?*

Children may be unsure how to find durations when they cross the hour boundary. Ask:
- *When do you arrive at school if you leave at '12 minutes to 8' and the journey lasts 15 minutes?*

STRENGTHENING UNDERSTANDING

Before the lesson, discuss real-life examples of duration (for example, TV guides). Ask: *Why might it be useful to know the start time, end time or duration of an event?*

GOING DEEPER

Challenge children to look at a local bus timetable. Ask: *Where can you travel to if you leave now and need to arrive at another stop before X am?*

KEY LANGUAGE

In lesson: start time, end time, duration
Other language to be used by the teacher: amount, finish, forwards, backwards, time taken

STRUCTURES AND REPRESENTATIONS

number line

RESOURCES

Mandatory: analogue clock manipulatives, laminated pictures of clock faces, digital clock

Optional: number lines

 In the eTextbook of this lesson, you will find interactive links to a selection of teaching tools.

Before you teach

- Can children use the vocabulary of sequence?
- What real-life experiences could you provide?

Discover

Pair work

ASK

- Question ❶ a): *What time is it at the moment? How do you know? Can you say the time another way? What would the time on a digital clock be? Is it am or pm? How do you know?*
- Question ❶ b): *What does queuing time mean? Is the time on the clock the start time or the end time?*

IN FOCUS Children have already explored finding durations, so they should be familiar with the idea of moving from a start time through a duration to an end time. Now that they are in Year 3, children will apply these concepts to times given to the nearest minute (and including digital notations).

PRACTICAL TIPS Provide children with real-life examples of duration, such as cooking instructions on food items. Ask children to consider what the end times might be, given a specific start time (or vice versa).

ANSWERS

Question ❶ a): Max will get on the dodgems at 2:53 pm or 7 minutes to 3.

Question ❶ b): Olivia should start queuing at 3:35 pm, or 25 minutes to 4.

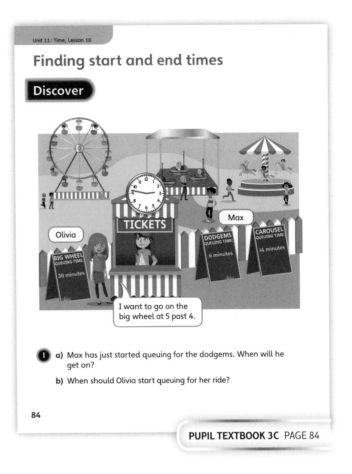

PUPIL TEXTBOOK 3C PAGE 84

Share

WAYS OF WORKING Whole class teacher led

ASK

- Question ❶ a): *What time is it in the picture?*
- Question ❶ a): *What will the clock look like when Max goes on the dodgems?*
- Question ❶ a): *If you know the start time and the duration, how can you find the end time? Is it forwards or backwards in time?*
- Question ❶ b): *If you know the end time and the duration, how can you find the start time? Is it forwards or backwards in time?*
- Question ❶ b): *Why does Sparks subtract 5 minutes first, then subtract 25 minutes to find the start time?*

IN FOCUS Ensure children are clear what they are being asked to do in this task. They should understand the difference between start time, duration and end time, and how they link together. Provide real clocks to help children visualise the problem. Draw their attention to how this question is similar to those in previous lessons.

STRENGTHEN Provide examples of problems where children have to find the start time, the duration or the end time. Encourage children to discuss what they need to find and the method they will use. Ask: *Do you add or subtract?* Ask children to work with durations that cross the hour. For example, ask: *Find the end time, if the start time is 4:48 and the duration is 25 minutes. Find the start time, if the end time is 3:16 and the duration is 55 minutes.*

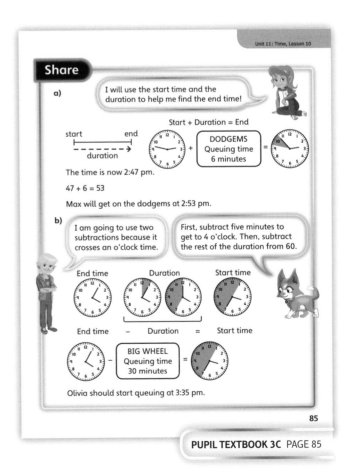

PUPIL TEXTBOOK 3C PAGE 85

Think together

WAYS OF WORKING Whole class teacher led (I do, We do, You do)

ASK

- Question ❶: *How will you use the start time and the duration to find the end time?*
- Question ❷: *How will you use the end time and the duration to find the start time?*
- Question ❷: *What do the shaded clock faces show?*
- Question ❸: *How can you use the number line to show how you found the end time?*

IN FOCUS Question ❶ scaffolds children's understanding of using the start time and duration to find the end time within an hour. Question ❷ asks children to find a start time, where the end time and the duration are known. Use the model that they learnt in the lesson and subtract the time in two stages: first they go back 9 minutes to 10 o'clock, then they go back another 16 minutes. Make sure children understand how to cross the hour to find the start and end time. This will enable them to work more efficiently, using more easily-recorded visual representations of time.

STRENGTHEN When children are working on questions ❶ and ❷, emphasise the link between the analogue clocks and a number line. In Year 2, children will have used a number line to find an end time. Strengthen their understanding by using a number line to find the end and start times. This will prepare children for question ❸ and increase their familiarity with the different visual representations of time.

DEEPEN In question ❸, deepen children's ability to reason, by asking: *What time will Bella go on the ride if the queue takes 22 minutes?* Pay attention to children who can model crossing the hour using the number line. Encourage children to use analogue clocks to answer the question as well. Ask: *Which method do you prefer? Why?*

ASSESSMENT CHECKPOINT At this point in the lesson, children should be able to calculate the start or end time, recognising the relationship that exists between start time, duration and end time. Children should be more confident in calculating the start or end time when crossing the hour.

ANSWERS

Question ❶: We can go on the carousel at 4:50 pm.

Question ❷: Luis started queuing at 9:44 am.

Question ❸ a): Bella will go on the helter-skelter at 4 minutes past 3 (or 15:04 or 3:04 pm).

Question ❸ b): They will get home at 6:34 pm.

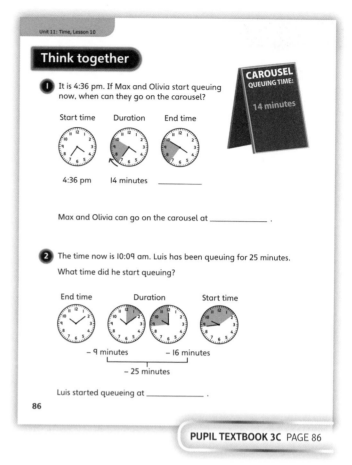

Think together

❶ It is 4:36 pm. If Max and Olivia start queuing now, when can they go on the carousel?

CAROUSEL QUEUING TIME: 14 minutes

Start time — Duration — End time

4:36 pm — 14 minutes — _____

Max and Olivia can go on the carousel at _____ .

❷ The time now is 10:09 am. Luis has been queuing for 25 minutes. What time did he start queuing?

End time — Duration — Start time

− 9 minutes — − 16 minutes

− 25 minutes

Luis started queueing at _____ .

86

PUPIL TEXTBOOK 3C PAGE 86

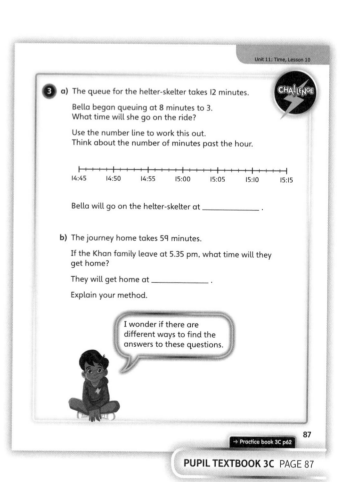

❸ a) The queue for the helter-skelter takes 12 minutes.

CHALLENGE

Bella began queuing at 8 minutes to 3.
What time will she go on the ride?

Use the number line to work this out.
Think about the number of minutes past the hour.

14:45 — 14:50 — 14:55 — 15:00 — 15:05 — 15:10 — 15:15

Bella will go on the helter-skelter at _____ .

b) The journey home takes 59 minutes.

If the Khan family leave at 5.35 pm, what time will they get home?

They will get home at _____ .

Explain your method.

I wonder if there are different ways to find the answers to these questions.

87

→ Practice book 3C p62

PUPIL TEXTBOOK 3C PAGE 87

Practice

WAYS OF WORKING Independent thinking

IN FOCUS When working independently on questions ❶ and ❷, children should continue to secure their understanding of the link between start time, duration and end time. Question ❸ requires children to calculate the start time when crossing the hour. A manipulative analogue clock can be provided to support their thinking.

STRENGTHEN When children are working on question ❹, support them in identifying whether they have to move forward to find the end time, or backwards to find the start time. Make sure they understand that the end time will always be after the start time, and use this to check and correct any errors that arise.

DEEPEN If children are confident in finding the length of time in question ❺, deepen their ability by asking: *Can you find different ways to show your answer?* In question ❻, children are provided with the opportunity to work with an open-ended investigative question. Children can choose the best representations to prove their ideas.

ASSESSMENT CHECKPOINT Children should be confident in finding durations of time. They should be able to use various representations to find and demonstrate durations of time visually. Get children to explain how they worked out the durations that cross the hour boundary. They should use this understanding to solve real-life problems independently.

ANSWERS Answers for the **Practice** part of the lesson appear in the separate **Practice and Reflect answer guide**.

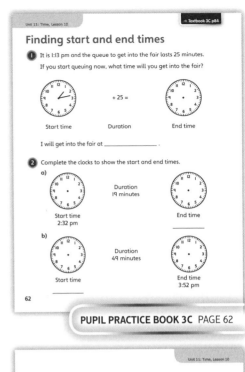

PUPIL PRACTICE BOOK 3C PAGE 62

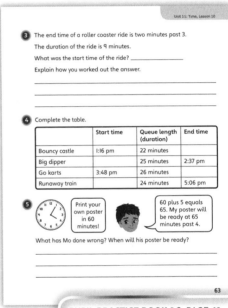

PUPIL PRACTICE BOOK 3C PAGE 63

Reflect

WAYS OF WORKING Pair work

IN FOCUS Give children an opportunity to develop their reasoning independently. Ask: *Which method do you prefer to use? Why did you choose this method?* Encourage children to compare their method with a partner. Ask: *Whose method is more efficient?*

ASSESSMENT CHECKPOINT Children should be able to identify a start and end time, and find the duration of time between them. Children should be using different types of representation fluently. Ask: *Do you use different representations when the duration is within an hour, to when the duration is across the hour?* Listen to children's reasoning as to why they chose a particular representation.

ANSWERS Answers for the **Reflect** part of the lesson appear in the separate **Practice and Reflect answer guide**.

After the lesson ⏸

- Are children confident in using the lesson's vocabulary?
- Can children confidently find a duration across the hour?
- Are they confident in choosing different types of representation to solve problems independently?

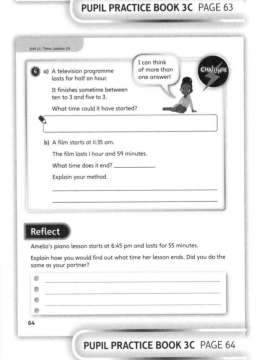

PUPIL PRACTICE BOOK 3C PAGE 64

Measuring time in seconds

Learning focus

In this lesson, children will learn to measure events (such as a race) in seconds.

Small steps

→ Previous step: Finding start and end times
→ **This step: Measuring time in seconds**
→ Next step: Turns and angles

NATIONAL CURRICULUM LINKS

Year 3 Measurement

- Estimate and read time with increasing accuracy to the nearest minute; record and compare time in terms of seconds, minutes and hours; use vocabulary such as o'clock, am/pm, morning, afternoon, noon and midnight.
- Compare durations of events [for example to calculate the time taken by particular events or tasks].

ASSESSING MASTERY

Children know how long a second is and how many seconds equal 1 minute. They can apply the information to estimate 1 minute, and time activities in seconds.

COMMON MISCONCEPTIONS

Children may think 1 second is any fast period of time, and that however quickly they count to 60, it is 1 minute. Ask:
- *How long does the second hand take to move once? Is it always the same?*

Children may mix up the three clock hands or the numbers on digital clocks, and so cannot identify seconds. Ask:
- *What part of the clock helps us count seconds? How can you tell?*

STRENGTHENING UNDERSTANDING

Give children a stopwatch and cards with numbers of seconds (such as 5 seconds, 15 seconds, 30 seconds, 45 seconds, 60 seconds). Children work in pairs, taking turns to pick up a card. One child starts the stopwatch, the other says 'Stop' when they think the time has passed. The child who gets closest wins 1 point.

GOING DEEPER

Show 100 m race results from a school race, county race and the Olympics. Ask: *How many seconds did the winners take? Estimate how long you might take. Have a race. How do the results compare with the estimates?*

KEY LANGUAGE

In lesson: measure, **seconds**, minutes, stopwatch
Other language to be used by the teacher: amount, time taken

STRUCTURES AND REPRESENTATIONS

bar model

RESOURCES

Mandatory: analogue and digital clocks that show hours, minutes and seconds

Optional: stopwatch

 In the eTextbook of this lesson, you will find interactive links to a selection of teaching tools.

Before you teach

- Do children know that a minute is 60 seconds?
- Have children seen a stopwatch in real life?

Discover

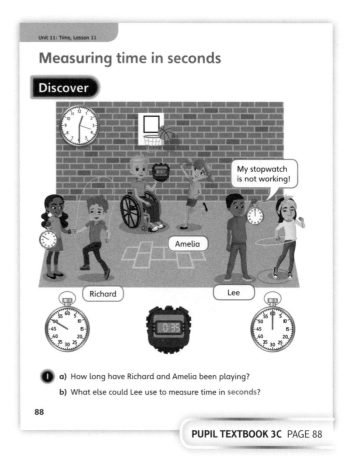

Unit 11: Time, Lesson 11

Measuring time in seconds

Discover

My stopwatch is not working!

Amelia

Richard

Lee

0:35

1 a) How long have Richard and Amelia been playing?

b) What else could Lee use to measure time in seconds?

88

PUPIL TEXTBOOK 3C PAGE 88

WAYS OF WORKING Pair work

ASK

- Question **1** a): *Where might you use seconds every day (hint: timers)? Where can you see the number of seconds on this clock?*
- Question **1** a): *Can you use a clock face to prove that there are 60 seconds in a minute? How?*
- Question **1** a): *There are 60 seconds in 1 minute. How many seconds until the end of a minute if 18 seconds have gone by?*

IN FOCUS Use the pictures to discuss some instances where a stopwatch may be used (for example, measuring the time in a race).

PRACTICAL TIPS Play a minute game in class. Say '*Go!*' and time 1 minute. Each child should close their eyes and silently use their own method to count in seconds; when they think 1 minute is up, they put their hand up. Keep looking at the clock and make a note of the children whose estimates are closest to 1 minute. Ask them to share their methods. Ask: *Can you improve your estimate?*

ANSWERS

Question **1** a): Richard has been playing for 50 seconds. Amelia has been playing for 35 seconds.

Question **1** b): Lee could measure seconds using the clock on the wall, by counting the marks as the second hand moves.

Share

Unit 11: Time, Lesson 11

Share

a) Seconds are used to measure short periods of time.

60 seconds = 1 minute

I second is about the length of time it takes to say 'I second'!

Richard has been playing for 50 seconds.

Amelia has been playing for 35 seconds.

b) The red hand counts round the clock in seconds.

I know that each mark on the clock face shows one second.

Lee could measure seconds using the clock on the wall, by counting the marks as the second hand moves.

89

PUPIL TEXTBOOK 3C PAGE 89

WAYS OF WORKING Whole class teacher led

ASK

- *What are seconds used for?*
- *How many seconds are there in 1 minute?*
- *Why do we use a stopwatch? How could we measure seconds if we didn't have a stopwatch?*
- *How do the two stopwatches in the picture differ?*
- *Do all clocks have a second hand? Why? Why not?*

IN FOCUS Ensure children are confident reading the stopwatches in the picture. Make sure children understand that there are 60 seconds in 1 minute, and they can show how this is measured on a stopwatch and an analogue clock. Ask: *How do a stopwatch and an analogue clock differ?*

STRENGTHEN Some children may not have enough experience measuring in seconds. You could ask them to check their heart rate for 30 seconds. Can they predict what their heart rate will be in 1 minute? Ask children to think of activities that could happen in 1 minute and how they can measure them (for example, the number of steps they could walk or the number of sit-ups they could do). Encourage children to set up their own tasks and record their findings.

Think together

Whole class teacher led (I do, We do, You do)

ASK

- Question ❶: *What is the start time? What is the end time?*
- Question ❶ a): *What does the shaded face show?*
- Question ❶ a): *How will you count the duration of time between the start and end times?*
- Question ❶ b): *How can you calculate the duration?*
- Question ❷: *How can you use the bar model to calculate the time left?*
- Question ❷: *Could you record it in a different way?*

IN FOCUS Questions ❶ and ❷ give children pictorial representations of measuring seconds, to scaffold their learning of start time, end time and duration. Provide plastic clocks or laminated stopwatch pictures to support their learning.

STRENGTHEN To strengthen understanding of question ❶, ask children to mark the start times and the end times. Ensure they understand that each mark on the stopwatch in part a) shows one second. Ask children to think about how this question differs from other questions they have solved in previous lessons. Ask: *What do you know? What do you have to find out?*

DEEPEN When solving question ❸, deepen children's understanding by asking them to show two different ways to work out the answers, for example counting up in multiples of 30 seconds.

ASSESSMENT CHECKPOINT Children should be able to recognise that there are 60 seconds in 1 minute. They should be confident converting minutes into seconds by using different representations including the bar model.

ANSWERS

Question ❶ a): Star jumps take 37 seconds,

Question ❶ b): Running takes 43 seconds

Question ❷: $60 - 48 = 12$

　　　　　　There are 12 seconds left.

Question ❸ a): 30 seconds

Question ❸ b): 90 seconds

Question ❸ c): 150 seconds

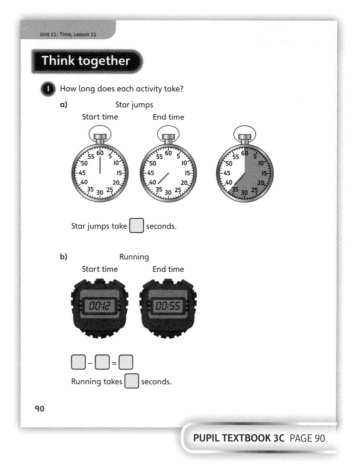

PUPIL TEXTBOOK 3C PAGE 90

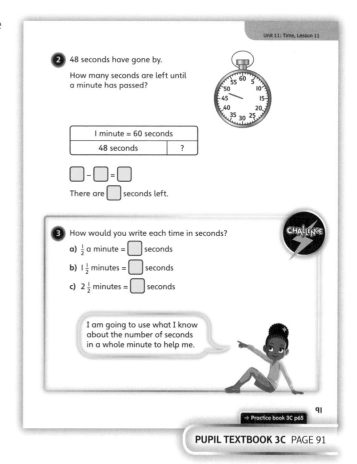

PUPIL TEXTBOOK 3C PAGE 91

122

Practice

WAYS OF WORKING Independent thinking

IN FOCUS Question ❶ gives children the opportunity to work with pictorial representations of time to develop their ability to measure time in seconds. Ask: *Which picture do you find the easiest to read? Which picture is the trickiest?*

Children should be familiar with the different ways used to measure seconds.

STRENGTHEN Question ❷ offers concrete examples of measuring time in seconds. Children use their knowledge of fractions to convert between minutes and seconds. If children are struggling with the abstract representation of time, provide the concrete and pictorial representations that they have been using before.

DEEPEN Provide children with blank stopwatch faces and ask them to show each of the times included in question ❹ . Repeat with an analogue clock.

ASSESSMENT CHECKPOINT At this point in the lesson children should be confident in estimating time in seconds and should know that there are 60 seconds in 1 minute. Children are able to convert minutes to seconds and vice versa. Look for children using the concrete and pictorial representations they have worked with to support their learning.

ANSWERS Answers for the **Practice** part of the lesson appear in the separate **Practice and Reflect answer guide**.

Reflect

WAYS OF WORKING Pair work

IN FOCUS The question revisits the misconception that counting to 60 is 1 minute, regardless of how slow or fast. Give children time to discuss with their partner how they would help Bella overcome her misconception. Provide children with a stopwatch or analogue clock and ask them to use these to justify their answers.

ASSESSMENT CHECKPOINT Children should recognise that there are 60 seconds in 1 minute. They should be able to estimate with confidence a minute, and understand that 1 minute is made of 60 equal intervals which are called seconds.

Children explore different ways of estimating 1 minute. Listen to children's reasoning as to why they chose the methods they did.

ANSWERS Answers for the **Reflect** part of the lesson appear in the separate **Practice and Reflect answer guide**.

After the lesson

- Are children confident of how many seconds are in 1 minute?
- Can children confidently estimate 1-minute intervals?
- Are they secure in converting from minutes to seconds and from seconds to minutes?

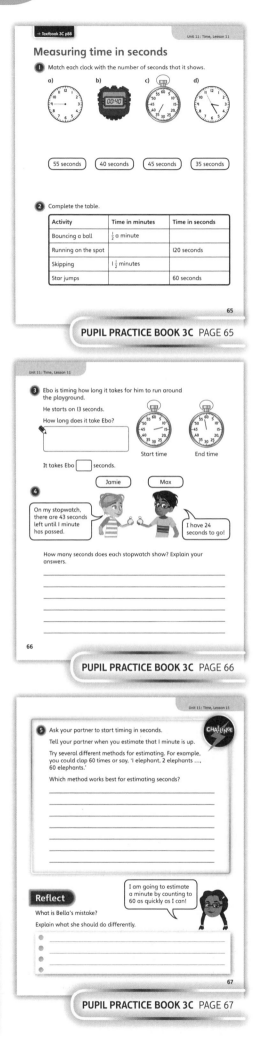

PUPIL PRACTICE BOOK 3C PAGE 65

PUPIL PRACTICE BOOK 3C PAGE 66

PUPIL PRACTICE BOOK 3C PAGE 67

End of unit check

> Don't forget the *Power Maths* unit assessment grid on p26.

WAYS OF WORKING Group work adult led

IN FOCUS

- Question **1** assesses children's ability to recognise the months that have 30 days. Ask: *How do you remember which months have 30 days and which months have 31 days?*
- Question **2** assesses children's ability to recognise the number of months in a year, the number of days in a year and the number of hours in a day. Ask: *What is a leap year?*
- Question **3** assesses children's ability to tell the time in different ways such as 'am' and 'pm', minutes past, minutes to, 12-hour and 24-hour time. It also provides an opportunity to discuss similarities and differences between times such as 16:58, and '2 minutes to 5' am. Ask: *How are these times the same and different?*
- Question **4** assesses children's ability to find the end time when given the start time and duration, and to use different representations to record the time. Ask: *What is the start time/end time? What does duration mean?*
- Question **5** assesses children's ability to recognise that there are 60 seconds in 1 minute, and to convert minutes into seconds. Ask: *How many seconds are there in 1 minute?*

ANSWERS AND COMMENTARY

Children will demonstrate mastery by knowing how many days there are in each month. Children use different ways to record the time, including using the 12-hour clock and 24-hour clock, digital and analogue clock, am and pm.

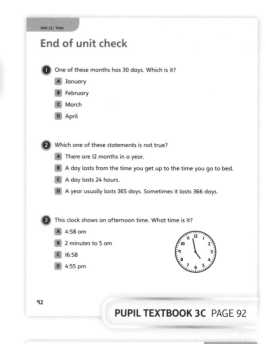

PUPIL TEXTBOOK 3C PAGE 92

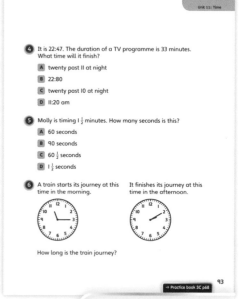

PUPIL TEXTBOOK 3C PAGE 93

Q	A	WRONG ANSWERS AND MISCONCEPTIONS	STRENGTHENING UNDERSTANDING
1	D	Choosing A, B or C may indicate a lack of understanding about the number of days in each month.	To help children gain fluency in their understanding and use of time:
2	B	Choosing A, C or D may indicate a lack of understanding about time.	• Make sure there are calendars in the classrooms showing clearly all the months of the year.
3	C	Choosing A or B may indicate a lack of understanding as to what am means. Choosing D may indicate that children are not able to read time to the nearest minute.	• Clearly label all representations of analogue and digital clocks around the classroom.
4	A	Choosing B or C may indicate that children lack experience in working with duration across an hour.	• Give access to 12-hour and 24-hour clocks throughout the day.
5	B	Choosing A may indicate children have for misread the question. C and D indicate a lack of understanding of how to find half of 1 minute in seconds.	• Provide train and bus timetables and TV guides. Use these to: find start/end times or durations of TV programmes; convert 12-hour time to 24-hour time and vice versa; and find the duration of journeys.
6	2 h 55 m	Other answers may indicate that children do not understand durations crossing one or more hours – for example, they may have added the start and end time hours and/or minutes.	

My journal

ANSWERS AND COMMENTARY

Question **1**:

For each time, children may record answers such as those shown below:

a) I know that the time is 25 minutes to 3 because:
- the hour hand has passed the 2 and is travelling towards the 3
- the minute hand is in the 'to' section of the clock.
- the minute hand is pointing at 7 which means 35 minutes past
- I can count 25 minutes to 3.

b) I know that the time is 17 minutes past 8 because:
- the minute hand is pointing 2 minutes away from 15 minutes past, so it is
- 17 minutes past 8
- the minute hand is in the 'past' section of the clock.

c) I know that the time is 9 minutes to 5 because:
- the minute hand is in the 'to' section of the clock
- the minute hand is pointing at 1 minute away from '10 minutes to'.

Encourage children to give reasons. Ask:
- *Where is the minute hand pointing to? Can you count the minutes?*
- *What part of the clock is the minute hand in, 'to' or 'past'? How do you know?*
- *What do the hour hands tell you on each clock face?*

Question **2**:

Answers should demonstrate that children can draw times on analogue clock faces and write the corresponding times in words.

Power check

WAYS OF WORKING Independent thinking

ASK

- *What did you know about reading and writing time before this unit?*
- *What new ideas and words have you learnt?*
- *How confident do you feel about reading and recording the time?*
- *Do you think you could look at a TV schedule at home and tell how long a programme lasts? What time does it start? What time does it end?*

Power play

WAYS OF WORKING Independent thinking or Pair work

IN FOCUS This game will assess children's ability to recognise times presented in different ways, and to identify the start and end times of 23-minute durations. It may help them to have the representations used in this unit at hand.

ANSWERS AND COMMENTARY If children are unable to follow the route accurately, give them opportunities to practise matching written times with pictorial and concrete representations of an analogue clock and a digital clock.

After the unit

- How will you encourage children to measure time beyond this unit? For example, using time in role play, etc.
- Is your classroom/school a 'time-rich' environment? Is there a calendar/digital clock/analogue clock in each room? How could resources be improved to deepen children's fluency and use of time?

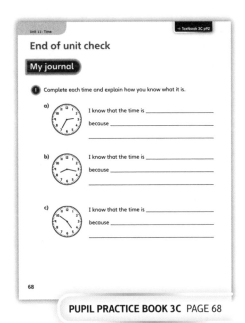

PUPIL PRACTICE BOOK 3C PAGE 68

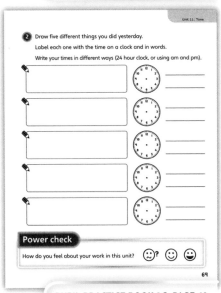

PUPIL PRACTICE BOOK 3C PAGE 69

PUPIL PRACTICE BOOK 3C PAGE 70

Strengthen and **Deepen** activities for this unit can be found in the *Power Maths* online subscription.

Unit 12
Angles and properties of shapes

Mastery Expert tip! "When I taught this unit, I used examples I could refer to within the school environment – square or rectangular tiles, vertical and horizontal lines around the classroom, parallel and perpendicular lines marked on the school playground. We turned quarter, half, three-quarter and full turns, varying the starting positions."

Don't forget to watch the Unit 12 video!

WHY THIS UNIT IS IMPORTANT

This unit explores the concept of right angles. Right angles are linked to the concepts of parallel, perpendicular, vertical and horizontal lines and are linked with the angle properties of 2D shapes. Vertical and horizontal lines of symmetry are also explored and, finally, children describe and construct 3D shapes.

Angles are introduced to children as a measure of a turn, establishing that a right angle is a quarter turn, two quarter turns make a half turn, three right angles make a three-quarter turn and four right angles make a full turn. Children will learn that angles less than a right angle are called acute angles and angles greater than a right angle (but less than two right angles) are called obtuse angles. Children will revise the names of 2D shapes. These include triangles (right-angled and isosceles), quadrilaterals (square, rectangle, rhombus, trapezium, parallelogram and kite), pentagons, hexagons and octagons. Children will revise the names of 3D shapes: cube, cuboid, pyramid, prism, cylinder, sphere and cone. This unit will provide an important foundation for further development of the concept of geometry in later years, such as measuring and drawing angles accurately and describing properties of 2D shapes in more detail.

WHERE THIS UNIT FITS

→ Unit 11: Time
→ **Unit 12: Angles and properties of shapes**
→ Unit 13: Mass

This unit builds on children's understanding of the names and some of the properties of 2D and 3D shapes. It extends children's basic comprehension of these shapes with an emphasis on identifying right angles, lines of symmetry, vertical and horizontal lines and parallel and perpendicular lines and edges.

Before they start this unit, it is expected that children:
- understand what is meant by a 2D shape and are able to recognise and name most of them
- understand what is meant by a 3D shape and are able to recognise and name most of them.

ASSESSING MASTERY

Children who have mastered this unit will understand that angles are a measure of a turn and will recognise acute and obtuse angles. Children will recognise and identify vertical and horizontal lines in diagrams and 2D shapes. Children will identify pairs of parallel or perpendicular lines in diagrams and 2D shapes. Children will begin to describe 2D and 3D shapes in terms of the properties of right angles, parallel and perpendicular edges and lines of symmetry.

COMMON MISCONCEPTIONS	STRENGTHENING UNDERSTANDING	GOING DEEPER
Children may not recognise right angles, symmetry or parallel lines when shapes are in different orientations.	Mark 2D shapes with their right angles and parallel/perpendicular lines and then turn them 45 degrees. Record both on squared paper.	Encourage children to consider 'always, sometimes, never' relating to right angles, and parallel and perpendicular lines in 2D shapes, especially in quadrilaterals.
Children mix up the terms parallel and perpendicular and horizontal and vertical.	Give plenty of opportunity to explore all these concepts in and around school.	Children explore changing a pair of parallel lines into a pair of perpendicular lines and vice versa by turning one line a quarter turn.

Unit 12: Angles and properties of shapes

WAYS OF WORKING

Use these pages with the whole class to revise the names and some of the properties of 2D and 3D shapes introduced in KS1; use the actual shapes rather than just the images on the page. Do children recognise any of the key language? Discuss where they may have heard some of these words previously.

STRUCTURES AND REPRESENTATIONS

2D shapes:

right-angled triangle   isosceles triangle   rhombus

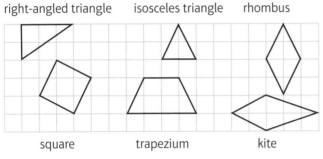

square   trapezium   kite

3D shapes:

cuboid   triangular prism   square-based pyramid

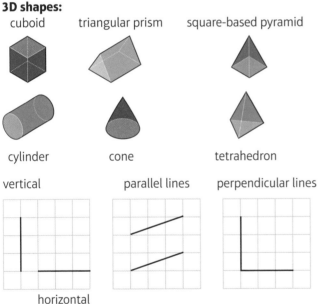

cylinder   cone   tetrahedron

vertical   parallel lines   perpendicular lines

horizontal

KEY LANGUAGE

There is some key language that children will need to know as part of the learning in this unit:

→ right angle, quarter turn, half turn, acute angle, obtuse angle

→ vertical, horizontal, parallel, perpendicular

→ triangle, quadrilateral, square, rectangle, trapezium, rhombus, kite, pentagon, hexagon

→ cube, cuboid, sphere, pyramid, prism, cylinder, cone, triangular prism, square-based pyramid, tetrahedron

→ describe, property, 2D, 3D, draw accurately, construct

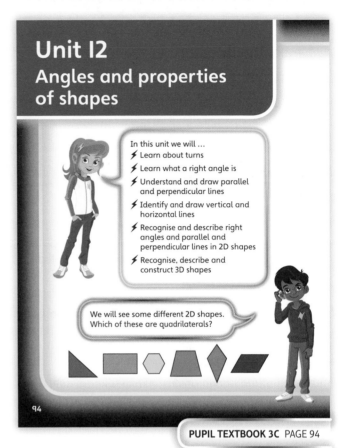

Unit 12
Angles and properties of shapes

In this unit we will ...
- ⚡ Learn about turns
- ⚡ Learn what a right angle is
- ⚡ Understand and draw parallel and perpendicular lines
- ⚡ Identify and draw vertical and horizontal lines
- ⚡ Recognise and describe right angles and parallel and perpendicular lines in 2D shapes
- ⚡ Recognise, describe and construct 3D shapes

We will see some different 2D shapes. Which of these are quadrilaterals?

94

PUPIL TEXTBOOK 3C PAGE 94

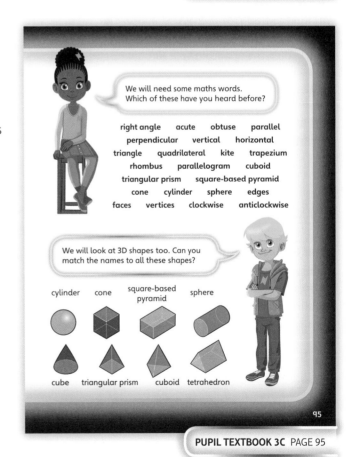

We will need some maths words. Which of these have you heard before?

right angle   acute   obtuse   parallel
perpendicular   vertical   horizontal
triangle   quadrilateral   kite   trapezium
rhombus   parallelogram   cuboid
triangular prism   square-based pyramid
cone   cylinder   sphere   edges
faces   vertices   clockwise   anticlockwise

We will look at 3D shapes too. Can you match the names to all these shapes?

cylinder   cone   square-based pyramid   sphere

cube   triangular prism   cuboid   tetrahedron

95

PUPIL TEXTBOOK 3C PAGE 95

Turns and angles

Learning focus

In this lesson, children understand angles as a measure of turn. Children learn that a right angle is a quarter turn, two right angles make a half turn, and four right angles make a whole turn.

Small steps

→ Previous step: Measuring time in seconds
→ **This step: Turns and angles**
→ Next step: Right angles in shapes

NATIONAL CURRICULUM LINKS

Year 3 Geometry – Properties of Shapes
- Recognise angles as a property of shape or a description of a turn.
- Identify right angles, recognise that two right angles make a half turn, three make three quarters of a turn and four a complete turn; identify whether angles are greater than or less than a right angle.

ASSESSING MASTERY

Children can follow rotations in steps of a quarter turn, both clockwise and anticlockwise. Children can explain the effect of turning two quarter turns, and how many right-angle turns are equivalent to a full turn.

COMMON MISCONCEPTIONS

Children may not recognise turns if they are presented in different orientations. Ask:
- *Face the window. Face this corner. Where will you be facing after a quarter turn? After a half turn?*

Children may struggle to sense which way is clockwise and which is anticlockwise, especially when given different starting positions. Ask:
- *If you turn clockwise, is that to the left or the right? What do you see first when you turn anticlockwise?*

STRENGTHENING UNDERSTANDING

Give children the opportunity to turn themselves, physically. Practise as a class: start facing the walls but then turn at a diagonal, facing a corner. Then use toy figures on a simple map to enact the turns. Practise turning clockwise and listing the things children see in order. Repeat with a turn anticlockwise. Give children a clock face with moveable hands to place on the floor in front of them.

GOING DEEPER

Use a simple treasure map on a grid (or ask children to draw one with four or five features marked). Ask children to write instructions to get from one feature to another, using the language of turns.

KEY LANGUAGE

In lesson: angle, **right angle**, turn, direction, quarter turn, half turn, complete turn, clockwise, anticlockwise

Other language used by the teacher: three-quarter turn, right-angle turn, whole turn, north, south, east, west

RESOURCES

Optional: toy figures, diagrams of eight-point compass (or chalks so this can be drawn on the playground), an object to represent the rover

 In the eTextbook of this lesson, you will find interactive links to a selection of teaching tools.

Before you teach ⏸

- Do children know the difference between clockwise and anticlockwise?
- Can children describe a half turn and a quarter turn?

Discover

WAYS OF WORKING Pair work

ASK

• Question ❶ a): *What feature is the rover facing?*
• Question ❶ a): *What will this button make the rover do?*
• Question ❶ a): *Imagine you are the rover. Which way could you turn first?*
• Question ❶ b): *Can you turn more than once?*

IN FOCUS The purpose of this activity is for children to develop an understanding of quarter turns in relation to half and whole turns.

Question ❶ a) focuses on combining two quarter turns to make a half turn.

Question ❶ b) develops an understanding that combining four quarter turns makes a whole (complete) turn.

PRACTICAL TIPS This could be enacted with a small toy vehicle, or toy robot. Alternatively, a child could take the place of the rover in a role play. There is an opportunity for taking this task into the hall or the playground, and labelling parts of the room according to the rover's environment, or drawing a 'map' for the rover on the playground in chalk. Children should experience turning two half turns in either direction to see that the end result is the same.

ANSWERS

Question ❶ a): To face the crater, the rover needs to make two quarter turns. It can turn either clockwise or anticlockwise. The final direction will be the same for a half turn.

Question ❶ b) To make a full turn, the rover should make four quarter turns in the same direction. It could turn clockwise or anticlockwise.

Share

WAYS OF WORKING Whole class teacher led

ASK

• Question ❶ a): *Can you show me what a right-angle turn clockwise would look like?*
• Question ❶ b): *How many turns do you need to make before you get back to where you started?*
• Question ❶ b): *Astrid has made a comment about adding fractions. Can you explain what she means?*

IN FOCUS Question ❶ a) demonstrates how two right-angle turns are equivalent to a half turn.

Question ❶ b) shows that four right-angle turns take you back to the original position.

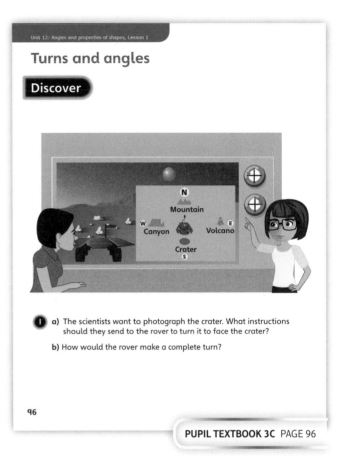

PUPIL TEXTBOOK 3C PAGE 96

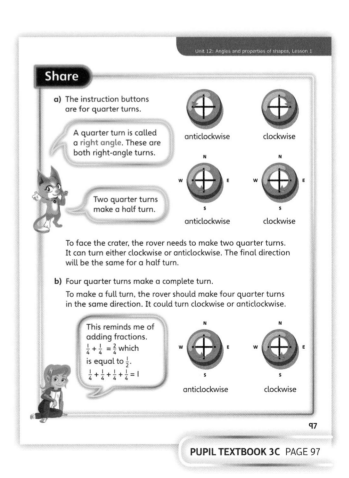

PUPIL TEXTBOOK 3C PAGE 97

Think together

WAYS OF WORKING Whole class teacher led (I do, We do, You do)

ASK

- Question ❶ : *Why are there two possible answers here?*
- Question ❷ : *What happens when the instruction is reversed?*
- Question ❸ : *Why is making a right-angle turn on this map trickier?*

IN FOCUS Question ❶ shows that a quarter turn clockwise has a different result from a quarter turn anticlockwise.

Question ❷ shows that a turn clockwise is reversed by the same turn anticlockwise.

STRENGTHEN Children could use a toy or make the turns themselves. They should practise making quarter turns, then two quarter turns in a sequence, then three and four turns in a sequence.

Children may struggle to remember and have a sense of which way a clockwise and an anticlockwise turn takes them. This should be practised from different starting positions. Place a clock face at their feet.

DEEPEN Challenge children to explain the relationship between a three-quarter turn in one direction, compared with a one quarter turn in the opposite direction. Ask them to explain how to reverse the turn instruction to get back to the start position. Question ❸ challenges children to make and understand turns using right angles which do not use vertical and horizontal lines, but instead the compass points NE, SE, SW and NE.

ASSESSMENT CHECKPOINT Children should now understand the language of quarter, half and whole turns, realising that a quarter turn clockwise will have a different result from a quarter turn anticlockwise. Children will be beginning to understand how instructions can be reversed to get back to the original position.

ANSWERS

Question ❶ : The rover could be facing the volcano or the canyon.

Question ❷ a): The rover is facing the mountain.

Question ❷ b): The rover is now facing the volcano again. A turn anticlockwise reverses the same turn clockwise.

Question ❸ a): The rover was facing the landing craft.

Question ❸ b): Make a quarter turn anticlockwise or make a three-quarter turn clockwise.

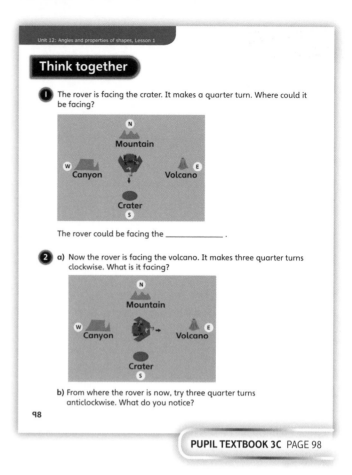

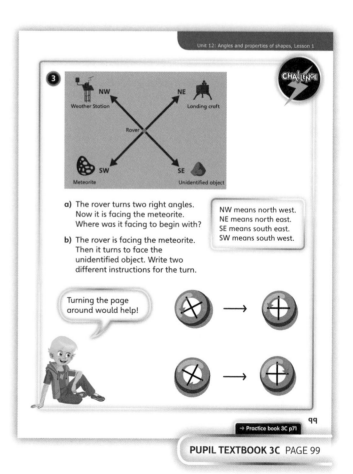

Practice

WAYS OF WORKING Independent thinking

IN FOCUS Questions ❶ and ❷ focus on quarter turns in different contexts. Question ❸ demonstrates that a quarter turn clockwise is the same as a three-quarter turn anticlockwise.

STRENGTHEN Allow children to use a toy figure to move according to each question and act out the turns.

DEEPEN Ask children to discuss and explain to each other what types of turn need to include clockwise and anticlockwise and when it does not matter. In pairs, one child gives an instruction and the other reverses it.

Question ❺ challenges children to apply their understanding of turns to the rotation of simple shapes.

THINK DIFFERENTLY Question ❹, with some compass points being on a 45 degree angle, tests understanding of right-angle turns from non-horizontal or non-vertical lines. It is usual to describe quarter, half or three-quarter turns as one instruction, rather than a half turn followed by a quarter turn, but accept these suggestions.

ASSESSMENT CHECKPOINT Children should now understand the language of quarter, half and whole turns, realising that a quarter turn clockwise will have a different result from a quarter turn anticlockwise. Children will be beginning to understand how instructions can be reversed to get back to the original position.

ANSWERS Answers to the **Practice** part of the lesson appear in a separate **Practice and Reflect answer guide**.

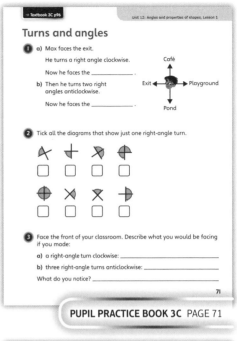

PUPIL PRACTICE BOOK 3C PAGE 71

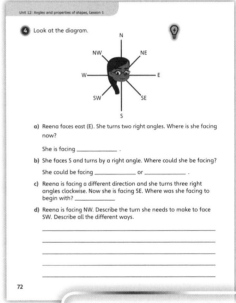

PUPIL PRACTICE BOOK 3C PAGE 72

Reflect

WAYS OF WORKING Independent thinking

IN FOCUS This challenges children to recognise the difference between clockwise and anticlockwise for a single right angle and how this differs for a half turn or whole turn.

ASSESSMENT CHECKPOINT If children can explain accurately the need to include direction (clockwise and anticlockwise) when making a quarter turn but not when making a half or full turn, they will have a good understanding of the language of turns and angles.

ANSWERS Answers to the **Reflect** part of the lesson appear in a separate **Practice and Reflect answer guide**.

After the lesson ⏸

- How many right-angle turns are required for a whole turn?
- Do you have any advice for how to remember the difference between clockwise and anticlockwise?

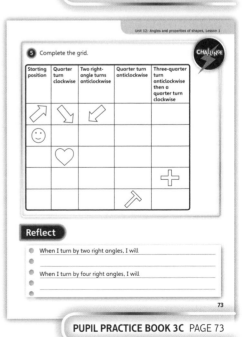

PUPIL PRACTICE BOOK 3C PAGE 73

Right angles in shapes

Learning focus

In this lesson, children develop their understanding of right angles to include the measure of an angle in a shape. They learn the symbol that indicates a right angle and are introduced to the idea of perpendicular lines.

Small steps

→ Previous step: Turns and angles
→ **This step: Right angles in shapes**
→ Next step: Comparing angles

NATIONAL CURRICULUM LINKS

Year 3 Geometry – Properties of Shapes
- Recognise angles as a property of shape or a description of a turn.
- Identify right angles, recognise that two right angles make a half turn, three make three quarters of a turn and four a complete turn; identify whether angles are greater than or less than a right angle.

ASSESSING MASTERY

Children can recognise right angles in shapes in different orientations, and can draw a pair of perpendicular lines to create a right angle.

COMMON MISCONCEPTIONS

Children may struggle to recognise right angles that are oriented diagonally – where neither line is horizontal or vertical. Ask:
- *How can you check whether this is a right angle or not? Does it help to turn the paper round?*

Children may not understand how the measure of turn is linked to the measure of an angle in a shape. Ask:
- *How can you check whether this angle is the same as, greater than or less than a quarter turn?*

STRENGTHENING UNDERSTANDING

Encourage children to use their reasoning skills to predict if an angle is a right angle, greater than a right angle or less than a right angle; then support children to make right-angle measures, or to use the corner of a 2D square to check. Help children to understand how to orient and read the measure in order to check the angle.

GOING DEEPER

Challenge children to use the reasoning of a grid to justify whether or not an angle is a right angle, using the properties of the grid to support their reasoning, especially when two diagonal lines form the angle.

KEY LANGUAGE

In lesson: right angle, angle, **perpendicular**, angle measurer, curved, straight, shape

Other language used by the teacher: square, rectangle, arrow, right-angled triangle, reflex angle, greater than (>), less than (<), predict, prediction, diagonally, measure of turn, quarter turn, half turn

STRUCTURES AND REPRESENTATIONS

2D shapes

RESOURCES

Mandatory: right-angle measurer (folded paper, ruler or 2D square or rectangle)

 In the eTextbook of this lesson, you will find interactive links to a selection of teaching tools.

Before you teach

- Can children find the angles in a shape?
- Do they know what right angle means?

Discover

WAYS OF WORKING Pair work

ASK

- Question ① a): *How can you recognise a right angle?*
- Question ① a): *Which parts of this shape could show a right angle?*
- Question ① a): *Which shapes cannot show a right angle? Why?*
- Question ① b): *What is the symbol for a right angle in a 2D shape?*

IN FOCUS This is the first time that children are asked to recognise right angles in a shape. Allow them to make a right-angle measurer by folding paper and show them how to use it to test which angles are right angles. Discuss together how children can tell that some of the angles are not right angles or that a shape will not contain right angles. Curved lines cannot make right angles.

PRACTICAL TIPS Use large 2D replicas of the shapes shown in the picture, allowing children to use the angle measurer to check these angles.

ANSWERS

Question ① a): Five shapes have at least one right angle (rectangle – 4; purple trapezium – 2; square – 4; right-angled triangle – 1; irregular hexagon – 5).

Question ① b): There should be squared angle marker in every right angle; lines meeting at a right angle are perpendicular.

Share

WAYS OF WORKING Whole class teacher led

ASK

- Question ① a): *How can the measurer be used to check this angle?*
- Question ① a): *How do you line up the measurer to check the angle accurately?*
- Question ① a): *Can you predict whether any of these angles are not right angles before you check?*
- Question ① b): *How many right-angle symbols do you need to show on the rectangle?*

IN FOCUS Question ① a) shows children how to use an angle measurer and how to check whether an angle is a right angle, greater than a right angle or less than a right angle. Children should be given the opportunity to discuss how they know that the circle, hexagon and isosceles trapezium do not have right angles.

Question ① b) shows children how to mark right angles using conventional notation.

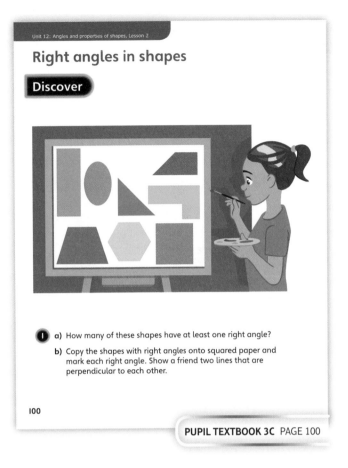

PUPIL TEXTBOOK 3C PAGE 100

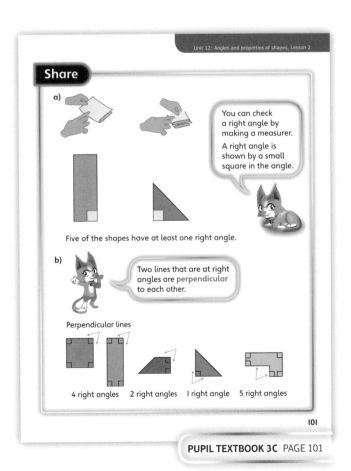

PUPIL TEXTBOOK 3C PAGE 101

Think together

WAYS OF WORKING Whole class teacher led (I do, We do, You do)

ASK

- Question **1** : *Can you measure the angle in a curve?*
- Question **2** : *Should you measure the angles inside or outside the shape?*
- Question **4** : *How could you use the pattern of the grid to decide where to draw the lines?*

IN FOCUS Questions **1** and **2** develop an understanding of recognising right angles in different orientations, and recognising non-examples (curved lines).

STRENGTHEN Encourage children to practise using a measurer, but also to make predictions before they measure so that the tool becomes a means of checking, and their predictions require some visual reasoning. Use large scale 2D shapes to make the task easier.

DEEPEN Challenge children to explain how to use a grid to find right angles in different orientations (diagonals). Question **4** challenges children to use the grid to decide where to draw right angles. This revisits the word perpendicular, introduced in the **Share** section and is covered more explicitly in a later lesson. The lines do not need to cross, and can be any length, but all should be drawn carefully, joining the dots not going between them.

ASSESSMENT CHECKPOINT Children should be able to use an informal paper angle measurer to check if an angle is a right angle, identify angles that are clearly not right angles and explain that curved lines cannot show right angles.

ANSWERS

Question **1** : There are 8 right angles on the hockey pitch.

Question **2** : A 2; B 4; C 0; D 3

Question **3** : Each shape has five internal right angles and one reflex angle that is a three-quarter turn. The external angle at the reflex is a right angle. It is more common to measure the internal angles of a shape.

Question **4** : Solutions are as shown below. The lines can be shorter and they do not need to cross the given line.

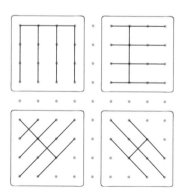

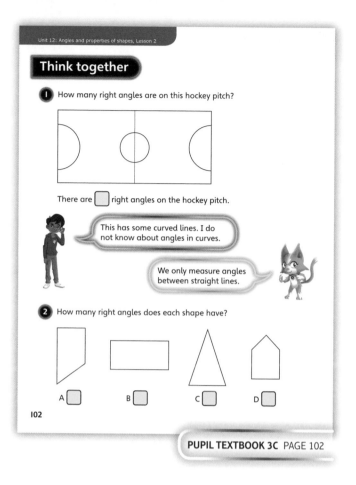

PUPIL TEXTBOOK 3C PAGE 102

PUPIL TEXTBOOK 3C PAGE 103

Practice

WAYS OF WORKING Independent thinking

IN FOCUS Question ❶ tests recognition of right angles, and the understanding that they cannot be formed by a curved line.

Question ❷ focuses on right angles in 2D shapes that are oriented in different ways.

Question ❹ focuses on forming pairs of perpendicular lines on a dotted grid when one line is given.

Question ❻ is a logic puzzle with clues involving recognition of right angles.

STRENGTHEN Encourage children to use visual reasoning and justify predictions before checking with an angle measurer. Examples on a slant could be turned to vertical/horizontal. Provide a variety of physical 2D shapes for children to identify the right angles in each. Ask: *Is this angle less than a right angle? Is it greater than a right angle?*

DEEPEN There are several solutions to question ❹ . Challenge children to find all the different solutions to each. There are a limited number if you insist the lines join the dots.

THINK DIFFERENTLY Question ❸ challenges children to identify plausible misconceptions about right angles.

ASSESSMENT CHECKPOINT Children should be able to identify correctly the internal right angles of a variety of 2D shapes and be able to show pairs of perpendicular lines on a grid, including those on a diagonal. They will be beginning to identify angles within shapes that are greater than or less than a right angle and will know that right angles cannot be formed on curved lines.

ANSWERS Answers to the **Practice** part of the lesson appear in a separate **Practice and Reflect answer guide**.

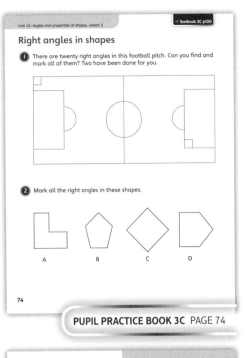

PUPIL PRACTICE BOOK 3C PAGE 74

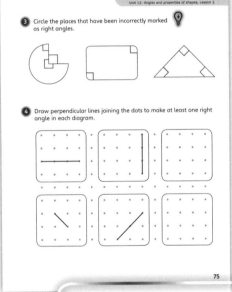

PUPIL PRACTICE BOOK 3C PAGE 75

Reflect

WAYS OF WORKING Independent thinking

IN FOCUS This is an open opportunity for children to demonstrate their understanding. Once complete, they should share their shape with others, and use the right-angle notation to identify the three right angles.

ASSESSMENT CHECKPOINT Children accurately show a shape with exactly three right angles and use the correct notation to denote them.

ANSWERS Answers to the **Reflect** part of the lesson appear in a separate **Practice and Reflect answer guide**.

After the lesson ⏸

- Can children recognise right angles in different orientations?
- Can children explain the link between right angles and pairs of perpendicular lines?
- Can children use an angle measurer to check predictions made based on visual reasoning on grids?

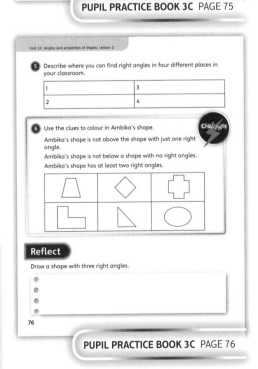

PUPIL PRACTICE BOOK 3C PAGE 76

135

Comparing angles

Learning focus

In this lesson, children learn how to recognise angles that are greater than, equal to or less than a right angle. They are introduced to the terms acute and obtuse.

Small steps

→ Previous step: Right angles in shapes
→ **This step: Comparing angles**
→ Next step: Drawing accurately

NATIONAL CURRICULUM LINKS

Year 3 Geometry – Properties of Shapes
- Identify right angles, recognise that two right angles make a half turn, three make three quarters of a turn and four a complete turn; identify whether angles are greater than or less than a right angle.
- Recognise angles as a property of shape or a description of a turn.

ASSESSING MASTERY

Children can identify acute and obtuse angles in relation to a right angle in different orientations, using visual reasoning and checking with a right-angle measurer. They can use reasoning to predict or justify whether an angle is greater or less than a right angle.

COMMON MISCONCEPTIONS

Children may think that an angle is a measure of the size of the space between two lines, and so may think that a given angle is larger if the lines extend further. Ask:
- *How could you compare the size of these two angles to see which is smaller/larger?*

STRENGTHENING UNDERSTANDING

Children could use two rods hinged together at a point, or a folded piece of card, to create angles greater than, equal to or less than a right angle in different orientations. They should start with a right angle, and close the rods (or card) in for an acute angle and open them further out for an obtuse angle. Children could also demonstrate the angles by creating an angle between their arms, or they could move the hands on a clock face to form right angles first, then obtuse or acute angles.

GOING DEEPER

Challenge children to make reasoned predictions before checking with a measure. They could use the properties of a given background (such as squared paper or a clock face) to justify their reasoning.

KEY LANGUAGE

In lesson: compare, angle, right angle, **acute**, **obtuse**, greater than (>), less than (<), equal to (=), turn, measure

Other language to be used by the teacher: predict, space, size, straight line, half turn, quarter turn, complete turn

STRUCTURES AND REPRESENTATIONS

Geoboard

RESOURCES

Optional: clock faces with moveable hands, a pair of hinged rods, pipe cleaners, two rulers or folded card to make angles, squared paper, geoboards and bands or square dotted paper to represent geoboards

 In the eTextbook of this lesson, you will find interactive links to a selection of teaching tools.

Before you teach

- Can children show you a right angle with their arms or a folded piece of paper?
- Do children know that a right angle is a quarter turn?

Discover

WAYS OF WORKING Pair work

ASK

- Question ❶: *Which angle do you need to measure in order to answer the question?*
- Question ❶: *Are you looking for roof angles less than or greater than a right angle?*
- Question ❶: *How can you measure each angle?*
- Question ❶: *Can you see any right angles?*

IN FOCUS Here, children's attention is drawn to the angle formed at the peak of the roof, and they consider how this angle relates to the pitch of the roof. Children may want to discuss the physical/engineering reasons that underlie the context, but should return to a comparison of the angle at the apex of each roof.

PRACTICAL TIPS Children could form the different angles of each roof by opening or leaning books to an approximation of the given angles. Alternatively, children could construct them from folded card, and place them above a box. This could form the basis of an interesting experiment in pouring water from a watering can to represent the rain.

ANSWERS

Question ❶ a): House C would be good in a snowy country.

Question ❶ b): Houses B and D would suit a dry country.

Comparing angles

Discover

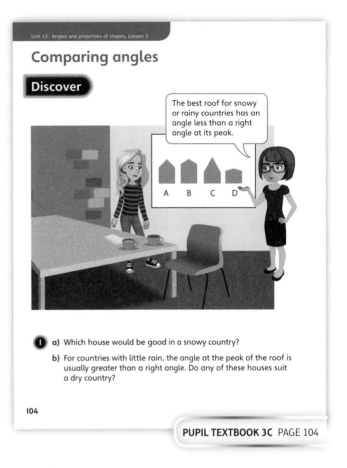

The best roof for snowy or rainy countries has an angle less than a right angle at its peak.

❶ a) Which house would be good in a snowy country?

b) For countries with little rain, the angle at the peak of the roof is usually greater than a right angle. Do any of these houses suit a dry country?

104

PUPIL TEXTBOOK 3C PAGE 104

Share

WAYS OF WORKING Whole class teacher led

ASK

- Question ❶: *Can you predict which roof angle is less than a right angle just by looking?*
- Question ❶: *How should you place a measurer to check your predictions?*
- Question ❶: *Are you looking for roof angles less than or greater than a right angle for this part of the question?*

IN FOCUS Question ❶ a) focuses on identifying the acute angle but without introducing this language.

Question ❶ b) focuses on identifying the two obtuse angles, but once again the language will be formally introduced by Sparks in **Think Together**.

Share

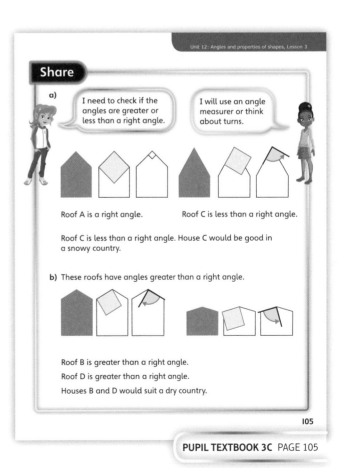

a)

I need to check if the angles are greater or less than a right angle.

I will use an angle measurer or think about turns.

Roof A is a right angle.   Roof C is less than a right angle.

Roof C is less than a right angle. House C would be good in a snowy country.

b) These roofs have angles greater than a right angle.

Roof B is greater than a right angle.
Roof D is greater than a right angle.
Houses B and D would suit a dry country.

105

PUPIL TEXTBOOK 3C PAGE 105

Think together

WAYS OF WORKING Whole class teacher led (I do, We do, You do)

ASK

- Question **1** : *Can you tell just by looking whether this angle is greater than or less than a right angle?*
- Question **1** : *Is an acute angle greater than or less than a right angle?*
- Question **2** : *Which numbers on a clock are at right angles to each other?*
- Question **2** : *Is the angle between two numbers next to each other on the clock less or more than a right angle?*

IN FOCUS Question **2** uses the angles between numbers on a clock face to identify acute and obtuse angles.

Question **3** asks children to show or make acute and obtuse angles on a geoboard.

STRENGTHEN Ask children to make predictions and check them using a right angle to compare with the given angle. Children should also practise forming different angles by opening the covers of a book, or pivoting their arms about a point. They could use geoboards to explore question **2** : it is helpful for children to see that the angles between 12 and 3, 3 and 6, 6 and 9, and 9 and 12 are all right angles. Link this with quarter turns and the fact that the angle between 12 and 6 is a half turn – as is the angle between all pairs of opposite numbers.

DEEPEN Challenge children to justify their reasoning about different or similar acute and obtuse angles represented on the geoboards in different orientations. Can children recognise when two angles are the same (rotations or reflections of one another)? Extend question **3** by asking children to start with the right angle in a different place on the board.

ASSESSMENT CHECKPOINT Children should be able to recognise, form or draw angles that are greater than, less than or equal to a right angle and explain the terms acute and obtuse in relation to a right angle.

ANSWERS

Question **1** : A and F are acute; B and D are obtuse; C and E are right angles.

Question **2** : A is a right angle; B is acute; C is acute; D is obtuse; E is a right angle; F is obtuse.

Question **3** : There are multiple solutions to this question. If children keep to the given right angle, then there are more acute than obtuse angles possible.

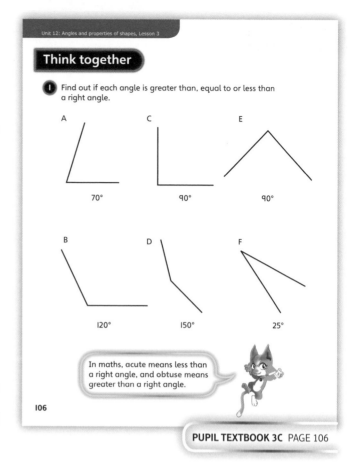

PUPIL TEXTBOOK 3C PAGE 106

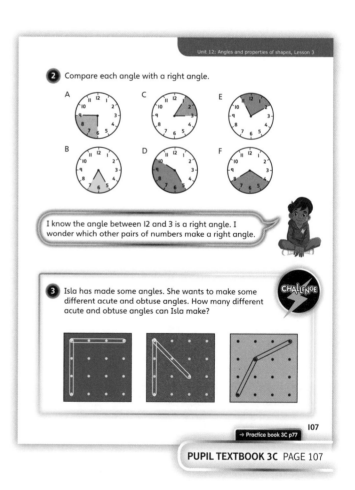

PUPIL TEXTBOOK 3C PAGE 107

Practice

WAYS OF WORKING Independent thinking

IN FOCUS The focus here is on recognising and drawing angles that are less than, greater than or equal to a right angle.

Question **5** asks children to make predictions about acute and obtuse angles and to justify their reasoning.

STRENGTHEN Encourage children to demonstrate acute and obtuse angles as turns, using pipe cleaners bent into the shapes or clock faces with moveable hands.

DEEPEN Challenge children to make generalisations about the angles between numbers on a clock face. For example: between consecutive/ alternate numbers the angles are acute; between three numbers (1 and 4, 2 and 5 and so on) the angle is a right angle; between more than three numbers the angle is obtuse; opposite numbers are on a straight line, or a half turn.

THINK DIFFERENTLY Question **4** will require children to form angles in various orientations to ensure they draw three different angles of each type that are not simply rotations or reflections.

ASSESSMENT CHECKPOINT Children should be able to recognise, form or draw angles that are greater than, less than or equal to a right angle and explain the terms acute and obtuse in relation to a right angle.

ANSWERS Answers to the **Practice** part of the lesson appear in a separate **Practice and Reflect answer guide**.

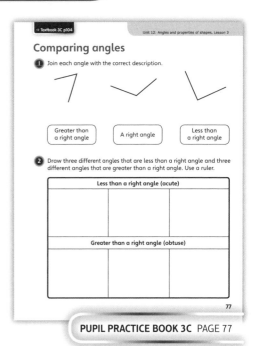

PUPIL PRACTICE BOOK 3C PAGE 77

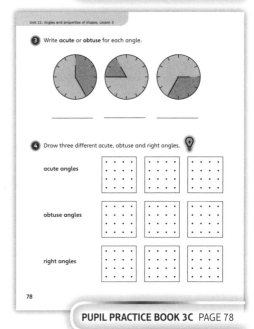

PUPIL PRACTICE BOOK 3C PAGE 78

Reflect

WAYS OF WORKING Independent thinking

IN FOCUS This section asks children to explore their understanding of angles in the school environment. Some children may look around their classroom, while others may visualise angles that are in another part of the school.

ASSESSMENT CHECKPOINT Can children justify their suggestions by comparing the angles with a right angle?

ANSWERS Answers to the **Reflect** part of the lesson appear in a separate **Practice and Reflect answer guide**.

After the lesson ⏸

- Can children recognise angles that are greater than, less than or equal to a right angle in different orientations?
- Do children understand the terms acute and obtuse, explaining them in comparison to a right angle?

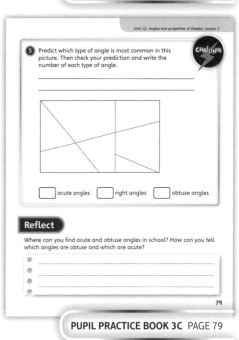

PUPIL PRACTICE BOOK 3C PAGE 79

Drawing accurately

Learning focus

In this lesson, children develop their ability to draw and measure accurately in centimetres and millimetres, and apply this to reasoning about 2D shapes.

Small steps

→ Previous step: Comparing angles
→ **This step: Drawing accurately**
→ Next step: Types of line (1)

NATIONAL CURRICULUM LINKS

Year 3 Geometry – Properties of Shapes
- Draw 2D shapes and make 3D shapes using modelling materials; recognise 3D shapes in different orientations and describe them.
- Identify horizontal and vertical lines and pairs of perpendicular and parallel lines.

ASSESSING MASTERY

Children can measure and draw accurately in centimetres and millimetres and use this skill to form and measure 2D shapes of given dimensions.

COMMON MISCONCEPTIONS

Children may not appreciate the importance of accuracy when drawing and measuring to form specific shapes. Ask:
- *Why is it important to measure the lines accurately when drawing a square?*

Children may not have mastered the ruler skills required. Ask:
- *Are you holding the ruler correctly to measure this line? Can you explain the mistake?*

STRENGTHENING UNDERSTANDING

Help children to measure single lines, and to mark accurately, by supporting their motor skills where necessary: for example, hold the ruler still once they have positioned it correctly.

GOING DEEPER

Challenge children to draw squares and rectangles of any given dimensions given as whole centimetres and millimetres.

KEY LANGUAGE

In lesson: measure, measurement, accurately, ruler, centimetre (cm), millimetre (mm), wide, width, length, predict, check, square, diagonal, opposite, corner

Other language to be used by the teacher: wide, long, rectangle, horizontal, vertical

STRUCTURES AND REPRESENTATIONS

2D shapes

RESOURCES

Mandatory: ruler, scissors, landscape A4 paper cut into 10 cm strips, squared paper

Optional: pre-cut 10 cm squares, plastic/wooden squares and rectangles

 In the eTextbook of this lesson, you will find interactive links to a selection of teaching tools.

Before you teach

- Do children know any common mistakes made when measuring with a ruler?
- Can children explain the difference between centimetres and millimetres?
- Can children draw a line, for example, 3 cm 5 mm long?

Discover

WAYS OF WORKING Pair work

ASK

- Question **1** a): *Where should you place the ruler to start the measurement?*
- Question **1** a): *How do you measure exactly 10 cm?*
- Question **1** a): *How many whole 10 cm squares can be made?*

IN FOCUS Question **1** a) develops the skill of measuring accurately from Unit 8. Here, children are challenged to follow instructions to form a square, which requires accurate measurement.

PRACTICAL TIPS The dimensions of the paper strips are designed to match the width of an A4 piece of paper presented horizontally. Show a piece of A4 paper held horizontally and explain that what is shown in the book is a 10 cm strip cut from this size paper. Cut out an approximate strip of depth 10 cm to demonstrate. Give each child an accurately cut 10 cm deep strip of A4 paper. If the mixed units of 29 cm 7 mm is a distraction for children, then the strips could be pre-cut to a width of 25 cm, for example, and the instructions adapted accordingly.

ANSWERS

Question **1** a): You can make two 10 cm squares. Use a ruler to measure 10 cm accurately across the top and bottom of the strip, make markers, draw a line and cut out the square.

Question **1** b): The piece of paper left over is 9 cm and 7 mm wide.

Share

WAYS OF WORKING Whole class teacher led

ASK

- Question **1** a): *Why do you need to measure and make a mark at the top and the bottom?*
- Question **1** a): *How can you make sure your square is 10 cm along each side?*
- Question **1** b): *How will you find out how wide the left over piece is?*

IN FOCUS This shows children a method for measuring accurately: make two opposing marks and then join them. This skill is transferable to other craft or design activities.

PUPIL TEXTBOOK 3C PAGE 108

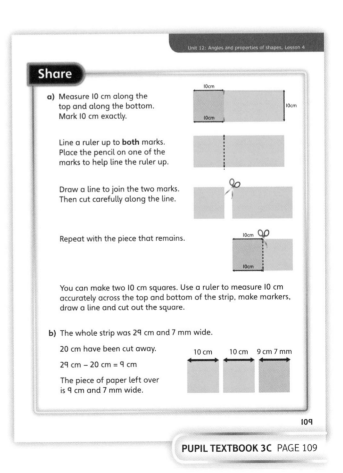

PUPIL TEXTBOOK 3C PAGE 109

Think together

WAYS OF WORKING **WAYS OF WORKING** Whole class teacher led (I do, We do, You do)

ASK

- Question **1** : *Which line will you measure and draw first?*
- Question **2** : *Which line will you cut first?*
- Question **2** : *Do you need to cut out each shape separately?*
- Question **4** : *Is Astrid correct?*

IN FOCUS Questions **1** and **2** focus on accurate measuring. Both use one of the 10 cm squares that were made previously, so it is important that these are accurate. If necessary provide pre-cut 10 cm squares.

Question **4** provides an opportunity for reasoning about the relative lengths of diagonals of squares.

STRENGTHEN Support children with their motor skills where necessary. Children should focus on the skill of measuring accurately, but may need someone to support the ruler while they draw lines to join points. When using squared paper, encourage children to keep to the vertical and horizontal grid lines for relevant sides.

DEEPEN Challenge children to draw squares on squared paper to explore whether both the diagonals of a square are the same length or different lengths and whether the diagonals are always longer than the sides. Children could also explore diagonals in rectangles.

ASSESSMENT CHECKPOINT Children should realise that accurate drawing and measuring is an important skill. They should be able to use a ruler correctly to make the necessary markers to draw and measure the length of the sides of squares and rectangles accurately.

ANSWERS

Question **1** : The lines (horizontal and vertical) should be measured and drawn accurately.

Question **2** : The cut-out shapes are: a 3×3 cm square; a 7×7 cm square; two 3×7 cm rectangles.

Question **3** : Triangle A: 5 cm, Triangle B: 3·6 cm.

Both triangles should be drawn accurately.

Question **4** : Square A: 4·2 cm, Square B: 9·9 cm.

PUPIL TEXTBOOK 3C PAGE 110

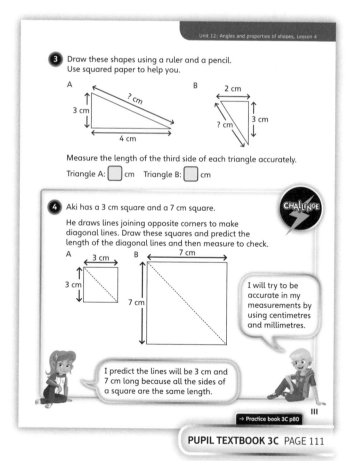

PUPIL TEXTBOOK 3C PAGE 111

Practice

WAYS OF WORKING Independent thinking

IN FOCUS Questions ❶ and ❸ focus on measuring and drawing in centimetres and millimetres.

STRENGTHEN Build children's confidence by measuring some given shapes or using given shapes as stencils, by marking a dot at each corner, and then joining the dots using a ruler; or keep to shapes with most lengths in whole centimetres. Children could measure the lengths of wooden/plastic squares and rectangles for further practice.

DEEPEN Question ❸ challenges children to enhance their accuracy in measuring. Question ❹ challenges children to form shapes of relative size to one another, using proportional reasoning.

For further practice, ask children to measure 2D squares and rectangles and then make accurate drawings of them. They could also explore right-angled triangles. Can children explain why they do not need to measure the diagonal side before they draw it?

THINK DIFFERENTLY In question ❸, children will need to think about where to start for these diagrams as they cannot always begin as before with the vertical/horizontal from the left. If the copies are not accurate encourage children to explain why they think this has happened.

ASSESSMENT CHECKPOINT Children should realise that accurate drawing and measuring is an important skill. They are able to use a ruler correctly to make the necessary markers to draw and measure the length of the sides of squares and rectangles accurately.

ANSWERS Answers to the **Practice** part of the lesson appear in a separate **Practice and Reflect answer guide**.

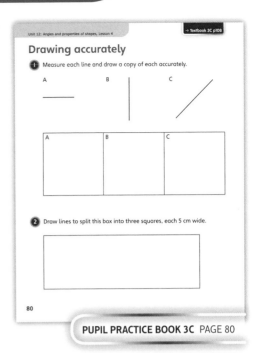

PUPIL PRACTICE BOOK 3C PAGE 80

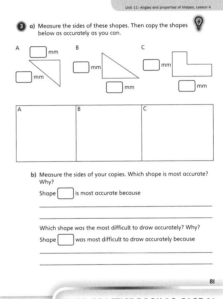

PUPIL PRACTICE BOOK 3C PAGE 81

Reflect

WAYS OF WORKING Independent thinking

IN FOCUS Children need to use the correct words to break the skill down into its key steps.

ASSESSMENT CHECKPOINT Do children's explanations take into account common errors, such as letting the ruler slip or measuring from the wrong mark?

ANSWERS Answers to the **Reflect** part of the lesson appear in a separate **Practice and Reflect answer guide**.

After the lesson ⏸

- Can children measure and join two opposing marks to form a given line?
- Are children able to apply their understanding of millimetres and centimetres to drawing 2D shapes?
- Where children are unsuccessful, what is causing the inaccuracies (measuring, using a ruler or a different reason)?

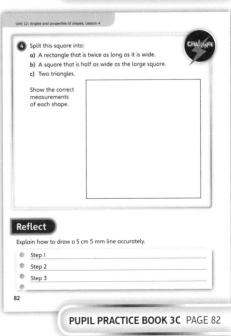

PUPIL PRACTICE BOOK 3C PAGE 82

Types of line ❶

Learning focus

In this lesson, children learn to identify and draw horizontal and vertical lines.

Small steps

→ **Previous** step: Drawing accurately
→ **This step: Types of line (1)**
→ Next step: Types of line (2)

NATIONAL CURRICULUM LINKS

Year 3 Geometry – Properties of Shapes

Identify horizontal and vertical lines and pairs of perpendicular and parallel lines.

ASSESSING MASTERY

Children can identify horizontal and vertical lines, construct horizontal and vertical lines, and recognise where lines are neither vertical nor horizontal. They are able to explain the relevance of horizontal and vertical lines in examples relating to their environment.

COMMON MISCONCEPTIONS

Children may find it difficult to remember which term relates to which property. **Horizon**tal is flat, like the **horizon; vert**ical stands up straight like **vert**ebrae in your back. Children may use the terms 'flat' or straight' instead. Ask:
• *How could you describe the two types of line without using the words 'horizontal' or 'vertical'?*
• *Can a straight line be neither horizontal nor vertical?*

STRENGTHENING UNDERSTANDING

Children could use a range of equipment, such as string, metre sticks or PE benches, to explore the concepts practically. They could try to balance a ball or marble on a table or a plank to keep it still (either horizontally or vertically). Discuss words which have the same roots.

GOING DEEPER

Provide a set of horizontal and non-horizontal lines which have a base line (similar to the ground in the **Discover** picture). Ask children to label those which are horizontal and to measure using a ruler those which are not horizontal to see how far one end needs to be moved in order to make it horizontal.

KEY LANGUAGE

In lesson: horizontal, vertical, straight, lower, higher, height, level, raised, lowered, right angle, line of symmetry, mirror line

Other language to be used by the teacher: plumb line, balanced, metre (m), centimetre (cm)

STRUCTURES AND REPRESENTATIONS

squared paper

RESOURCES

Optional: plumb line, PE equipment, marbles, mirrors, clear pictures of a flat and straight horizon

 In the eTextbook of this lesson, you will find interactive links to a selection of teaching tools.

Before you teach ⏸

• Do children know what it means to sit up straight?
• Do children know what the horizon is?

Discover

Pair work

ASK

- Question ❶ a): *What is the same and what is different about the shelves?*
- Question ❶ a): *Why are shelves designed to be a certain way?*
- Question ❶ b): *How could the shelf be adjusted to make it work better?*

IN FOCUS Children will need to compare the shelves in the picture, and begin to search for an accurate way to describe the type of line they will come to know as horizontal.

PRACTICAL TIPS This context could be adapted in a number of ways. Children could explore horizontal surfaces by looking at when a ball balances motionless on a plank, or they could try walking around with a tennis ball balanced on a racket.

Alternatively, children could look at shelves in different parts of the school and judge why they are all level. Show children pictures of the horizon where there is a clear straight and level line between sea and sky, or land and sky; explain that this is called the horizon, which can help you remember that the word horizontal means level and flat, left to right (or right to left).

ANSWERS

Question ❶ a): The books stand upright on the horizontal shelf but have fallen over on the other shelf.

Question ❶ b): The shelf can be fixed by raising one end to 1 m 55 cm, or lowering the other to 1 m 50 cm.

Share

WAYS OF WORKING Whole class teacher led

ASK

- Question ❶ a): *How do know that one shelf is not horizontal?*
- Question ❶ b): *In how many different ways could the shelf be fixed?*

IN FOCUS This might be the first time children have used the word horizontal. They may need to explore its meaning in terms of their experience of other level situations, such as balancing on a beam, climbing a hill, rolling down a hill or riding a bike.

PUPIL TEXTBOOK 3C PAGE 112

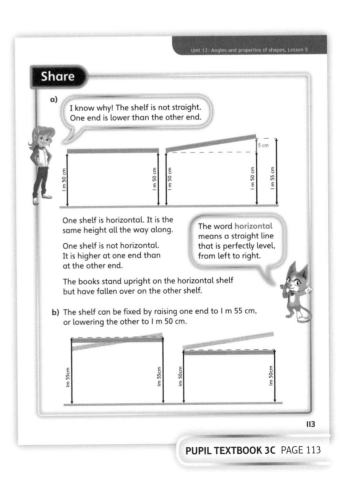

PUPIL TEXTBOOK 3C PAGE 113

Think together

WAYS OF WORKING Whole class teacher led (I do, We do, You do)

ASK

- Question ❶ : *What do horizontal and vertical mean?*
- Question ❶ : *Which are the horizontal parts of the fence? Which are the vertical parts of the fence?*
- Question ❷ : *What causes a plumb line to hang vertically?*
- Question ❸ : *Are lines of symmetry always vertical?*

IN FOCUS Question ❷ demonstrates a method for testing for vertical lines in the environment, and deepens children's understanding of vertical as straight down due to gravity.

Question ❸ applies the concept of vertical and horizontal lines to the context of symmetry in simple polygons. Note that if shapes were turned a quarter turn, then the vertical symmetry lines would become horizontal, and vice versa. This is picked up in **Practice** question ❺ .

STRENGTHEN Explore the language of straight across and straight down in physical terms, by dropping or rolling a ball, and balancing objects.

DEEPEN Challenge children to explore the relationship between gravity and our understanding of horizontal and vertical lines. Ask children to find examples around school where objects that should be vertical or horizontal are not (fence falling down, bent netball post, pictures hung crookedly) and where objects are deliberately not vertical or horizontal for a particular purpose (ramps for example).

ASSESSMENT CHECKPOINT If children are able to recognise both horizontal and vertical lines of symmetry in question ❸ and choose the correct term (vertical or horizontal) to describe the line of symmetry, then they will show good understanding.

ANSWERS

Question ❶ : Fence A has vertical posts and horizontal crosspieces; fence B has vertical posts but crosspieces are not horizontal; fence C has horizontal crosspieces but the posts are not vertical.

Question ❷ : Explore and identify vertical and non-vertical lines using a plumb line around school; children could check door frames, table legs, the backs of chairs, whether walls are vertical, and so on.

Question ❸ a): The triangle, the kite and the trapezium (A, E, F) have horizontal symmetry; the rectangle and the rhombus (B, D) have both vertical and horizontal symmetry; the parallelogram (C) has no lines of symmetry.

Question ❸ b): Children will design different shapes with horizontal lines of symmetry.

PUPIL TEXTBOOK 3C PAGE 114

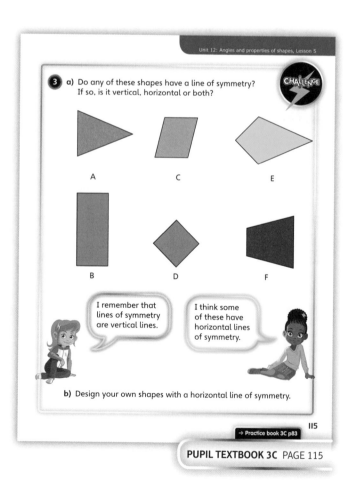

PUPIL TEXTBOOK 3C PAGE 115

Practice

WAYS OF WORKING Independent thinking

IN FOCUS Questions **1** and **2** are about recognising horizontal and vertical lines, and identifying lines which are neither.

Question **3** requires children to draw the given lines.

Question **4** looks for vertical and horizontal lines of symmetry.

Question **6** challenges children to use their measuring skills to show whether or not the lines are vertical or horizontal. Children could predict and then use measuring to test their predictions.

STRENGTHEN Explore horizontal and vertical lines with practical equipment such as string, metre rules, or by aligning PE benches.

DEEPEN Challenge children to apply their measuring skills to prove which lines are or are not vertical or horizontal by measuring from the top and bottom and from the left and right. Ask children to design artwork with vertical and horizontal lines and some lines that are neither horizontal nor vertical.

THINK DIFFERENTLY Question **5** challenges children to think back to the lesson on right-angle turns to change the mirror line from a horizontal to a vertical, or vertical to horizontal, by turning the shape a right-angle quarter turn clockwise or anticlockwise.

ASSESSMENT CHECKPOINT Children should now be able to draw and identify lines that are vertical, horizontal or neither and use this skill to describe lines of symmetry in simple polygons.

ANSWERS Answers to the **Practice** part of the lesson appear in a separate **Practice and Reflect answer guide**.

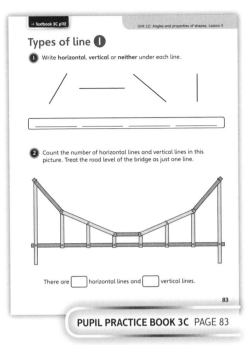

PUPIL PRACTICE BOOK 3C PAGE 83

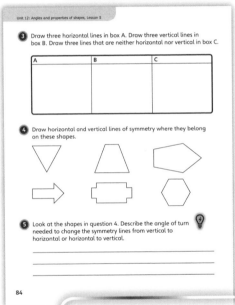

PUPIL PRACTICE BOOK 3C PAGE 84

Reflect

WAYS OF WORKING Independent thinking

IN FOCUS Children should discuss and justify their ideas, based on reasoning about the physical properties of horizontal and vertical lines and surfaces. They could consider where it is necessary, helpful or not important for items to be vertical or horizontal.

ASSESSMENT CHECKPOINT Can children link the technical words to the properties of horizontal and vertical lines?

ANSWERS Answers to the **Reflect** part of the lesson appear in a separate **Practice and Reflect answer guide**.

After the lesson

- Have children developed a good understanding of the two types of line in relation to everyday experience?
- Can children apply their measuring skills to construct and identify horizontal and vertical lines?

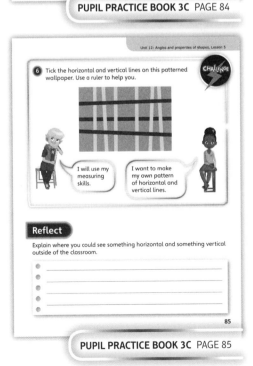

PUPIL PRACTICE BOOK 3C PAGE 85

Types of line ❷

Learning focus

In this lesson, children learn to identify and construct parallel and perpendicular lines.

Small steps

→ Previous step: Types of line (1)
→ **This step: Types of line (2)**
→ Next step: Recognising and describing 2D shapes

NATIONAL CURRICULUM LINKS

Year 3 Geometry – Properties of Shapes

Identify horizontal and vertical lines and pairs of perpendicular and parallel lines.

ASSESSING MASTERY

Children can explain that parallel lines are a constant distance apart, and even if the lines continued indefinitely they would never cross. Children can construct parallel lines that meet this property. They also understand that perpendicular lines intersect at right angles, and can construct a range of lines perpendicular to another line.

COMMON MISCONCEPTIONS

Children may assume that parallel lines must be of identical length. Ask:
• *How can you tell if these two lines are parallel?*

Children may assume that any two lines which do not intersect are parallel. Ask:
• *Would these two lines cross if they were continued?*

Children may confuse the two terms. Explain:
• *The word parallel has the letter 'l' twice in the middle, which itself shows a pair of parallel lines.*

STRENGTHENING UNDERSTANDING

Explore parallel and perpendicular lines through drawing, observing the environment around school, art activities such as weaving, and looking at pieces of modern art (for example, the work of Piet Mondrian).

GOING DEEPER

Can children form parallel lines by reasoning about a shape or a background; for example by measuring regular intervals or using the squares or dots on grid paper (especially for non-horizontal or non-vertical lines)?

KEY LANGUAGE

In lesson: parallel, perpendicular, right angle, distance, ruler, concertina, angle, sign, describe, diagram

Other language to be used by the teacher: measure, identical length, constant distance, construct, intersect, extend, extended

RESOURCES

Mandatory: ruler, paper for folding, square paper, square dotted paper

Optional: examples of modern art that contain parallel and perpendicular lines (Piet Mondrian); circles (see **Practice Book**, question ❺) with 3–10 dots

 In the eTextbook of this lesson, you will find interactive links to a selection of teaching tools.

Before you teach

• Can children use their hands or arms to show a right angle?
• Do children know how to measure the distance between two lines accurately?

Discover

ASK

- Question **1** : *How can the folds be made accurately?*
- Question **2** : *What sorts of lines will the creases make?*

IN FOCUS Children will need to visualise what the creases will look like, before folding and checking for themselves. There may be a need for a discussion around why there could be differences, if some people fold more accurately than others.

PRACTICAL TIPS Children could fold their own sheets of scrap paper, trying to match the concertina Isla is folding. Challenge children to line up the bottom edge with the first fold so that the lines are equally spaced.

Alternatively, children could explore the situation by lining up pencils so they are all facing the same direction, or placing cones in a line so that they form stripes that would never cross.

ANSWERS

Question **1** a): When Isla unfolds the paper, she will see parallel lines made by the folds.

Question **1** b): When Max opens his paper, it will have parallel lines like Isla's, but also perpendicular lines where he has folded his paper in half.

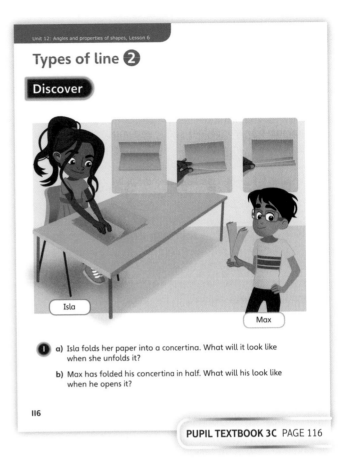

Types of line ②

Discover

1 a) Isla folds her paper into a concertina. What will it look like when she unfolds it?

  b) Max has folded his concertina in half. What will his look like when he opens it?

116

PUPIL TEXTBOOK 3C PAGE 116

Share

ASK

- Question **1** a): *How could you use measuring to check if your creases are parallel?*
- Question **1** a): *Would these creases still be parallel if you turned the page a quarter turn?*
- Question **1** b): *How many horizontal/vertical lines will there be when the paper is opened up?*
- Question **1** b): *At what angle do the lines on Max's paper cross?*

IN FOCUS Children will need to understand that parallel lines are a constant distance apart and would never intersect (cross over), even if extended indefinitely.

Children will also need to understand that perpendicular lines are related to right angles. They either *meet* at a right angle (more often found in 2D shapes) or *cross over* each other at a right angle.

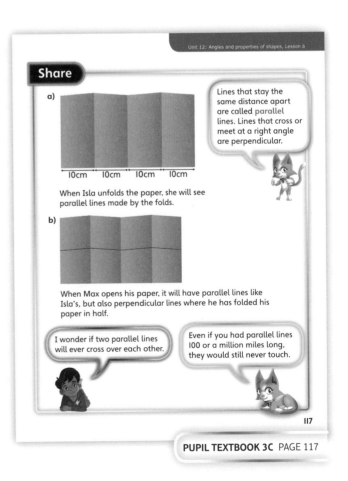

PUPIL TEXTBOOK 3C PAGE 117

Think together

Think together

WAYS OF WORKING Whole class teacher led (I do, We do, You do)

ASK

• Question ❶ : *What types of line can you see in this picture?*
• Question ❶ : *How do you think the artist created this picture?*
• Question ❸ : *How can you tell if lines are parallel or perpendicular?*

IN FOCUS Question ❶ shows vertical and horizontal parallel lines, which then form many pairs of perpendicular lines. By discussing this picture, children will learn that: pairs of parallel lines can be at different distances apart from other pairs; parallel lines can be vertical or horizontal; perpendicular lines can join in the middle of a line not just at the ends, and that perpendicular lines can cross.

Question ❸ a) addresses several misconceptions: sometimes children think that parallel lines must be the same length; that if lines do not actually cross then they must be parallel; and that lines actually have to cross to be perpendicular.

STRENGTHEN Explore parallel lines in different orientations and of different lengths through drawing or lining up strips of paper or straight objects. In question ❸ a), ask children to copy the lines onto squared paper, or use a pair of rulers or rods on the page to continue the lines as far as is necessary, to see if the pairs are parallel, perpendicular or neither.

DEEPEN Question ❸ b) challenges children to use the grid to justify how to draw lines parallel to diagonal lines. Can children spot how to do this by either using the diagonals of the squares or by using the ratio of squares up to squares across?

ASSESSMENT CHECKPOINT Children should be able to use the images in this lesson to explain what they understand about parallel and perpendicular lines and know which word describes each pair of lines. Children should explain that lines can be parallel or perpendicular even when the lines are not vertical or horizontal.

ANSWERS

Question ❶ : There are both vertical and horizontal parallel lines. The vertical lines are all perpendicular to the horizontal lines, and vice versa.

Question ❷ : A ruler has a constant width so will produce parallel lines that are a ruler width apart.

Question ❸ a): A shows parallel lines (they can be on a diagonal)
B shows parallel lines (they need not be the same length)
C does not show parallel lines, as they would cross over if continued further
D shows perpendicular lines because they would cross at right angles if continued further.

Question ❸ b): Various answers are possible. For example: Use the sides of a ruler; count the squares; use the diagonals of the squares.

PUPIL TEXTBOOK 3C PAGE 118

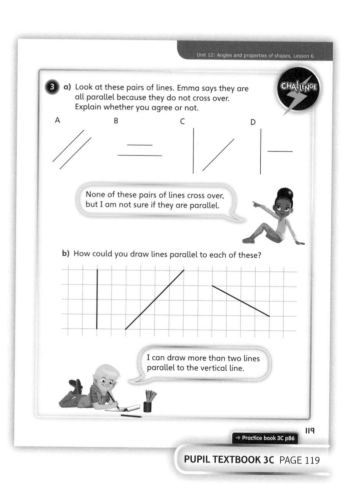

PUPIL TEXTBOOK 3C PAGE 119

Practice

WAYS OF WORKING Independent thinking

IN FOCUS Question ❶ focuses on recognising and drawing parallel and perpendicular lines.

Question ❷ focuses on the construction of parallel and perpendicular lines without a grid to support the drawing.

STRENGTHEN Explore parallel and perpendicular lines by using physical equipment (such as rods, rulers of the same and of different lengths, walking along lines of a football pitch or netball court), or lying down to make a pair of parallel or perpendicular lines with a partner.

DEEPEN Question ❺ challenges children to explore parallel and perpendicular lines by joining dots around a circle. Challenge children to find as many possibilities as they can and to explain why perpendicular lines cannot be shown on the six-dot circle. Children could also explore circles with three, four, five, seven, nine and ten dots.

THINK DIFFERENTLY Question ❹ tackles a problem where the distance between two lines is not measured accurately.

ASSESSMENT CHECKPOINT Answers to questions ❶ b) and ❷ will indicate the level of understanding of the difference between parallel and perpendicular lines.

ANSWERS Answers to the **Practice** part of the lesson appear in a separate **Practice and Reflect answer guide**.

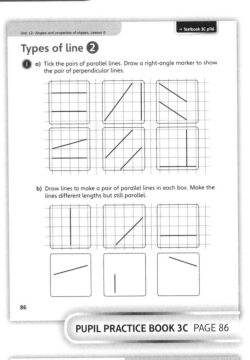

PUPIL PRACTICE BOOK 3C PAGE 86

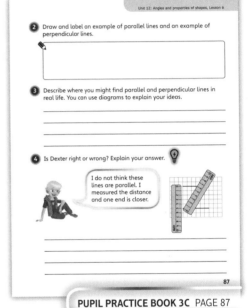

PUPIL PRACTICE BOOK 3C PAGE 87

Reflect

WAYS OF WORKING Pair work

IN FOCUS Children should write their own responses and then compare these with those of their partner. Children could then try to justify their decision, or adopt their partner's reasoning if convinced.

ASSESSMENT CHECKPOINT Do children's responses demonstrate a clear understanding of the fundamental properties of both types of line and address some of the misconceptions?

ANSWERS Answers to the **Reflect** part of the lesson appear in a separate **Practice and Reflect answer guide**.

After the lesson ⏸

- Are children able to explain clearly the difference between parallel and perpendicular lines?
- Can children construct both kinds of line with reasonable accuracy, and justify their method?
- What further opportunities will you give children to reinforce the language covered in this lesson?

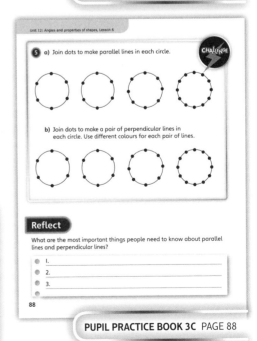

PUPIL PRACTICE BOOK 3C PAGE 88

Recognising and describing 2D shapes

Learning focus

In this lesson, children apply their understanding of types of line and angle to the properties of 2D shapes.

Small steps

→ Previous step: Types of line (2)
→ **This step: Recognising and describing 2D shapes**
→ Next step: Recognising and describing 3D shapes

NATIONAL CURRICULUM LINKS

Year 3 Geometry – Properties of Shapes

Draw 2D shapes and make 3D shapes using modelling materials; recognise 3D shapes in different orientations and describe them.

ASSESSING MASTERY

Children can describe common 2D shapes using their angle and line properties, including an understanding of vertical and horizontal symmetry.

COMMON MISCONCEPTIONS

Children may rely on recognising common representations of shapes, and may not recognise a shape in a different orientation, or shapes which do not look like the regular versions they are used to. Ask:
• *What is true of all rectangles/hexagons/quadrilaterals? How can you check if this is a square?*

Children may think that if a shape has two pairs of parallel sides, then it must be a square or a rectangle. Ask:
• *Does this shape (rhombus or parallelogram) have two pairs of parallel sides? How can you tell that it is not a rectangle or a square?*

STRENGTHENING UNDERSTANDING

Explore polygons using constructions such as geoboards, stencils or tangible representations of the shape. Trace around 2D shapes by placing them in different orientations, marking the right angles in each and identifying the pairs of parallel or perpendicular sides.

GOING DEEPER

Challenge children to explore the properties of parallel and perpendicular lines in different polygons. Ask leading questions such as: *Do all quadrilaterals have a pair of parallel sides? Can you draw a trapezium with perpendicular sides? Can a triangle have parallel sides? Could the equal angles in a kite be right angles?*

KEY LANGUAGE

In lesson: 2D shapes, quadrilateral, pentagon, parallel, perpendicular, acute angle, line of symmetry

Other language to be used by the teacher: kite, parallelogram, trapezium, rhombus, symmetrical, obtuse angle, right angle, hexagon, polygon

STRUCTURES AND REPRESENTATIONS

2D shapes

RESOURCES

Mandatory: sticks or pencils of equal length

Optional: plastic or wooden 2D shapes, sorting table

 In the eTextbook of this lesson, you will find interactive links to a selection of teaching tools.

Before you teach

• Can children draw four different triangles?
• Do children know what is the same and what is different about squares, rectangles and pentagons?

Discover

WAYS OF WORKING Pair work

ASK

- Question ❶ a): *What is a quadrilateral? What are parallel lines?*
- Question ❶ a): *How can you check whether any of the lines are parallel?*
- Question ❶ b): *What could you do to check if this is true for all sizes of this shape?*

IN FOCUS Children are searching the picture for as many properties as they can, based on their understanding of types of 2D shape, types of line and types of angle. Recap on the meaning of the terms parallel, perpendicular, vertical and horizontal, and the names of quadrilaterals. Which properties prove that the shape being studied is a rectangle? Discuss what is the same and what is different about a range of rectangles to ascertain that all rectangles, including squares, always have two pairs of parallel and equal length sides, and that adjacent sides are perpendicular.

PRACTICAL TIPS This activity could be re-created as part of a PE lesson. The shapes could be modelled using matchsticks, lolly sticks or base 10 equipment, or rectangular shapes placed end to end.

ANSWERS

Question ❶ a): The children have made a rectangle. It has two pairs of parallel sides.

Question ❶ b): All rectangles, including squares, have two pairs of parallel lines..

Share

WAYS OF WORKING Whole class teacher led

ASK

- Question ❶ a): *Can you explain why a rectangle is a type of quadrilateral?*
- Question ❶ b): *Would the opposite sides still be parallel if you turned the rectangle?*
- Question ❶ b): *Would the opposite sides still be parallel if the rectangles were smaller or larger?*

IN FOCUS Children are exploring the idea that a rectangle must always have two pairs of parallel lines (sides). The justification is that opposite sides are of equal length, so the lines joining them must be a constant distance apart. It may also be worth discussing that, as all the angles are right angles, the adjacent sides are perpendicular.

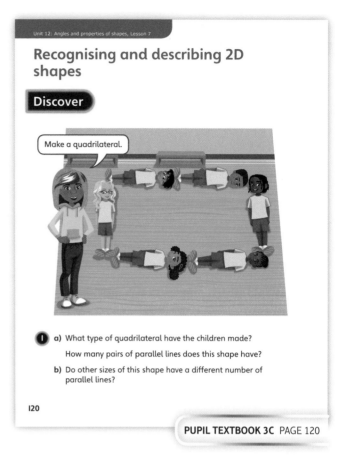

Recognising and describing 2D shapes

Discover

Make a quadrilateral.

❶ a) What type of quadrilateral have the children made? How many pairs of parallel lines does this shape have?

b) Do other sizes of this shape have a different number of parallel lines?

120

PUPIL TEXTBOOK 3C PAGE 120

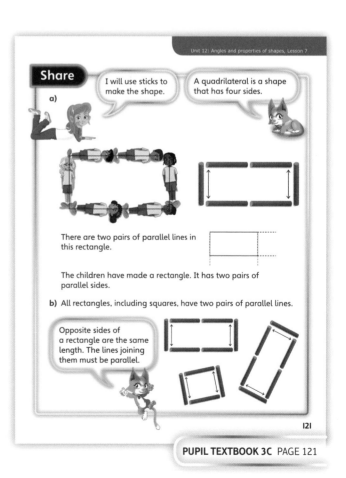

Share

I will use sticks to make the shape.

A quadrilateral is a shape that has four sides.

a)

There are two pairs of parallel lines in this rectangle.

The children have made a rectangle. It has two pairs of parallel sides.

b) All rectangles, including squares, have two pairs of parallel lines.

Opposite sides of a rectangle are the same length. The lines joining them must be parallel.

121

PUPIL TEXTBOOK 3C PAGE 121

Think together

Whole class teacher led (I do, We do, You do)

ASK

- Question ❶ : *How can you recognise and check for perpendicular lines?*
- Question ❷ : *How many sides does a quadrilateral have?*
- Question ❸ a): *Can you make a quadrilateral with ten people, which has all sides of equal length?*
- Question ❸ b): *What shape could be in this section of the diagram? Is this shape in the right place?*

IN FOCUS Question ❷ focuses on quadrilaterals and identifying the one with no parallel or perpendicular sides. Six children could make a rectangle again, a kite, a right-angled trapezium, an isosceles trapezium or a parallelogram.

Question ❸ b) requires reasoning about symmetry in shapes presented in a sorting table. Discuss the properties of the shapes that should be in each section.

STRENGTHEN Encourage children to explore making the different shapes using sticks. Remind children that they can make shapes with acute or obtuse angles. Provide 2D shapes for them to use as aids.

DEEPEN Encourage children to go one step further with questions ❷ and ❸ : explore Ash's pondering in question ❷ , recording the possibilities on squared paper. Adapt the headings in the sorting table of question ❸ b), to test for other properties such as: has no obtuse angles or has one pair of parallel lines. In question ❸ b), ask: *Which shapes cannot be made with ten sticks?*

ASSESSMENT CHECKPOINT All questions will help to check that children are beginning to recognise the properties that make a shape distinct from other shapes. Ask children to explain how they know a shape is *not* a rectangle, is *not* a quadrilateral, *is* a rectangle, and so on.

ANSWERS

Question ❶ : There are four pairs of perpendicular lines (at the vertices).

Question ❷ a): The children could make a: rectangle, kite (1, 1, 2, 2), trapezium (1, 1, 1, 3), and a parallelogram (1, 2, 1, 2).

Question ❷ b): The kite has no parallel or perpendicular lines.

Question ❸ a): Various answers are possible, the following are not possible: rectangles (no acute angles); squares (no acute angles and ten sticks cannot make four equal sides); rhombi (ten sticks cannot make four equal sides).

Question ❸ b): Various answers are possible. A could be an irregular, symmetrical polygon with sides the same length but angles not all the same; B could be a non-isosceles trapezium; C could be a rhombus, square or other regular polygon; D could be an isosceles trapezium, an isosceles triangle or a kite.

PUPIL TEXTBOOK 3C PAGE 122

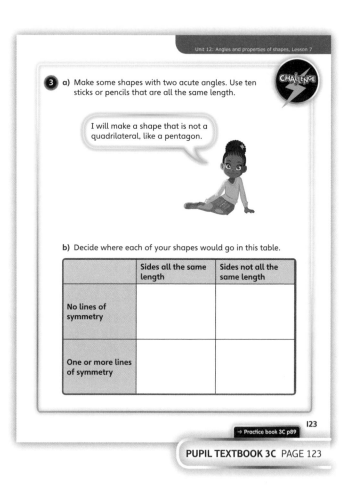

PUPIL TEXTBOOK 3C PAGE 123

Practice

WAYS OF WORKING Independent thinking

IN FOCUS Questions **1** and **2** focus on recognition of the names of common 2D shapes in different orientations and proportions, with a focus on quadrilaterals in question **2**.

Question **3** focuses on symmetry in polygons. Most children will only draw vertical or horizontal lines and may not include them all but, at this stage, this is acceptable.

Question **5** requires logical reasoning using knowledge of the different properties of 2D shapes.

STRENGTHEN Explore the properties of shapes using geoboards or string to form the outline of the shapes.

DEEPEN Challenge children to invent their own properties puzzle, using clues similar to the ones in question **5**.

THINK DIFFERENTLY Question **4** requires children to think about the properties of shapes as they design suitable but different shapes that will fulfil the given criteria. Ask pairs of children to check each other's work. Ask: *Are the shapes different or the same one turned? Do they all match the properties required?*

ASSESSMENT CHECKPOINT Children should be able to name many of the common 2D shapes covered in this unit and describe some of them in relation to their angle and line properties. Question **5** will support this assessment.

ANSWERS Answers for the **Practice** part of the lesson appear in the separate **Practice and Reflect answer guide**.

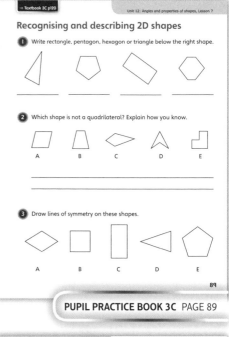

PUPIL PRACTICE BOOK 3C PAGE 89

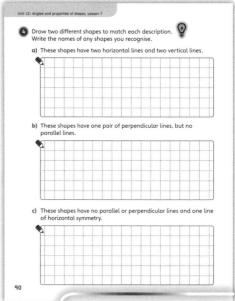

PUPIL PRACTICE BOOK 3C PAGE 90

Reflect

WAYS OF WORKING Independent thinking

IN FOCUS Children should use this opportunity to show the depth of their knowledge of the properties of shapes, including reference to three of these properties: parallel lines, perpendicular lines, number of right angles, vertical/horizontal symmetry or the fact that it is a quadrilateral.

ASSESSMENT CHECKPOINT Do children apply their knowledge of types of lines and angles, and the correct names, to the properties of a rectangle?

ANSWERS Answers to the **Reflect** part of the lesson appear in a separate **Practice and Reflect answer guide**.

After the lesson ⏸

- Can children apply their knowledge of types of line, types of angle and symmetry to recognition and description of 2D shapes?
- How could you help children to reinforce the names of 2D shapes and their properties in curriculum areas such as art, DT and computing?

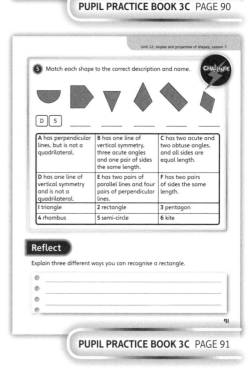

PUPIL PRACTICE BOOK 3C PAGE 91

Recognising and describing 3D shapes

Learning focus

In this lesson, children identify and sort 3D shapes based on properties of faces, vertices and edges. They deepen their understanding of cubes and cuboids, and also describe the shapes and dimensions of faces of different 3D shapes.

Small steps

→ Previous step: Recognising and describing 2D shapes
→ **This step: Recognising and describing 3D shapes**
→ Next step: Constructing 3D shapes

NATIONAL CURRICULUM LINKS

Year 3 Geometry – Properties of Shapes

Draw 2D shapes and make 3D shapes using modelling materials; recognise 3D shapes in different orientations and describe them.

ASSESSING MASTERY

Children can describe and visualise the faces of 3D shapes from 2D representations. They can name and describe a range of 3D shapes, including prisms and cuboids. Children can sort and classify shapes according to their properties.

COMMON MISCONCEPTIONS

Children may confuse prisms with pyramids. Ask:
• *What is the same and what is different about a triangular-based pyramid and a triangular prism?*

Children may find it difficult to visualise individual faces from a 2D representation of a 3D shape. Ask:
• *What shape is the face opposite to this one? What shape are the faces on a cuboid?*

STRENGTHENING UNDERSTANDING

Handling models of 3D shapes, and exploring them in different orientations, is essential. Use equipment to build 3D shapes that will unfold to reveal the faces. Explore prisms: all have rectangular faces and two identical end faces that give the prism its name. Define 3D as an object with three dimensions (such as height, width and length), as opposed to 2D, which has only two dimensions (width and length usually).

GOING DEEPER

Challenge children to describe similarities as well as differences when comparing different 3D shapes. Use a range of sorting circles or sorting tables to prompt reasoning about properties of 3D shapes.

KEY LANGUAGE

In lesson: cuboid, cube, prism, pyramid, vertices, face, edge, square, rectangle, shape, size, opposite, sorting circles, parallel, perpendicular, symmetrical

Other language to be used by the teacher: vertex, sphere, square-based pyramid, triangular-based pyramid, triangular prism, cone, cylinder, rectangular

STRUCTURES AND REPRESENTATIONS

3D shapes

RESOURCES

Mandatory: 3D shapes to handle (cuboid, cube, prisms, pyramids, sphere, cone, cylinder)

Optional: range of cardboard boxes in different proportions; 3D shapes that open out into nets, 3D shapes represented as solid shapes and as wireframe models

 In the eTextbook of this lesson, you will find interactive links to a selection of teaching tools.

Before you teach

• Do children know the names of any 3D shapes?
• Can children find the faces/edges/vertices of a shape?

Discover

Recognising and describing 3D shapes

WAYS OF WORKING Pair work

ASK

- Question **1** a): *How could you describe the faces of a cube precisely?*
- Question **1** a): *What is the difference between a cube and a cuboid?*
- Question **1** b): *How can you check the properties of a 3D shape accurately?*

IN FOCUS Children explore the properties of cubes and cuboids in terms of the length of their edges and the shapes of their faces. They use careful measuring to identify these properties and find out whether a shape is a cube or a cuboid.

PRACTICAL TIPS Children could explore the faces of cardboard boxes in different proportions. This could be done with eyes closed, so children try to judge whether a box is cube or cuboid without looking. They could then check by measuring the edges of any faces that could be square. Measuring opposite faces will enable children to understand that opposite faces of a cuboid are identical.

ANSWERS

Question **1** a): Ambika can measure all the sides of her gift to find out if it is a cube.

Question **1** b): All the faces of Ambika's gift are rectangles. The opposite faces are exactly the same shape and size. Ambika's gift is a cuboid.

Discover

I think my present is a cube.

Ambika

Zac

25 cm
22 cm
20 cm

1 a) How can Ambika find out if her gift is a cube?

   b) Ambika then describes the faces of her gift. Is it a cube?

124

PUPIL TEXTBOOK 3C PAGE 124

Share

WAYS OF WORKING Whole class teacher led

ASK

- Question **1** a): *Why is it important to measure the edges?*
- Question **1** a): *What do you know about the length of the edges of a cube?*
- Question **1** b): *What shape are the faces of a cube/cuboid?*
- Question **1** b): *What is special about the opposite faces of a cuboid?*

IN FOCUS In question **1** a), children are deepening their understanding of a cube as having all edges the same length, and all faces as squares.

In question **1** b), children explore how to describe individual faces of a cuboid and recognise that opposite faces are identical.

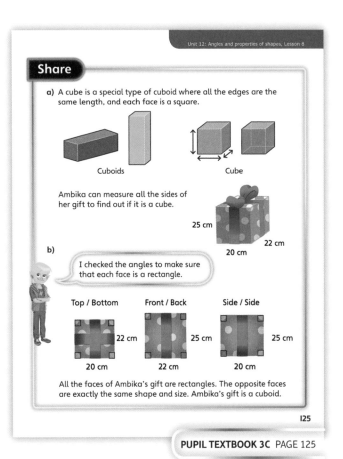

Share

a) A cube is a special type of cuboid where all the edges are the same length, and each face is a square.

Cuboids

Cube

Ambika can measure all the sides of her gift to find out if it is a cube.

25 cm
22 cm
20 cm

b)

I checked the angles to make sure that each face is a rectangle.

Top / Bottom   Front / Back   Side / Side

22 cm   25 cm   25 cm
20 cm   22 cm   20 cm

All the faces of Ambika's gift are rectangles. The opposite faces are exactly the same shape and size. Ambika's gift is a cuboid.

125

PUPIL TEXTBOOK 3C PAGE 125

Think together

WAYS OF WORKING Whole class teacher led (I do, We do, You do)

ASK

- Question ❶ : *Do only cubes have square faces? What other shapes could have one or more square faces?*
- Question ❷ : *How can you tell a prism from a pyramid?*
- Question ❸ : *What is true of all prisms?*

IN FOCUS Question ❶ focuses on the faces of a cuboid where two opposite faces are squares. This tackles a misconception that only cubes have square faces.

Question ❸ covers a range of common 3D shapes, and prompts children to sort them in to the sorting circles based on their properties. Children should be taught that shapes that do not fit into either circle must be put outside, but still within the rectangle that surrounds the sorting circles.

STRENGTHEN Children should handle models of the common 3D shapes in order to fully explore the properties in a concrete way, but should be encouraged to do so after reasoning from the 2D representations. Some children may need to use stickers to keep track of the faces/edges/vertices as they count them. Some children will need support in question ❸ to realise that cubes, cuboids and cylinders are also classed as prisms.

DEEPEN Challenge children to sort shapes in different ways by altering the headings of the sorting circles in question ❸, using properties such as Has an odd number of rectangular faces or Has no parallel edges.

ASSESSMENT CHECKPOINT Responses to question ❸ should indicate a good level of understanding of a range of 3D shapes and their properties, recognising that cubes, cuboids and cylinders are also classed as prisms.

ANSWERS

Question ❶ : There are four 12×24 cm faces and two 12×12 cm square faces.

Question ❷ : The shape is a triangular prism. There are five faces, six vertices and nine edges.

Question ❸ :

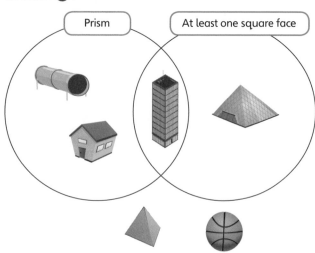

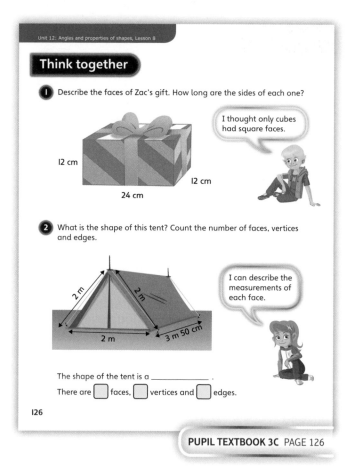

PUPIL TEXTBOOK 3C PAGE 126

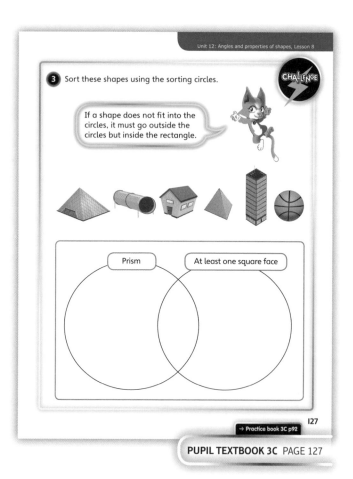

PUPIL TEXTBOOK 3C PAGE 127

Practice

WAYS OF WORKING Independent thinking

IN FOCUS Question ❹ requires children to complete a table based on properties of prisms. It should show that all prisms have more than one rectangular face (the exception being cylinders). Take the opportunity to discuss the differences between prisms and pyramids, as both non-prisms in this question are actually pyramids. Only a truncated pyramid has more than one rectangular face, and not every pyramid has a rectangular face. Children may need reminding that a square is a special type of rectangle. None of the common shapes would fit into the Not a prism / Has more than one rectangular face section.

STRENGTHEN Encourage children to make reasoned predictions about given faces and properties of shapes, before checking the predictions by handling 3D models or by measuring edges.

DEEPEN Challenge children to sort shapes into different sorting circles or tables by choosing their own headings. Extend question ❺ to compare other shapes. Ask: *What is the same? What is different?*

THINK DIFFERENTLY Question ❸ requires children to use reasoning skills to match the cuboids to the correct set of faces.

ASSESSMENT CHECKPOINT Responses to these questions will assess whether children can name common 3D shapes, describe them using the shape and number of their faces, and sort them according to their properties.

ANSWERS Answers for the **Practice** part of the lesson appear in the separate **Practice and Reflect answer guide**.

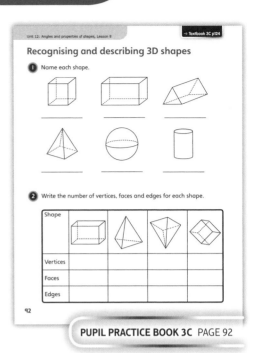

PUPIL PRACTICE BOOK 3C PAGE 92

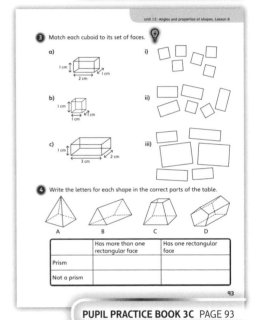

PUPIL PRACTICE BOOK 3C PAGE 93

Reflect

WAYS OF WORKING Independent thinking

IN FOCUS This task looks simple, but children will need to make sure that their checklist includes enough information so that it does not also encompass other shapes. For example, a shape with six faces and edges all the same length could be a pentagon-based pyramid.

ASSESSMENT CHECKPOINT Can children use the properties of a cube to identify it definitively?

ANSWERS Answers to the **Reflect** part of the lesson appear in a separate **Practice and Reflect answer guide**.

After the lesson

- Are children able to describe individual faces of a 3D shape?
- Can children explain the properties of a cuboid that is not a cube, including reference to opposite faces?
- Are children confident in sorting 3D shapes according to different criteria relating to their properties?

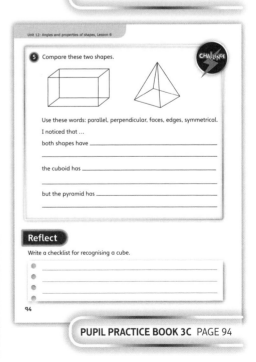

PUPIL PRACTICE BOOK 3C PAGE 94

Constructing 3D shapes

Learning focus

In this lesson, children learn to construct 3D shapes by considering their properties in relation to different construction materials.

Small steps

→ Previous step: Recognising and describing 3D shapes
→ **This step: Constructing 3D shapes**
→ Next step: Measuring mass (1)

NATIONAL CURRICULUM LINKS

Year 3 Geometry – Properties of Shapes

Draw 2D shapes and make 3D shapes using modelling materials; recognise 3D shapes in different orientations and describe them.

ASSESSING MASTERY

Children can describe different ways to construct 3D shapes from different construction materials, by reasoning about their properties.

COMMON MISCONCEPTIONS

Children may not recognise that the same cuboid could be represented in different orientations. Ask:
• *Which cuboid is the same as this one, but has been turned around?*

Children may not understand that different construction materials are based on different properties. Ask:
• *What features of a 3D shape are sticks and marshmallows good at representing? Why is it not possible to make a cone, cylinder or sphere with these construction materials?*

STRENGTHENING UNDERSTANDING

All children would benefit from having access to the different construction materials in order to build the different shapes. Children should be shown how to make connecting edges with sticks and vertices with the marshmallows..

GOING DEEPER

Challenge children to think of innovative ways to construct, for example, a cylinder. Children should not be pushed to formal consideration of nets, but their inventiveness should be encouraged.

KEY LANGUAGE

In lesson: cube, length, direction, angle, features, vertices, faces, edges, sphere, pyramid

Other language to be used by the teacher: cuboid, prism, cone, cylinder, sphere, vertex

STRUCTURES AND REPRESENTATIONS

3D shapes

RESOURCES

Mandatory: multilink cubes, construction materials

Optional: sticks and marshmallows, modelling clay, snap-together construction materials, wireframe models

 In the eTextbook of this lesson, you will find interactive links to a selection of teaching tools.

Before you teach ⏸

• Which 3D shapes can children construct?
• What materials have children used before to make 3D shapes?

Discover

Pair work

ASK

- Question ❶ a): *How many cubes does each child have?*
- Questions ❶ a) and ❶ b): *What do you need to think about before you start using the multilink cubes?*
- Question ❶ a): *How can you identify a cube?*
- Question ❶ b): *Would this be the same shape if I turned it around like this?*

IN FOCUS Question ❶ a) challenges children to form a larger cube from the limited numbers available to Lee or Bella. Some children may mistakenly identify a 1x4 arrangement as a cube.

Question ❶ b) pushes children to consider how the same cuboid can be represented in different orientations, and to distinguish which properties of two cuboids make them distinct or identical.

PRACTICAL TIPS Ideally, all children should have access to linking cubes, so that they can test out their ideas. However, in this case, it is also important that children have a chance to consider their ideas before trying out the materials.

ANSWERS

Question ❶ a): Bella can make a cube by using all of her smaller cubes. It has a length of 2 units in every direction.

Question ❶ b): Lee is not correct: he can only make two different cuboids.

Share

Whole class teacher led

ASK

- Question ❶ a): *Can you prove that Bella's shape is definitely a cube?*
- Question ❶ b): *Why are some of Lee's shapes not really different?*

IN FOCUS Question ❶ a) focuses on the property that a cube has edges of equal length.

Question ❶ b) focuses on how cuboids can be represented in different orientations.

Some children may argue that Lee could make many different cuboids if he did not have to use all six cubes every time. This is an interesting point to clarify and a good extension for children to explore.

Constructing 3D shapes

Discover

Lee

Bella

❶ a) Who can make a cube by putting together their smaller cubes?

b) Lee thinks he can make five different cuboids using all of his small cubes. Is he correct?

128

PUPIL TEXTBOOK 3C PAGE 128

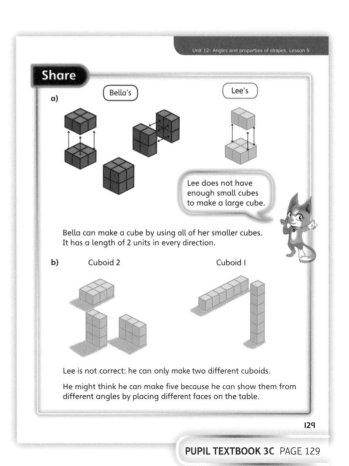

Share

a) Bella's | Lee's

Lee does not have enough small cubes to make a large cube.

Bella can make a cube by using all of her smaller cubes. It has a length of 2 units in every direction.

b) Cuboid 2 | Cuboid 1

Lee is not correct: he can only make two different cuboids.

He might think he can make five because he can show them from different angles by placing different faces on the table.

129

PUPIL TEXTBOOK 3C PAGE 129

Think together

ASK

- Questions ❶ and ❷ : *What is the same and what is different about these sets of construction materials?*
- Questions ❶ , ❷ and ❸ : *What is the same about the shapes that you cannot make from these materials?*

IN FOCUS All questions focus on the different ways of building shapes using different materials. Children are asked to consider which materials are appropriate and which are not when constructing specific 3D shapes. The marshmallows are used to connect the sticks to form edges and vertices. Small balls of modelling clay could replace the marshmallows.

STRENGTHEN Give children access to different types of construction materials to build and experiment with.

DEEPEN Challenge children to produce a list or table identifying which 3D shapes can and cannot be made from the different construction materials shown or available in class.

ASSESSMENT CHECKPOINT Are children able to explain which materials can be used to construct a prism and why cubes cannot be used for this purpose? Can they explain the difficulty in constructing shapes that have any curved surfaces?

ANSWERS

Question ❶ : You need 6 squares to make the faces of a cube.

You need 12 sticks to make the edges of a cube.

You need 8 marshmallows to make the vertices of a cube.

Question ❷ a): The children can make a cube with every set; a pyramid can be made from snap-together construction materials and sticks/marshmallows; a pyramid cannot be made from multilink cubes.

Question ❷ b): A sphere cannot be made from any of the materials due to its curved surface.

Question ❸ a): The triangular prism can be made from snap-together construction materials or sticks and marshmallows; the cylinder cannot be made from any of these materials because of its curved edge; the linking cubes cannot make either shape.

Question ❸ b): The answer depends on the length of the prism: a triangular prism needs two triangles and three (or six or nine, etc.) squares; or at least nine sticks and six marshmallows. Other answers are possible.

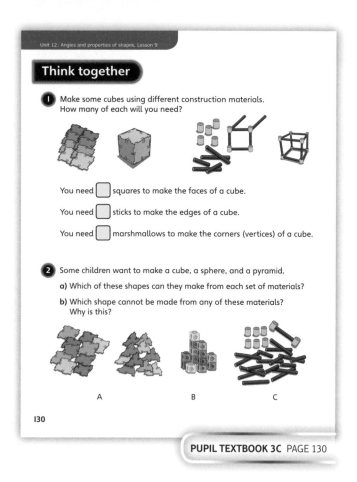

PUPIL TEXTBOOK 3C PAGE 130

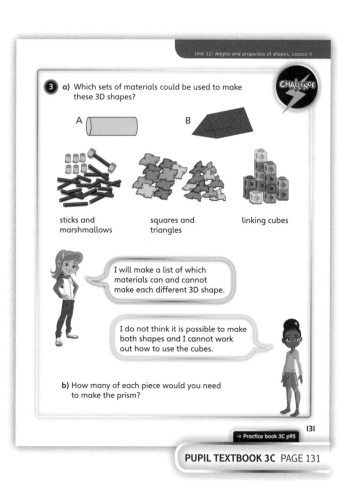

PUPIL TEXTBOOK 3C PAGE 131

Practice

WAYS OF WORKING Independent thinking

IN FOCUS Question ❶ focuses on recognising how many cubes have been used to build a 3D shape given as a 2D representation.

Question ❸ requires children to link the number of edges and vertices to the amount of construction material they will need.

STRENGTHEN Encourage children to form an idea of how to build shapes before trialling their ideas with construction materials.

DEEPEN Question ❻ challenges children to explain the pattern that appears in the table, based on a comparison of the shapes. The answers will depend on the length of each prism, but the number of sticks should be a multiple of the number of sides on the end piece, assuming each end piece has equal length sides.

THINK DIFFERENTLY Question ❺ requires children to use the language and terminology of edges and vertices to describe a construction. As all sides are not the same length, they will have to think about how many short and how many long sticks they will need.

ASSESSMENT CHECKPOINT Are children able to explain which materials can and cannot be used to construct specific shapes? Can they explain the difficulty in constructing shapes that have any curved surfaces?

ANSWERS Answers to the **Practice** part of the lesson appear in a separate **Practice and Reflect answer guide**.

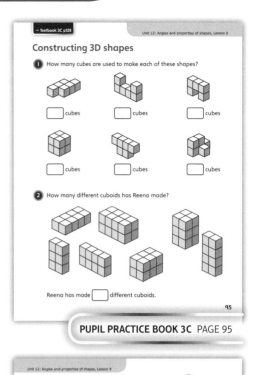

PUPIL PRACTICE BOOK 3C PAGE 95

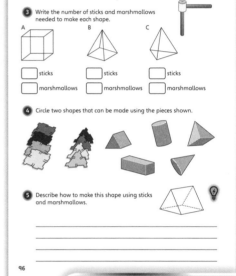

PUPIL PRACTICE BOOK 3C PAGE 96

Reflect

WAYS OF WORKING Pair work

IN FOCUS Children should discuss and compile a list by looking back through the unit. Children should then decide individually which three things they feel are the most important.

ASSESSMENT CHECKPOINT Are children able to pick out the concepts they understood well, and concepts they may need to do more work on? Did children pick out new concepts or concepts they were already comfortable with?

ANSWERS Answers to the **Reflect** part of the lesson appear in a separate **Practice and Reflect answer guide**.

After the lesson

- Can children justify decisions about how to construct 3D shapes, based on the properties of the shapes and of the materials?
- Are children able to recognise shapes when they are presented in different orientations?
- What did children learn in this unit that could be useful in DT, science or art?

PUPIL PRACTICE BOOK 3C PAGE 97

End of unit check

Don't forget the *Power Maths* unit assessment grid on p26.

WAYS OF WORKING Group work adult led

IN FOCUS

- Question **1** assesses children's ability to identify a shape with just one right angle.
- Question **2** assesses children's ability to identify an obtuse angle shown using the hands of a clock face.
- Question **3** assesses children's ability to identify the vertical lines in letter shapes.
- Question **4** assesses children's ability to identify vertical or horizontal lines of symmetry in order to identify the shape that does not have a line of symmetry.
- Question **5** assesses children's ability to identify the shape with no pairs of parallel sides.
- Question **6** is a SATs-style question relating to the faces of a cuboid.

ANSWERS AND COMMENTARY

Children who have mastered the concepts in this unit will be able to define these terms: right angle, parallel lines, perpendicular lines, vertical and horizontal. Children will be able to use these terms to describe some of the properties of 2D and 3D shapes.

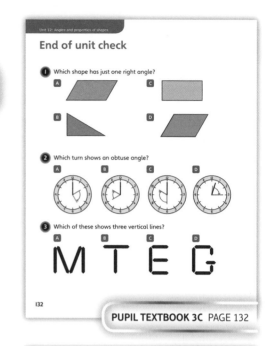

PUPIL TEXTBOOK 3C PAGE 132

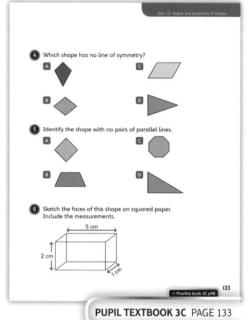

PUPIL TEXTBOOK 3C PAGE 133

Q	A	WRONG ANSWERS AND MISCONCEPTIONS	STRENGTHENING UNDERSTANDING
1	B	A or D suggest that the child is not sure how to identify right angles; C suggests that the child did not read the question carefully as C has more than one right angle.	Many of the misconceptions in this unit will be because children cannot remember which word is which. Help them to remember with these tips:
2	C	A or D suggest that the child does not know that the angle between three numbers on a clock face is exactly 90 degrees. B suggests confusion between acute and obtuse angles.	• acute, obtuse or right angle? (Acute contains the word cute which usually describes something small, so it is the smallest type of angle; right angles can stand up*right*);
3	D	A suggests that the child has not counted accurately, or confusion between vertical and diagonal lines. B or C suggest confusion between horizontal and vertical lines.	• horizontal or vertical? *Horizont*al is flat like the *horizon*; *vert*ical stands up straight like *vert*ebrae in your back;
4	C	A, B or D suggest that the child is not able to recognise vertical or horizontal lines of symmetry.	• parallel or perpendicular? The word parallel has double *ll* in the middle, which looks like a pair of parallel lines; parallel lines are like train tracks – they will never touch or cross; perpendicular lines can be made from a pair of parallel lines by turning one line a quarter turn.
5	D	A, B or C suggest confusion between parallel and perpendicular lines.	
6		Have children drawn six faces in three pairs?	

My journal

WAYS OF WORKING Independent thinking

ANSWERS AND COMMENTARY

Question ❶ a) and b): Ensure children think about which shape to start with and whether they could make some shapes on a different rotation to the ones shown. Ensure children explain how they lined up the ruler.

Question ❷ a): Children could use the grid lines to draw diagonals.

Question ❷ b): Children could use the vertical and horizontal grid lines to create a right angle or simply use the end of their ruler.

Question ❷ c): Children should draw a right-angled trapezium.

Question ❷ d): Children should draw a pentagon with one right angle.

Power check

WAYS OF WORKING Independent thinking

ASK

- Can you explain the difference between parallel and perpendicular lines?
- Are you confident describing 2D and 3D shapes?
- Can you draw a right-angled triangle?

Power play

WAYS OF WORKING Pair work

IN FOCUS Children should explore whether a shape can be split physically into two identical halves. Children may suggest slicing through to make identical halves, which would represent a plane of symmetry. This is acceptable, and an interesting discussion point, but this concept is not introduced until KS3.

ANSWERS AND COMMENTARY This puzzle is open-ended as there are many possibilities, especially if you allow the idea of slicing through the cubes horizontally or vertically. Most T shapes cannot be physically split, but they are all vertically symmetrical. A squared C or U shape can only be physically split where there is an even number of cubes in the middle section, but, again, they are still symmetrical. Asymmetrical shapes are easily constructed where there is a different number of cubes on each layer, as in the shape at the far right of the page.

After the unit ⏸

- What will you do differently next time you teach this unit?
- How well did children respond to the new words introduced in this unit? How can you continue reinforcing these words in future lessons?

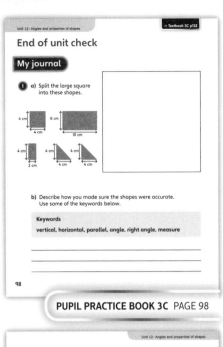

PUPIL PRACTICE BOOK 3C PAGE 98

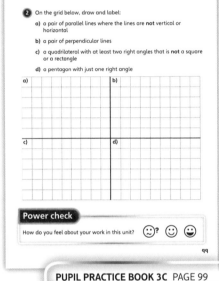

PUPIL PRACTICE BOOK 3C PAGE 99

PUPIL PRACTICE BOOK 3C PAGE 100

Strengthen and **Deepen** activities for this unit can be found in the *Power Maths* online subscription.

Unit 13
Mass

Mastery Expert tip! "Throughout this unit, make sure you do lots of practical weighing and measuring. This hands-on learning is vital to achieve mastery!"

Don't forget to watch the Unit 13 video!

WHY THIS UNIT IS IMPORTANT

This unit is important because it strengthens children's knowledge of mass: an important area of learning which has many real-life applications.

First, children will learn how to measure and read a scale, focusing upon unmarked intervals. Next, different masses will be compared and ordered. Following this, children will learn to add and subtract different amounts, using a range of strategies. Finally, they will apply their knowledge to real-life problems – an important skill for children to learn in order to work towards mastery.

WHERE THIS UNIT FITS

→ Unit 12 – Angles and properties of shapes
→ **Unit 13 – Mass**
→ Unit 14 – Capacity

This unit involves the application of skills such as addition and subtraction in a measures context. Children will have covered these strategies in Key Stage 1, and in previous Year 3 units, but will require support when applying them. Measures were covered in Year 2 Unit 14, in which weight, volume and temperature were the focus.

Before they start this unit, it is expected that children:
- can use scales to compare, estimate and measure the mass of an object
- are able to measure mass in grams and kilograms
- can count in hundreds to link grams to kilograms.

ASSESSING MASTERY

Children who have mastered this unit will be able to read scales accurately, including when there are missing intervals. Children should also be able to apply their understanding to solve problems involving mass. Finally, ideas and methods will be explained effectively, using the correct mathematical vocabulary and representations.

COMMON MISCONCEPTIONS	STRENGTHENING UNDERSTANDING	GOING DEEPER
Children may confuse grams and kilograms and not add them up separately, or convert once they meet the 1,000 g barrier.	Use place value counters to represent different amounts.	Solve problems involving grams and kilograms, in which children must convert the amounts.
Children may work out missing intervals incorrectly or think you cannot find a value between masses such as 1 kg and 2 kg.	Practice weighing objects on a range of scales.	Challenge children to find midpoints between two intervals. Provide children with some multi-step word problems. Can they explain their steps and solutions?
Children may solve problems incorrectly, applying the wrong calculations through misinterpretation.	Ask children to represent calculations in a bar model or use the column method.	

Unit 13: Mass

WAYS OF WORKING

Use these pages to introduce the unit focus to children. Talk through the key learning points that the characters mention and the key vocabulary.

STRUCTURES AND REPRESENTATIONS

Number line: The number line is effective when looking at scales and finding missing intervals. Children can count on and back too.

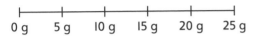

| 0 g | 5 g | 10 g | 15 g | 20 g | 25 g |

Bar model: The bar model helps children gain a visual understanding of word problems involving measures.

1 kg 500 g	
1 kg 300 g	200 g

Part-whole models: The part-whole model allows children to convert between units of measure effectively.

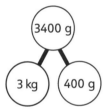

KEY LANGUAGE

There is some key language that children will need to know as part of the learning in this unit:

→ mass, weigh, measure, grams (g), kilograms (kg)
→ interval, scale

PUPIL TEXTBOOK 3C PAGE 134

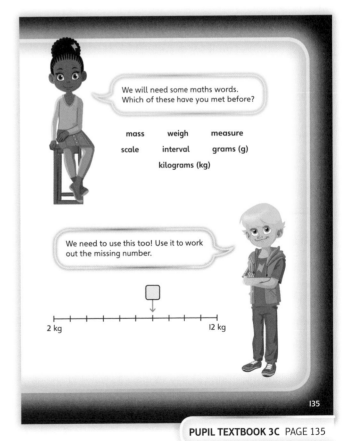

PUPIL TEXTBOOK 3C PAGE 135

Measuring mass ❶

Learning focus

In this lesson, children will learn how to read a range of scales relating to mass, including those with missing intervals.

Small steps

→ Previous step: Constructing 3D shapes
→ **This step: Measuring mass (1)**
→ Next step: Measuring mass (2)

NATIONAL CURRICULUM LINKS

Year 3 Measurement

Measure, compare, add and subtract: lengths (m/cm/mm); mass (kg/g); volume/capacity (l/ml).

ASSESSING MASTERY

Children can read scales quickly, using the correct method to find a missing interval. Furthermore, they will show a strong understanding of grams and kilograms.

COMMON MISCONCEPTIONS

Children may make errors when working out a missing interval. Ask:
• *What is the method you use to work out a missing interval?*

Children may not understand the value of grams and kilograms. Ask:
• *How many grams are in a kilogram? Can you think of something that weighs 1 gram and 1 kilogram?*

STRENGTHENING UNDERSTANDING

Children may need support when finding missing intervals. Ask children to provide missing interval questions for a partner and to explain the method they followed to find each answer. Summarise the correct methods at the end as a group.

Children may need support when finding the difference between intervals or when dividing. Use number lines to support learning.

GOING DEEPER

Go deeper by doing some practical activities such as weighing balls of modelling clay on scales. Experiment with balls and parachutes: find out what happens when different masses are attached to the parachutes.

Give children a range of misread intervals. Ask them to reason why the mistakes were made.

KEY LANGUAGE

In lesson: mass, measure, interval, grams (g), kilograms (kg), scale
Other language to be used by the teacher: difference, divide, dial

STRUCTURES AND REPRESENTATIONS

number line

RESOURCES

Mandatory: weighing scales, modelling clay
Optional: number lines, parachute

 In the eTextbook of this lesson, you will find interactive links to a selection of teaching tools.

Before you teach

• What did children cover in mass in Year 2?
• Are all children able to find differences?
• Do children have division strategies they can use?

Discover

WAYS OF WORKING Pair work

ASK

- Question **1** a): *What method did you use to work out the value of each interval?*
- Question **1** b): *What method did you use?*
- Question **1** b): *How can you check your answer is correct?*

IN FOCUS This question really gets children thinking about the missing intervals on scales. Encourage them to come up with step-by-step instructions to explain how to work them out.

PRACTICAL TIPS Give children dial scales and modelling clay, so they can measure mass in a practical context.

ANSWERS

Question **1** a): To work out what each interval represents, the steps are:
- Find the difference between the two marked amounts.
- Count the number of intervals.
- Divide the difference by this number.

Question **1** b): 20 g, 130 g, 600 g.

Unit 13: Mass, Lesson 1

Measuring mass **1**

Discover

1 Luis is measuring some clay for a sculpture.

   a) How can you work out what each interval represents?

   b) What is the mass of each piece of clay?

136

Share

WAYS OF WORKING Whole class teacher led

ASK

- Question **1** a): *What does interval mean?*
- Question **1** a): *Let's say the three steps aloud as a class. Does this method match the one you used to solve the problem?*

IN FOCUS Children will be reminded that 1,000 g equals 1 kg. This is a good opportunity to reinforce this knowledge. Ask: *What is 2 kg in grams? How about 5 kg? 8 kg?*

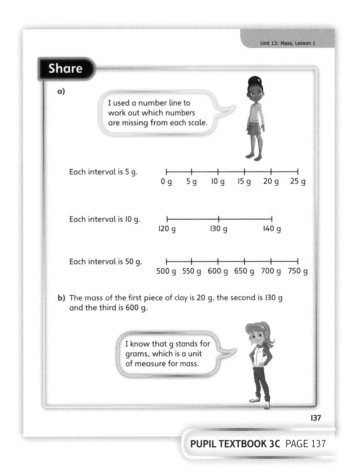

Unit 13: Mass, Lesson 1

Share

a)

I used a number line to work out which numbers are missing from each scale.

Each interval is 5 g.
0 g 5 g 10 g 15 g 20 g 25 g

Each interval is 10 g.
120 g 130 g 140 g

Each interval is 50 g.
500 g 550 g 600 g 650 g 700 g 750 g

b) The mass of the first piece of clay is 20 g, the second is 130 g and the third is 600 g.

I know that g stands for grams, which is a unit of measure for mass.

137

Think together

WAYS OF WORKING Whole class teacher led (I do, We do, You do)

ASK

- Question **2** : *How did you find the missing interval?*
- Question **2** : *Is there a representation that would help?*

IN FOCUS Question **2** a) shows intervals of 250 g. This may prove a challenge for some children. Ask children to think of an effective strategy to work out what the interval is. Some may see that there is a half-way mark, which has to be 500 g. Children can then halve again to find 250 g.

STRENGTHEN Children will benefit from counting practice. Count in 5s, 10s, 20s, 25s, 50s and 100s.

ASSESSMENT CHECKPOINT Question **1** will allow you to assess whether children can interpret and read the scales. Look for children who can confidently work out intervals on scales and explain their methodology.

ANSWERS

Question **1** : 225 g, 375 g, 450 g

Question **2** a):

Question **2** b):

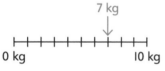

Questions **3** a) and b):

Objects you would measure in grams	Objects you would measure in kilograms
pen (6 g)	table (50 kg)
T-shirt (120 g / 140 g)	bicycle (10 kg)
ring (6 g)	suitcase (3 kg)
spoon (25 g)	
mobile phone (120 g / 140 g)	

PUPIL TEXTBOOK 3C PAGE 138

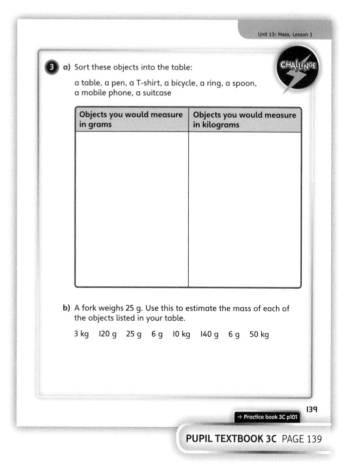

PUPIL TEXTBOOK 3C PAGE 139

Practice

WAYS OF WORKING Independent thinking

IN FOCUS Question ❷ will involve children reasoning, using their knowledge of grams and kilograms. Encourage them to be clear with their answers, and to use the correct vocabulary.

STRENGTHEN To support understanding in this section, give children similar problems to those in the first question. Use number lines, which will help children break down the scales and intervals.

DEEPEN Ask children to find things around the classroom and calculate their mass using scales. You could have different scales with different intervals, so they see the difference when the same object is weighed on different scales.

THINK DIFFERENTLY Question ❸ will require children to first find the correct answer and then explain where Andy went wrong in the example.

ASSESSMENT CHECKPOINT Question ❹ is an effective way to see if children can relate masses to real-life objects. Assess children on whether they have an understanding of mass in situations such as food labels or weighing fruit in a supermarket.

ANSWERS Answers for the **Practice** part of the lesson appear in the separate **Practice and Reflect answer guide**.

Reflect

WAYS OF WORKING Independent thinking

IN FOCUS This question gives children the opportunity to draw and label their own number line in order to understand the intervals on a scale.

ASSESSMENT CHECKPOINT This will allow you to assess children's understanding of using number lines to work out missing intervals.

ANSWERS Answers for the **Reflect** part of the lesson appear in the separate **Practice and Reflect answer guide**.

After the lesson ⏸

• Do any children need more practice with reading scales?
• Can children count in 5s, 10s, 20s, 25s, 50s and 100s?

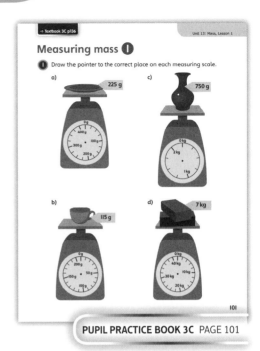

PUPIL PRACTICE BOOK 3C PAGE 101

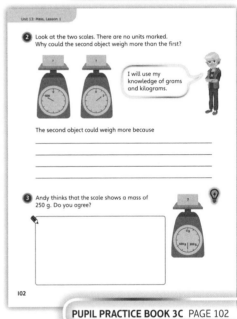

PUPIL PRACTICE BOOK 3C PAGE 102

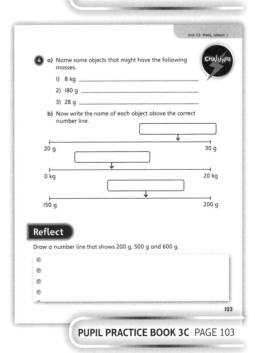

PUPIL PRACTICE BOOK 3C PAGE 103

171

Measuring mass ②

Learning focus

In this lesson children will learn how to read a range of scales in which kg and g are mixed. They will also find midpoints between intervals.

Small steps

→ Previous step: Measuring mass (1)
→ **This step: Measuring mass (2)**
→ Next step: Measuring mass (3)

NATIONAL CURRICULUM LINKS

Year 3 Measurement

Measure, compare, add and subtract: lengths (m/cm/mm); mass (kg/g); volume/capacity (l/ml).

ASSESSING MASTERY

Children can understand the values of grams and kilograms. Children can represent values using place value counters and work out missing intervals using number lines.

COMMON MISCONCEPTIONS

Children may think that you cannot find anything between values such as 3 kg and 4 kg, because there are no whole numbers between them. Ask:

• *Is there a smaller unit you could use?*

Children may mix up grams and kilograms. Ask:
• *Which is larger? Which should you write first in your answer – the grams or kilograms?*

STRENGTHENING UNDERSTANDING

Children may need support when finding missing intervals between values such as 3 kg and 4 kg. Show them on a number line and practise counting in 100s, 200s and 500s.

You may also want to represent kilograms with weights (place value counters would also work), asking children to find different ways to make them; for example 10 × 100 g = 1 kg.

GOING DEEPER

Go deeper by asking children to find midpoints between intervals. This will call on children's knowledge of finding the values of the intervals and then finding half-way points between two of them.

You may want to continue doing some practical activities such as weighing balls of modelling clay on scales.

KEY LANGUAGE

In lesson: mass, measure, scale, interval, grams (g), kilograms (kg),

Other language to be used by teacher: midpoint, difference, divide, dial

STRUCTURES AND REPRESENTATIONS

number line

RESOURCES

Mandatory: weighing scales, modelling clay

Optional: number lines, place value counters

 In the eTextbook of this lesson, you will find interactive links to a selection of teaching tools.

Before you teach

• Are children confident in measuring grams and kilograms separately?
• How can any common misconceptions from Lesson 1 be addressed in this lesson?

Discover

ASK

- Question ❶ a): *Do you need to focus on the kilograms or grams to work out the answer?*
- Questions ❶ a) and b): *Could you use a smaller unit to help you?*

IN FOCUS Question ❶ b) will require some deeper thinking from children. Expect to hear some children saying the answer is 6 $\frac{1}{2}$ kg or 6 $\frac{3}{4}$ kg (children are likely to call on their knowledge of basic fractions). Focus learning by asking children if there is a smaller unit they could use.

PRACTICAL TIPS Explain the method for working out missing intervals and display the three steps on your maths learning wall: find the difference between the two amounts; count the number of intervals; divide the difference by the number of intervals.

Use number lines to help children count the value of grams between two 1 kg points. Use place value counters to help children visualise 100 and 1,000 values together.

ANSWERS

Question ❶ a): The mass of the bag of carrots is 1 kg 300 g.

Question ❶ b): There are 1,000 g in 1 kg; there are 10 intervals on the scale.
1,000 divided by 10 is 100; so each interval is 100 g.
The mass of the pumpkin is 6 kg 800 g.

Share

ASK

- Question ❶ a): *Can you count aloud in steps of 100 g? What happens when you get to 900 g?*
- Question ❶ b): *What does interval mean?*
- Question ❶ b): *Let's say the three steps aloud as a class. How could you use a number line to solve question ❶ b)?*

IN FOCUS Question ❶ introduces children to working with mixed grams and kilograms. This helps them to recognise and record mass value within the context of weighing different objects. Help children by modelling how different amounts can be represented: use weights or place value counters on a part-whole model to help with this.

PUPIL TEXTBOOK 3C PAGE 140

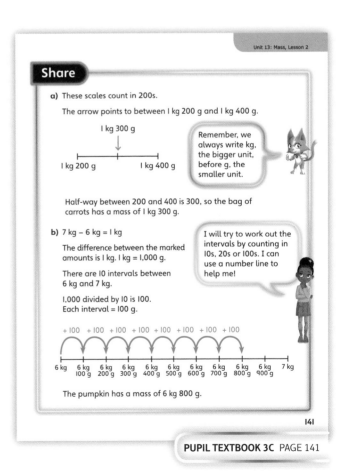

PUPIL TEXTBOOK 3C PAGE 141

Think together

Whole class teacher led (I do, We do, You do)

ASK

• Question **2** : *Can you count the intervals first?*
• Question **3** : *How can you work out the midpoint? What calculation do you need to do?*

IN FOCUS Question **2** shows the same amount represented on two different scales. Make learning real here by showing children that this happens in real life: not every scale is the same. You could do some practical measuring using a range of scales.

STRENGTHEN Ask children to count in 5s, 10s, 20s, 25s, 50s, 100s, 200s and 250s up to and past 1 kg. First count in grams (for example, 800 g, 900 g, 1,000 g, 1,100 g, 1,200 g); then count in mixed grams and kilograms (for example, 800 g, 900 g, 1 kg, 1 kg 100 g, 1 kg 200 g).

For question **3**, support children by asking them to find midpoints. This will require them to:
• find the interval value;
• find half of the interval value;
• add it on to the previous interval value.

DEEPEN For question **3**, children will have to find midpoints between marked intervals. This will certainly deepen learning in this lesson. Ask children to explain their methods clearly. Can they explain their methods? Show them that they must find the difference between the intervals, halve the amount and then add this onto the previous interval.

ASSESSMENT CHECKPOINT Use question **1** to assess whether children notice that the number of intervals are different on each scale. Listen carefully to their explanations and how they work each mass out.

ANSWERS

Question **1** a): The onions have a mass of 3 kg 400 g.

Question **1** b): The peas have a mass of 400 g.

Question **2** a): The mass of the bag of potatoes is 1 kg 500 g.

Question **2** b): Each scale has a different number of intervals between the marked amounts: on the first scale each interval represents 200 g; on the second, each interval represents 250 g.

Question **3** a): 4 kg 700 g

Question **3** b): 4 kg 500 g

Question **3** c): 1 kg 950 g

Question **3** d): 10 kg 875 g

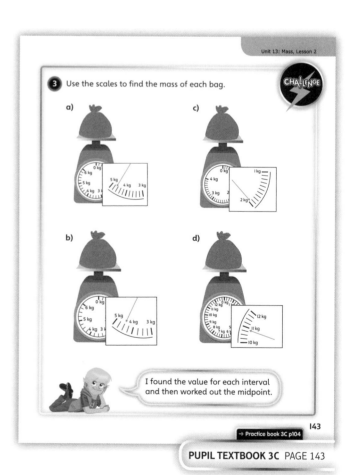

Practice

WAYS OF WORKING Independent thinking

IN FOCUS Questions ❶ and ❷ allow children to practise reading different scales. Question ❸ allows children to focus their learning by estimating answers on scales without interval lines. If children need support with question ❸ , suggest that they mark the half-way point; then the quarter-way and three-quarter-way points.

STRENGTHEN Ask children to work out the answers and then check these by counting around the scale in the interval value they have worked out. For instance, in question ❶ , children may find that the first scale has intervals of 500 g. Ask children to point to each interval and count around in 500s until they get to the answer. Use number lines or counters for support.

DEEPEN Question ❸ is a great activity for deepening learning; in this question, children are required to estimate amounts on a number line. After children have completed their answers, ask them if there are any other possibilities. This will deepen learning as they are applying knowledge of measure whilst using their estimation skills. Question ❹ challenges children to explore mass between whole kilograms as a word problem.

ASSESSMENT CHECKPOINT Questions ❶ and ❷ will allow you to see which children can read scales confidently, working out midpoints. For a more thorough assessment, ask children to explain why they matched each scale to the mass it shows.

ANSWERS Answers for the **Practice** part of the lesson appear in the separate **Practice and Reflect answer guide**.

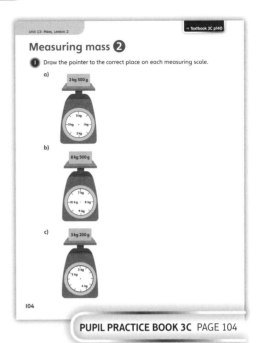

PUPIL PRACTICE BOOK 3C PAGE 104

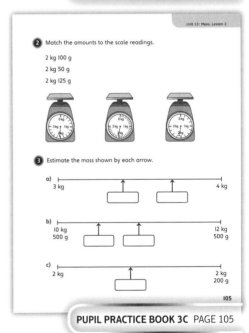

PUPIL PRACTICE BOOK 3C PAGE 105

Reflect

WAYS OF WORKING Independent thinking

IN FOCUS In this activity, encourage children to write their explanation in clear steps.

ASSESSMENT CHECKPOINT This will allow you to assess whether children can successfully find midpoints between intervals.

ANSWERS Answers for the **Reflect** part of the lesson appear in the separate **Practice and Reflect answer guide**.

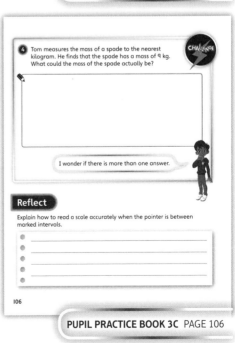

PUPIL PRACTICE BOOK 3C PAGE 106

After the lesson ⏸

- Are children secure at working with grams and kilograms together to find a mass value?
- How can you provide opportunities for children to further their skills at reading mass values on different scales, across the curriculum?

Measuring mass ❸

Learning focus

In this lesson, children will learn how to convert amounts in grams to values in both kilograms and grams.

Small steps

→ Previous step: Measuring mass (2)
→ **This step: Measuring mass (3)**
→ Next step: Comparing masses

NATIONAL CURRICULUM LINKS

Year 3 Measurement

Measure, compare, add and subtract: lengths (m/cm/mm); mass (kg/g); volume/capacity (l/ml).

ASSESSING MASTERY

Children can quickly convert and represent the amounts using representations such as the part-whole model. Children have a solid understanding of place value, and confidently convert amounts such as 1,009 g.

COMMON MISCONCEPTIONS

Children may have some place value misconceptions; for example, thinking 2,011 g = 2 kg 110 g. Ask:
• *Can you represent the amount using the weights (1 kg, 100 g, 10 g, 1 g), or place value counters?*

Some children may not be confident with using 0 as a place holder. Ask:
• *Why do you need to include a 0 in 1,022 g?*

STRENGTHENING UNDERSTANDING

Children may need reminding that 1 kg = 1,000 g (it would be useful to display this fact on a learning wall).

Provide children with a range of weights, so they can represent amounts with them and support their conversion mastery.

GOING DEEPER

Go deeper by asking children to represent amounts in different ways. For example: 1,340 g could be: 1 kg + 300 g + 40 g; or 1 kg + 100 g + 100 g + 100 g + 10 g + 10 g + 10 g + 10 g.

KEY LANGUAGE

In lesson: mass, measure, scale, grams (g), kilograms (kg)

Other language used by the teacher: interval, difference, divide, dial, balance

STRUCTURES AND REPRESENTATIONS

number line, place value counters, part-whole model

RESOURCES

Mandatory: weighing scales, weights

Optional: modelling clay, number lines

 In the eTextbook of this lesson, you will find interactive links to a selection of teaching tools.

Before you teach

• Do all children know that 1 kg = 1,000 g?
• Could conversion examples be made into a display?
• Have you got some weights ready for practical work?

Discover

ASK

• Question ❶ a): *Can you point to the thousands digit in 3,400 g and 3,500 g?*
• Question ❶ a): *How could you write your answer?*
• Question ❶ b): *How can you work out what each interval is worth?*

IN FOCUS Question ❶ a) introduces children to converting between grams and kilograms. Encourage children to recall the fact that 1 kg = 1,000 g. See if children can identify which digit represents each 1,000 g: they can do this by pointing to the 3 in 3,400 g. Look at the balance together and encourage children to add the kilograms and grams separately. Children should spot that 3,400 g is equal to 3 kg 400 g.

PRACTICAL TIPS For this activity, display some conversions on your learning wall, so children have a reference. This will help to scaffold learning. Part-whole models work well when separating larger amounts into grams and kilograms.

ANSWERS

Question ❶ a): The mass of the bike is 3 kg 400 g; Bella's guess is correct.

Question ❶ b):

3 kg 400 g

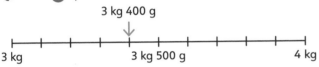

3 kg   3 kg 500 g   4 kg

Share

ASK

• Question ❶ a): *What amount would need to be added to the balance to make Richard's guess correct?*
• Question ❶ b): *Can you point to Richard's amount on your scale?*

IN FOCUS Question ❶ b) allows children to think about the relationship between grams and kilograms on a scale, giving them a context to work out the value of each interval and how many grams are found in 1 kg.

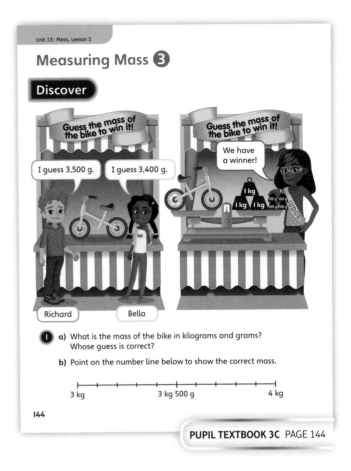

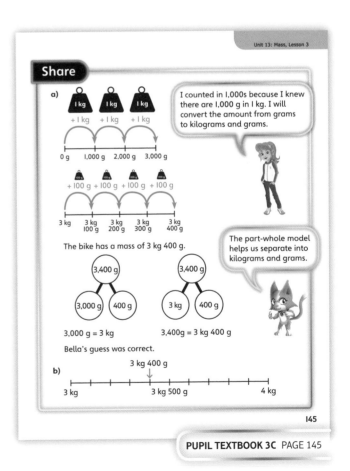

Think together

ASK

- Question **1** : *How can you convert 4 kg 1 g into grams only?*
- Question **2** : *How many ways can you find which include one or more kilogram weights?*

IN FOCUS Question **1** requires children to convert 943 g into kilograms and grams. Listen closely to children's reasoning. Some may suggest that there are no kilograms, so the answer does not change; this shows confidence and a firm understanding of place value in the context of mass. Others may suggest that there are 9 kg and 430 g: these children will probably need some support.

Question **2** requires children to represent amounts with different weights. Encourage children to find more than one answer.

STRENGTHEN Revise knowledge of place value before asking children to do conversions in Question **1** . Remind children of using 0 as a place holder. Use place value grids to support less confident children.

DEEPEN In question **3** , ask children which values they found challenging. Children may identify 1 kg 3 g and 1 kg 30 g as being tricky because they look similar; they should realise that they need to understand place value in order to recognise the difference between these values. Develop children's understanding further by asking them to make their own matching game involving similar amounts.

ASSESSMENT CHECKPOINT Question **1** will allow you to assess whether children can convert between kilograms and grams. They will need to call upon their knowledge of place value in some of the questions. Look carefully at how children convert 4 kg 1 g.

ANSWERS

Question **1** :

Result in grams	Result in kilograms and grams
a) 1,232 g	1 kg 232 g
b) 1,567 g	1 kg 567 g
c) 2,432 g	2 kg 432 g
d) 4,001 g	4 kg 1 g
e) 943 g	(0 kg) 943 g

Question **2** : There are a range of answers for this question. For example, 6 kg 700 g can be made using six 1 kg weights and seven 100 g weights, or five 1 kg weights and seventeen 100 g weights.

Question **3** : 5 kg 643 g – 5,643 g; 1 kg 3 g – 1,003 g; 1 kg 30 g – 1,030 g; 1 kg 100 g – 1,100 g

PUPIL TEXTBOOK 3C PAGE 146

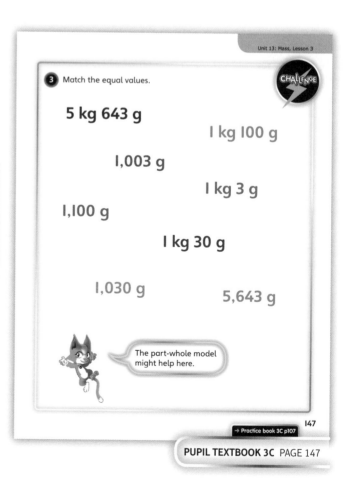

PUPIL TEXTBOOK 3C PAGE 147

Practice

WAYS OF WORKING Independent thinking

IN FOCUS Question ❶ is an effective way to represent converting between kilograms and grams. The weights shown next to the part-whole models should help to scaffold learning.

STRENGTHEN Children should practise converting amounts such as: 1 kg 200 g, 1 kg 20 g and 1 kg and 2 g. Use part-whole models to enable children to gain confidence with this way of modelling mass values. Ask children to tell you what the difference is between these amounts. This activity will greatly improve children's understanding of place value.

DEEPEN Question ❺ will deepen learning by making children think about converting kilograms into grams and vice versa. Children will show mastery of the lesson if they can represent amounts in different ways. Repeat the activity for other amounts such as 5,640 g.

THINK DIFFERENTLY Question ❹ is all about place value. Children will have to use their knowledge from the previous two lessons to work out the missing intervals and then reason why Lee is incorrect.

ASSESSMENT CHECKPOINT Question ❸ can be used to assess children's understanding. Children will have to draw on their knowledge of reading scales and apply it to the learning in this lesson.

ANSWERS Answers for the **Practice** part of the lesson appear in the separate **Practice and Reflect answer guide**.

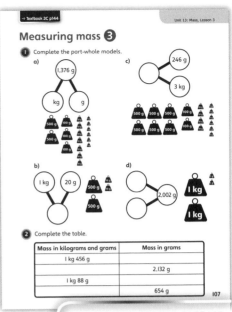

PUPIL PRACTICE BOOK 3C PAGE 107

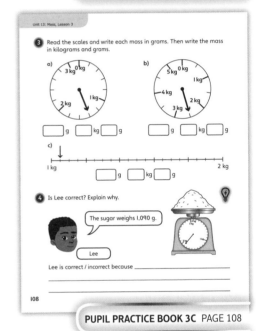

PUPIL PRACTICE BOOK 3C PAGE 108

Reflect

WAYS OF WORKING Independent thinking

IN FOCUS This activity will get children thinking about maths in real-life situations. Prompt children to look at the mass values of products the next time they go to the supermarket (this is a good home-learning activity).

ASSESSMENT CHECKPOINT Reflecting on real-life contexts will allow you to assess whether children can think about the importance of mass value in everyday situations. Children may think that only kilograms are used when we are estimating, or that they do not need to be overly accurate.

ANSWERS Answers for the **Reflect** part of the lesson appear in the separate **Practice and Reflect answer guide**.

After the lesson ⏸

- Are all children secure at converting kilograms into grams and vice versa?
- Can children represent amounts in different ways?
- How will you link this lesson to the following one (comparing masses) as well as across the curriculum?

PUPIL PRACTICE BOOK 3C PAGE 109

Comparing masses

Learning focus

In this lesson, children will compare masses by ordering them on a number line and by using <, > and =.

Small steps

→ Previous step: Measuring mass (3)
→ **This step: Comparing masses**
→ Next step: Adding and subtracting masses

NATIONAL CURRICULUM LINKS

Year 3 Measurement

Measure, compare, add and subtract: lengths (m/cm/mm); mass (kg/g); volume/capacity (l/ml).

ASSESSING MASTERY

Children can quickly order amounts and the use the correct language, such as: greater, more than, less than. Children can solve some problems involving ordering amounts.

COMMON MISCONCEPTIONS

Children may assume an amount in grams is larger than kilograms; for example: 1,245 g > 2 kg 100 g. Ask:
• *Can you convert the grams to kilograms to help you decide?*

Children might confuse the signs < and >. Ask:
• *What is wrong with this sentence: 1 kg < 100 g?*

STRENGTHENING UNDERSTANDING

Recap on the content and skills of converting amounts practised in the previous lesson.

GOING DEEPER

Deepen learning by asking children to order the mass of real-life objects. It is important that children can feel heavier and lighter objects: ask them to hold different objects and arrange themselves in a line of ascending order of mass. This will deepen learning by allowing children to discuss their object's value with others and will encourage peer correction if they fail to order correctly.

KEY LANGUAGE

In lesson: mass, scale, grams (g), kilograms (kg), weigh

Other language to be used by the teacher: measure, interval, difference, greater than (>), less than (<), equal to (=), compare, divide, dial, more than, order

STRUCTURES AND REPRESENTATIONS

number line, place value counters

RESOURCES

Mandatory: weighing scales, weights

Optional: modelling clay, number lines

 In the eTextbook of this lesson, you will find interactive links to a selection of teaching tools.

Before you teach

• Do all children have a sound knowledge of converting grams and kilograms?
• Is the key vocabulary on display in your classroom?
• Do children know what the signs <, >, and = mean?

Discover

Pair work

ASK

- Question ❶ a): *Would it help to convert grams to grams and kilograms for the pineapple?*
- Question ❶ a): *Is the item with the largest mass also the biggest item?*
- Question ❶ b): *Did you give your answer in both grams and kilograms? Why?*

IN FOCUS Question ❶ a) shows mass in grams and also kilograms and grams, which children will have seen before. In this question, children need to compare these masses in both grams and kilograms and grams, in a real-life context.

PRACTICAL TIPS Bring in a pineapple and a pumpkin so children can physically compare them. Discuss why we need scales to measure two objects which are close in weight value.

ANSWERS

Question ❶ a): The pineapple has the greater mass (1 kg 243 g > 1 kg 230 g).

Question ❶ b): The melon could weigh 1 kg 231 g, 1 kg 232 g, 1 kg 233g, 1 kg 234 g, 1 kg 235g, 1 kg 236 g, 1 kg 237 g, 1 kg 238 g, 1 kg 239 g, 1 kg 240 g, 1 kg 241 g or 1 kg 242 g.

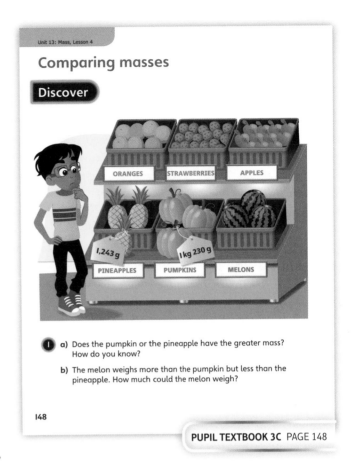

Comparing masses

Discover

1 a) Does the pumpkin or the pineapple have the greater mass? How do you know?

b) The melon weighs more than the pumpkin but less than the pineapple. How much could the melon weigh?

148

PUPIL TEXTBOOK 3C PAGE 148

Share

Whole class teacher led

ASK

- Question ❶ a): *When comparing the amounts, did you look at the kilograms or grams first?*
- Question ❶ b): *Why do you think there is more than one answer?*

IN FOCUS In question ❶ a), children may convert the mass of the pumpkin into grams. Explain that this is correct but is a less efficient method of working.

In question ❶ b), children are presented with a number line. Explain that number lines can be useful when asked to find the possible numbers between two numbers.

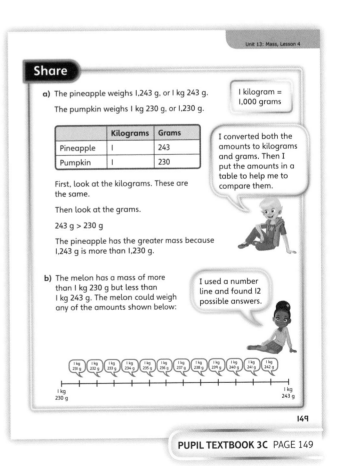

Share

a) The pineapple weighs 1,243 g, or 1 kg 243 g.
The pumpkin weighs 1 kg 230 g, or 1,230 g.

1 kilogram = 1,000 grams

	Kilograms	Grams
Pineapple	1	243
Pumpkin	1	230

First, look at the kilograms. These are the same.

Then look at the grams.

243 g > 230 g

The pineapple has the greater mass because 1,243 g is more than 1,230 g.

I converted both the amounts to kilograms and grams. Then I put the amounts in a table to help me to compare them.

b) The melon has a mass of more than 1 kg 230 g but less than 1 kg 243 g. The melon could weigh any of the amounts shown below:

I used a number line and found 12 possible answers.

1 kg 231 g, 1 kg 232 g, 1 kg 233 g, 1 kg 234 g, 1 kg 235 g, 1 kg 236 g, 1 kg 237 g, 1 kg 238 g, 1 kg 239 g, 1 kg 240 g, 1 kg 241 g, 1 kg 242 g

1 kg 230 g ———— 1 kg 243 g

149

PUPIL TEXTBOOK 3C PAGE 149

Think together

ASK

- Question **1** : *What do the signs < and > mean?*
- Question **2** : *Why are the scales incorrect?*

IN FOCUS Question **2** allows children to convert the amounts and then work out which scales are incorrect. There are some amounts that will require a good knowledge of place value: for example, in question **2** c), 1 kg 3 g is very similar to 1,001 g.

STRENGTHEN Children may find it helpful to use a table to convert, compare and order masses, as shown below:

Kilograms	Grams

DEEPEN In question **2** , ask children to explain why the scales are incorrect. Can they suggest an amount which would make each scale correct? Some children may point out that although **2** d) is correct, in reality they would almost be balanced because the difference between each side is only 2 g; this shows a good understanding of place value in the context of mass.

ASSESSMENT CHECKPOINT Question **3** can be used to assess whether children can compare more than two amounts. Assess children's ability to find ways to compare the amounts and to explain their answers clearly and concisely.

ANSWERS

Question **1** : 1 kg 456 g < 1,500 g

1211 g < 1 kg 215 g

1090g > 1 kg 9 g

2 kg 211 g > 2 kg 210 g

Question **2** : Scales A, B and C are not working correctly.

Question **3** : 754 g, 1 kg 9 g, 1,090 g, 1 kg 91 g, 1,098 g, 1,432 g, 1 kg 900 g

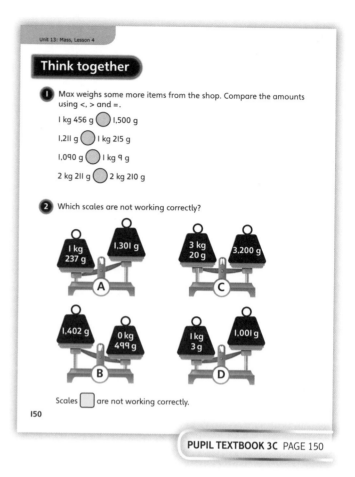

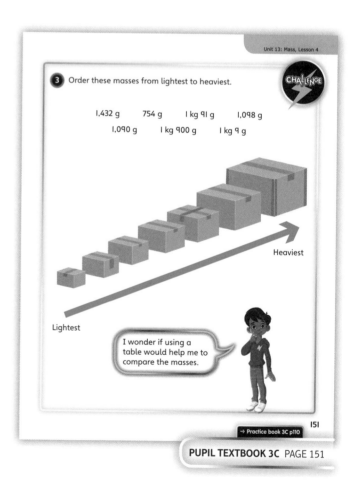

Practice

WAYS OF WORKING Independent thinking

IN FOCUS Question **5** requires children to have a good understanding of place value. Ask children to convert the amounts and then find the lowest value. After this, they should be able to complete the question.

STRENGTHEN Ask children to practise ordering everyday objects from home and in the classroom, such as bags of flour, tins of soup, pegs, pencils and so on.

DEEPEN An important learning point in this lesson is that just because an object is bigger, it is not necessarily heavier. Children need to understand this in order to answer question **1**. Demonstrate this with a small metal weight and a large cushion. You could also ask children to say which is heavier: 100 feathers or 100 bricks.

THINK DIFFERENTLY Question **4** provides an opportunity for reasoning and problem solving. Ask children to explain their answers; they should be able to give a range of values for B, C and D.

ASSESSMENT CHECKPOINT Question **1** will allow you to assess whether children can compare amounts using the <, > and = signs.

ANSWERS Answers for the **Practice** part of the lesson appear in the separate **Practice and Reflect answer guide**.

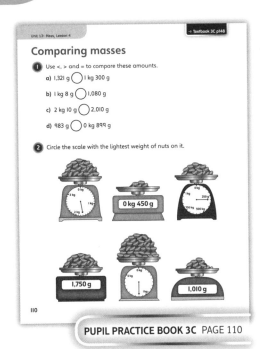

PUPIL PRACTICE BOOK 3C PAGE 110

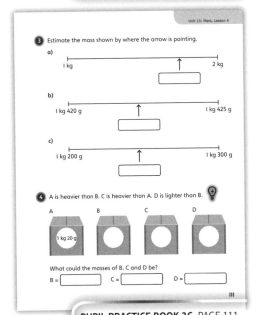

PUPIL PRACTICE BOOK 3C PAGE 111

Reflect

WAYS OF WORKING Pair work

IN FOCUS This activity will get children thinking about efficient methods of ordering. Children should realise that they always need to look at the kilograms, then the 100s of grams, then the 10s of grams and then the 1s.

ASSESSMENT CHECKPOINT Listen carefully to children's reasoning: they should be explaining that once Max has checked the kilograms and realised they are equal, he only needs to look at the hundreds of grams to see which mass is bigger.

ANSWERS Answers for the **Reflect** part of the lesson appear in the separate **Practice and Reflect answer guide**.

After the lesson

- Are all children secure in their knowledge of comparing and converting mass values?
- How can you provide further opportunities across the curriculum for comparing a range of objects?

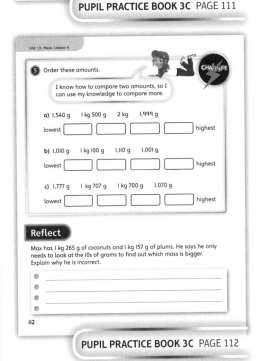

PUPIL PRACTICE BOOK 3C PAGE 112

Adding and subtracting masses

Learning focus

In this lesson, children will add and subtract masses, which include mixed units, using a range of strategies. They will continue to convert mass values between grams and kilograms.

Small steps

→ Previous step: Comparing masses
→ **This step: Adding and subtracting masses**
→ Next step: Problem solving – mass

NATIONAL CURRICULUM LINKS

Year 3 Measurement

Measure, compare, add and subtract: lengths (m/cm/mm); mass (kg/g); volume/capacity (l/ml).

ASSESSING MASTERY

Children can use efficient strategies to add and subtract mixed-value masses. They should be able to explain their methods and give reasons for why they have used a particular method.

COMMON MISCONCEPTIONS

Children may not add the kilograms and grams separately. Ask:
• *Can you add kilograms if they cross the 1,000 barrier?*

Children may not convert the grams to kilograms. For example, they may write 1,200 g. Ask:
• *Do you need to convert grams? Why not?*

STRENGTHENING UNDERSTANDING

To highlight the importance of conversion before carrying out an operation, ask children if they can add 1 kg 100 g to 1,500 g without converting. Then remind children how to convert grams to kilograms if needed.

Use representations such as the number line to support understanding of addition and subtraction.

GOING DEEPER

Deepen learning by challenging children to solve missing number problems. Ask questions such as:
• *On a balancing scale, if a vase weighs 1 kg 500 g on the heavier side and there are 3 toy cars weighing 375 g on the lighter side, how many more cars do you need to make the scales balance?*

KEY LANGUAGE

In lesson: mass, weigh, scale, grams (g), kilograms (kg)

Other language to be used by the teacher: measure, scale, interval, difference, divide, dial, add, subtract, more than, difference, take away, plus, minus, sum, total, inverse

STRUCTURES AND REPRESENTATIONS

number line, bar model, column addition

RESOURCES

Mandatory: weighing scales

Optional: modelling clay, number lines

 In the eTextbook of this lesson, you will find interactive links to a selection of teaching tools.

Before you teach

• Are all children secure in addition and subtraction operations?
• How will you support children who find counting on a number line difficult?

Discover

WAYS OF WORKING Pair work

ASK

- Question ❶ a): *What are the key words that help you identify which operation to use?*
- Question ❶ b): *What strategies could you use to work this out?*

IN FOCUS Question ❶ a) requires children to focus their attention on the language of the question and correctly identify the words that indicate which operation they should use to work out the answer.

In question ❶ b), some children may think 'more … than' means they should add. Explain this question in the context of more than as finding a difference between two values.

PRACTICAL TIPS Addition and subtraction in a real-life context is important for learning. Do some practical measuring of mass in the classroom and then ask children to add more mass, or take some away. This could be done in a cooking and nutrition lesson.

ANSWERS

Question ❶ a): 1 kg 500 g + 2 kg 250 g = 3 kg 750 g

Alex and Zac buy 3 kg 750 g of flour altogether.

Question ❶ b): 2 kg 250 g – 1 kg 500 g = 750g

Alex buys 3 kg 750 g more flour than Zac.

PUPIL TEXTBOOK 3C PAGE 152

Share

WAYS OF WORKING Whole class teacher led

ASK

- Question ❶ a): *Did you remember to add the grams and kilograms separately?*
- Question ❶ b): *Which strategy did you find the most efficient: using a number line or using the column method?*

IN FOCUS Question ❶ encourages children to use different strategies, in particular the column method and using a number line to add and subtract. Discuss how Flo has used the number line to find the difference between both numbers and the nearest kilogram as an efficient method to find the total difference. Ask children which strategy they find more efficient (this is a great whole class talking point).

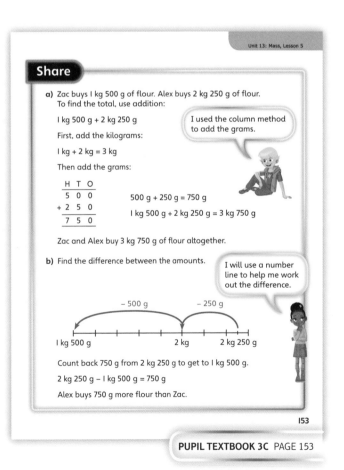

PUPIL TEXTBOOK 3C PAGE 153

Think together

Whole class teacher led (I do, We do, You do)

ASK

- Question ❶ : *Can you explain your chosen method?*
- Question ❸ : *How is the column method useful for solving these problems?*
- Question ❸ : *How can you use the inverse operation to check your answers?*

IN FOCUS In question ❶, point out that the answers could be written in grams or kilograms (depending on which way children convert). Encourage children to convert to kilograms: it makes the amounts more manageable (also children are not expected to add 4-digit numbers in Year 3).

STRENGTHEN Provide children with more activities similar to question ❷. Practising with the number line is an important skill for children; at first, they may need to make multiple jumps.

DEEPEN In question ❷, ask children to explain what operation is needed for each number line. They will have to think carefully about the missing number problems. Children should realise that, on the first two number lines, they must add the two amounts, however, on the third number line, they must do a subtraction. This is a good discussion point, and children will demonstrate a deeper understanding if they can explain this.

ASSESSMENT CHECKPOINT Question ❶ can be used to assess whether children can add and subtract amounts which require a conversion first.

ANSWERS

Question ❶ a): 2,423 g + 1 kg 221 g = 3 kg 644 g

Question ❶ b): 2 kg 800 g + 200 g = 3 kg

Question ❶ c): 1,950 g + 5 kg 100 g = 7 kg 50 g

Question ❷ a): The difference is 750 g

Question ❷ b): The difference is 1 kg 300 g

Question ❷ c): The starting mass is 2 kg 800 g

Question ❸ a): 1 kg 500 g + **750 g** = 2,250 g

Question ❸ b): **1 kg 150 g** + 2 kg 100 g = 3 kg 250 g

Question ❸ c): **3 kg 800 g** – 1,900 g = 1 kg 900 g

Question ❸ d): 3 kg 500 g – **900 g** = 2 kg 600 g

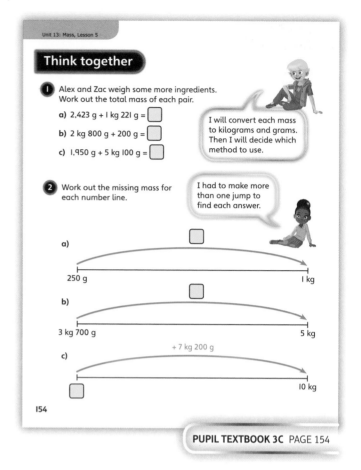

PUPIL TEXTBOOK 3C PAGE 154

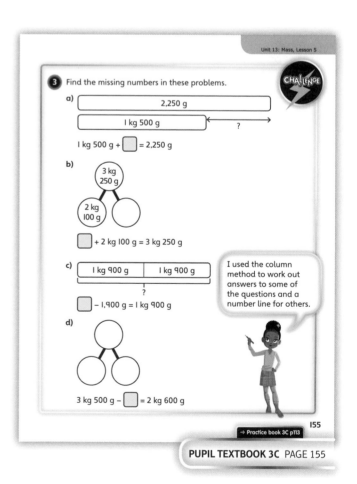

PUPIL TEXTBOOK 3C PAGE 155

Practice

WAYS OF WORKING Independent thinking

IN FOCUS Questions ❶ and ❺ help encourage children to use a range of strategies when adding and subtracting in the context of mass. The column method is a good strategy, but make sure children realise that it is not always the most efficient: they may find the bar method or using a number line is quicker. Questions ❶ and ❷ explore number lines and bar models to provide practice in the use of these strategies.

STRENGTHEN Allow children to practise addition and subtraction strategies, such as using number lines for questions similar to those calculations in question ❸. Ask children to come up with their own problems for the class to solve together.

DEEPEN In question ❸, challenge children to add or subtract more than two amounts. This will deepen children's learning as they work with what they have learnt and apply it when solving a multi-step number sentence.

ASSESSMENT CHECKPOINT Question ❷ will give you an insight into which children understand how addition and subtractions can be visually represented using bar models.

ANSWERS Answers for the **Practice** part of the lesson appear in the separate **Practice and Reflect answer guide**.

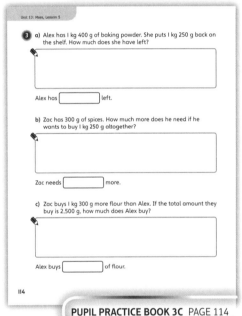

PUPIL PRACTICE BOOK 3C PAGE 113

PUPIL PRACTICE BOOK 3C PAGE 114

Reflect

WAYS OF WORKING Pair work

IN FOCUS This activity allows the sharing of ideas and methods. Children will have to explain their methods: a great learning point in itself.

ASSESSMENT CHECKPOINT Look carefully at children's explanations of methods. Do they understand why some methods are more efficient than others?

ANSWERS Answers for the **Reflect** part of the lesson appear in the separate **Practice and Reflect answer guide**.

After the lesson ⏸

- How will you build on this lesson with practical activities across the curriculum which involve the addition and subtraction of masses?
- Are all children secure in solving missing number problems? Do some need further support?
- Do children know how to add, and find the difference between, two masses given as a combination of grams, and kilograms and grams?

PUPIL PRACTICE BOOK 3C PAGE 115

Problem solving – mass

Learning focus

In this lesson, children will use all of the knowledge and strategies they have learnt in this unit to solve problems involving mass.

Small steps

→ Previous step: Adding and subtracting masses
→ **This step: Problem solving – mass**
→ Next step: Measuring capacity (1)

NATIONAL CURRICULUM LINKS

Year 3 Measurement

Measure, compare, add and subtract: lengths (m/cm/mm); mass (kg/g); volume/capacity (l/ml).

ASSESSING MASTERY

Children can solve problems effectively, using suitable strategies such as choosing the correct method of addition or subtraction. Children can explain how they solved the problem clearly and using the correct vocabulary.

COMMON MISCONCEPTIONS

Children may misinterpret the question and carry out an incorrect calculation. Ask:
• *How can you check your answer?*

Children may not be able to show the question using a visual representation. Ask:
• *Can you draw a bar model to help you solve the problem?*

STRENGTHENING UNDERSTANDING

Ask children to construct bar models to represent the problems. This should help them understand what is required to find a solution.

GOING DEEPER

To deepen learning, give children some answers (for example, 4 kg 20 g) and ask them to create multi-step problems to match them; asking children to explain their method for constructing and solving their problems will help to consolidate their understanding of the different ways to solve problems.

KEY LANGUAGE

In lesson: mass, scale, interval, grams (g), kilograms (kg)

Other language to be used by the teacher: measure, difference, divide, dial, problem

STRUCTURES AND REPRESENTATIONS

number line, place value counters, bar model, part-whole model, column addition

RESOURCES

Optional: weighing scales, modelling clay, number lines

 In the eTextbook of this lesson, you will find interactive links to a selection of teaching tools.

Before you teach

• Can a classroom display support problem solving with mass values?
• Are all children secure in operations such as multiplication and division?

Discover

Unit 13: Mass, Lesson 6

Problem solving – mass

Discover

WAYS OF WORKING Pair work

ASK
- Question **1** a): *Which method could you use?*
- Questions **1** a) and b): *How many steps are in this problem?*

IN FOCUS Question **1** b) focuses on subtraction. Children may have used the column method to find the solution to question **1** a); you may want to model finding the difference on a number line as a more efficient mental strategy.

PRACTICAL TIPS For this activity, encourage children to use a range of strategies to work out the answers, and use bar models to highlight how you can find the difference between two values. Afterwards, share the different methods.

ANSWERS

Question **1** a): 3 × 500 g = 1,500 g

1,500 g – 1,300 g = 200 g

Zac has 200 g of flour left.

Question **1** b): 200 g – 125 g = 75 g

Zac has 75 g of flour left now.

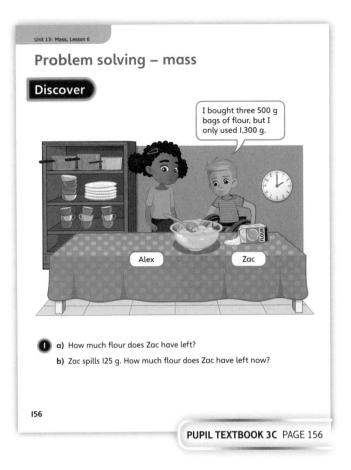

1 a) How much flour does Zac have left?

b) Zac spills 125 g. How much flour does Zac have left now?

156

PUPIL TEXTBOOK 3C PAGE 156

Share

WAYS OF WORKING Whole class teacher led

ASK
- Question **1** a): *How does the bar model help?*
- Question **1** b): *How does the number line help?*
- Questions **1** a) and b): *Are there any other methods you could use?*

IN FOCUS For both parts of the question, encourage children to work methodically and in clear steps. Children should record their workings in a series of number sentences. Some children may need the bar model and number line to be explained to them, to help them understand the problems.

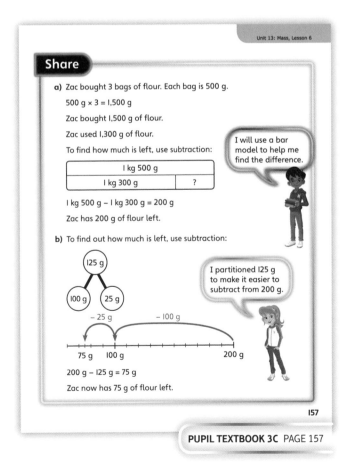

PUPIL TEXTBOOK 3C PAGE 157

Think together

WAYS OF WORKING Whole class teacher led (I do, We do, You do)

ASK

- Question ❶ : *How could the scale help you work out the problem?*
- Question ❸ : *Which object do you think you should work out first? Why?*
- Question ❸ : *How could you find out what one robot is worth?*

IN FOCUS In questions ❶ and ❷ , children may work out the intervals on the scale and then use it as a number line to help them work out the answer. This is a good strategy and should be encouraged.

STRENGTHEN Use question ❸ to explore the various calculation steps with learners who need more support and scaffolding. Ask children what they should find out first. If they are unsure, you may want to point at the two robots on the second scale and ask how they could work out what one robot might be worth.

In question ❷ , remind children that they can work out 40 × 3 by using place value knowledge (some may start with a written method).

DEEPEN Question ❸ can be used to deepen learning because it allows children to break down a problem clearly. Ask children to create their own similar problem.

ASSESSMENT CHECKPOINT Question ❸ is a good indication of which children have mastered the lesson. Those who have will demonstrate a clear understanding of the question and will be able to use appropriate strategies to work out the answers.

ANSWERS

Question ❶ : 1 kg 100 g – 50 g = 1,050 g
1,050 g – 275 g = 775 g
The mass of the flour is 775 g.

Question ❷ : 15 g × 2 = 30 g
40 g × 3 = 120 g
The total mass is 150 g.
The pointer will be pointing to 150 g.

Question ❸ : A robot weighs 1,050 g (2,100 g ÷ 2 = 1,050 g)
3 robots weigh 3,150 g (1,050 g × 3 = 3,150 g)
2 wagons weigh 1,000 g (4,150 g – 3,150 g = 1,000 g)
The mass of 1 wagon is 500 g
(1,000 g ÷ 2 = 500 g).

PUPIL TEXTBOOK 3C PAGE 158

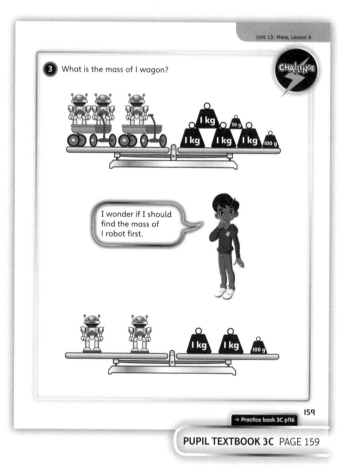

PUPIL TEXTBOOK 3C PAGE 159

Practice

WAYS OF WORKING Independent thinking

IN FOCUS Question ❶ allows children to practise adding mass values using a number line. In question ❷, encourage children to explore the problem using a representation such as the bar model. This is important as it gives children a visual understanding of the question.

STRENGTHEN Run intervention in which children practise calculation strategies. Apply these strategies to word problems and use the bar model to represent them.

DEEPEN After completing question ❹, challenge children to create similar problems. This will deepen learning as children will need to think carefully about their own problems – this will involve both creativity and logic.

ASSESSMENT CHECKPOINT Question ❸ can be used to see if children can extract the right information from the word problem in order to complete the bar model. This question will also test their understanding of mixed-value masses.

ANSWERS Answers for the **Practice** part of the lesson appear in the separate **Practice and Reflect answer guide**.

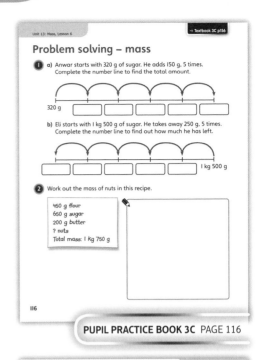

PUPIL PRACTICE BOOK 3C PAGE 116

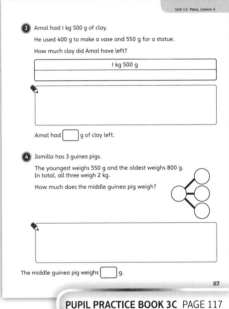

PUPIL PRACTICE BOOK 3C PAGE 117

Reflect

WAYS OF WORKING Pair work

IN FOCUS This activity consolidates learning in the lesson. Children will have to use their knowledge of problem solving in order to create a question to match a given answer. Encourage children to think of a multi-step question.

ASSESSMENT CHECKPOINT Ask children to swap their books with a partner and solve each other's questions. Look for multi-step questions which are correct.

ANSWERS Answers for the **Reflect** part of the lesson appear in the separate **Practice and Reflect answer guide**.

After the lesson ⏸

- Are all children secure in the aims for each lesson and ready for the **End of unit check**?
- Could children recognise and explain what approach they were taking to solve each problem?
- What were the main misconceptions children had during this lesson? How did you resolve them?

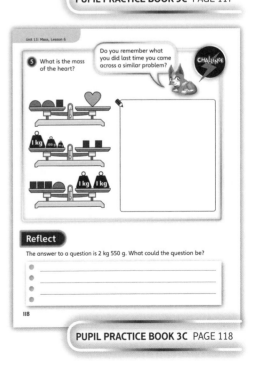

PUPIL PRACTICE BOOK 3C PAGE 118

End of unit check

> Don't forget the *Power Maths* unit assessment grid on p26.

WAYS OF WORKING Group work adult led

IN FOCUS

This **End of unit check** will allow you to focus on children's understanding of measuring mass and whether they can apply their knowledge in order to solve problems.

Look carefully at the answer that is given for question **5** : it will tell you if children can read two scales and then find the sum of the amounts.

The final question here is a SATs-style question. Talk through the question and, after children have answered it, explore answers.

Encourage children to think through or discuss this section before writing their answer in **My journal**.

ANSWERS AND COMMENTARY

Children should be secure with reading a range of scales and finding missing intervals. They should also be able to convert between grams and kilograms. Children should be confident when calculating answers to addition and subtraction questions involving mass, and should be able to check their strategies. Finally, they should apply their learning when solving problems.

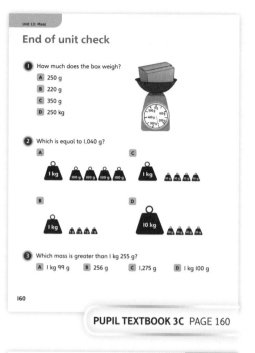

PUPIL TEXTBOOK 3C PAGE 160

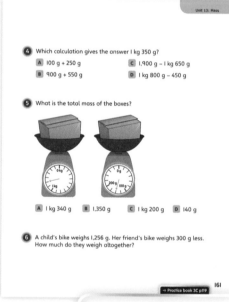

PUPIL TEXTBOOK 3C PAGE 161

Q	A	WRONG ANSWERS AND MISCONCEPTIONS	STRENGTHENING UNDERSTANDING
1	A	D suggests that the child has not read the units at the top of the scale.	Give children support with real-life contexts for measuring mass: • Ask children to convert measurements from grams to kilograms and vice versa. • Display the key vocabulary of the unit in your classroom. • Ask children to match word problems with representations such as bar models and number lines.
2	C	Any other answer suggests that children are not secure with the fact that 1 kg = 1,000 g or that they do not fully understand place value.	
3	C	B may suggest that children are struggling to convert and then compare amounts.	
4	D	B suggests that children have some difficulty crossing the kilogram barrier.	
5	A	D may suggest that children have only looked at the second scale and hasn't interpreted the question fully.	
6	2,212 g	Have children followed both steps of the problem?	

My journal

WAYS OF WORKING Independent thinking

ANSWERS AND COMMENTARY

Question **1** : Children should realise that they have to look at the balance first to work out the mass of the pineapple. They can then take this away from the value on the first scale, to leave the mass of the pear.

The calculations are as follows:

500 g + 200 g + 50 g + 5 g = 755 g

1 kg 300 g – 755 g = 545 g

Children are likely to use the column method for the addition and the number line for the subtraction.

If children are finding it difficult to write an explanation, ask: *Should you find the total amounts of each side of the scale first?*

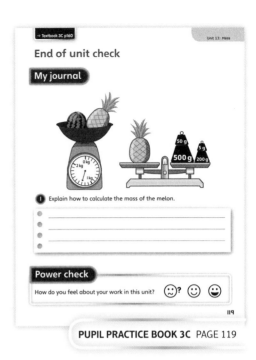

→ Textbook 3C p160   Unit 13: Mass

End of unit check

My journal

1 Explain how to calculate the mass of the melon.

Power check

How do you feel about your work in this unit?   :)?   :)   :D

119

PUPIL PRACTICE BOOK 3C PAGE 119

Power check

WAYS OF WORKING Independent thinking

ASK

- *What visual representation helped you in this unit?*
- *What do you know now that you did not at the start of the unit?*
- *Can you write down what new words you have learnt and what they mean?*

Power play

WAYS OF WORKING Pair work

IN FOCUS Use this **Power play** to assess children's addition, subtraction and problem-solving skills (involving masses). Can children explain their methods or any strategies they used?

ANSWERS AND COMMENTARY If children can do the **Power Play**, it means they can use learnt strategies to find solutions. Listen to the explanations of their strategies and note down any children who may need further support. Children should be encouraged to go deeper with this **Power play** by creating their own similar game.

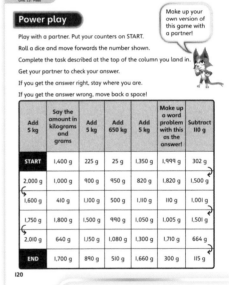

Unit 13: Mass

Power play

Make up your own version of this game with a partner!

Play with a partner. Put your counters on START.

Roll a dice and move forwards the number shown.

Complete the task described at the top of the column you land in.

Get your partner to check your answer.

If you get the answer right, stay where you are.

If you get the answer wrong, move back a space!

Add 5 kg	Say the amount in kilograms and grams	Add 5 kg	Add 650 kg	Add 5 kg	Make up a word problem with this as the answer!	Subtract 110 g
START	1,400 g	225 g	25 g	1,350 g	1,999 g	302 g
2,000 g	1,000 g	900 g	950 g	820 g	1,820 g	1,500 g
1,600 g	410 g	1,100 g	500 g	1,110 g	110 g	1,001 g
1,750 g	1,800 g	1,500 g	990 g	1,050 g	1,005 g	1,501 g
2,010 g	640 g	1,150 g	1,080 g	1,300 g	1,710 g	664 g
END	1,700 g	890 g	510 g	1,660 g	300 g	115 g

120

PUPIL PRACTICE BOOK 3C PAGE 120

After the unit

- Are all children secure in converting mass units, finding an interval value and applying the correct method when working out multi-step problems?
- How will you link this unit to other areas of the curriculum, for example weighing materials in art and design?

Strengthen and **Deepen** activities for this unit can be found in the *Power Maths* online subscription.

Unit 14
Capacity

Mastery Expert tip! "I found it valuable to make the links between this unit and the work children have done in number and calculating. Thinking of the scale as a number line helped the children to apply their understanding of number to the context of capacity."

Don't forget to watch the Unit 14 video!

WHY THIS UNIT IS IMPORTANT

This unit explores capacity and comes after other units about measure. It asks children to interpret a range of scales and apply their knowledge of place value and the number system. Children will learn to compare and order measurements, and convert between millilitres and mixed units of litres and millilitres. They will then use knowledge of all four operations to solve problems involving capacity.

WHERE THIS UNIT FITS

→ Unit 13: Mass

→ **Unit 14: Capacity**

This unit builds on from children's previous work in measures involving length and mass. Children should already have experience in reading and interpreting a range of scales and converting between units of measure, which will help them in this unit. Children will learn to compare, calculate and solve problems in the context of capacity. Children will need to apply their knowledge of the number system and calculating, in order to solve capacity word problems.

Before they start this unit, it is expected that children:
• understand place value in 3-digit numbers
• know how to add and subtract 3-digit numbers
• know multiplication facts for the 2, 5 and 10 times-tables.

ASSESSING MASTERY

Children will be able to use and interpret a variety of scales in order to measure amounts. They will be able to work with mixed units and convert between litres and millilitres. Children will be able to add and subtract capacities that cross the litre boundary; and they will be able to solve problems using addition, subtraction, multiplication and division. Children will understand that the capacity of a container is how much it holds when full.

COMMON MISCONCEPTIONS	STRENGTHENING UNDERSTANDING	GOING DEEPER
Children may struggle to interpret scales where not all divisions are labelled. They may make errors in place value, particularly when measuring and calculating in mixed units and converting between litres and millilitres.	Make the links to the work on calculations and the number system clear to children. Encourage children to think of the scales as number lines, and to represent them horizontally as well as vertically. Allow children to explore with capacity equipment by measuring, comparing and calculating capacities practically.	Encourage children to write their own capacity word problems that they can try on a partner. You could challenge them by specifying what operations their problem should include. Ask: *Can you write a problem with three or four steps?*

Unit 14: Capacity

WAYS OF WORKING

Use these pages to introduce what children will be covering in this unit. Ask children if they have done anything similar in other units. Children may be able to make links between this unit and their work on length and mass.

Talk through the bar model to ensure children understand what it represents. You could start with easier examples, using number bonds to 100, such as: *How does 35 + ? = 100 relate to 350 + ? = 1,000?* Discuss how a subtraction such as 100 ? = 45 would be represented and how that relates to 1,000 – ? = 450.

Talk through the part-whole model, using it to practise the same number bonds to 100 used in the bar model, such as: *35 + ? = 100; 100 - ? = 45.* Ask: *How many multiples of 5 pairs can you write in 3 minutes? Can you then relate this to multiples of 10 bonds to 1,000?*

Finally go through the key vocabulary with children. Ask: *Do you recognise any words? Can you explain what they mean? Which words are new?* Practise counting up and back in steps of 100 and 1,000.

STRUCTURES AND REPRESENTATIONS

Bar model:

350	?
1,000	

Part-whole model: **Scales:**

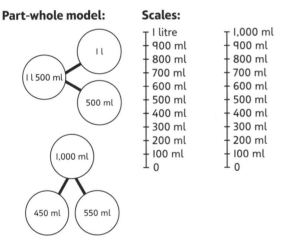

Number lines:

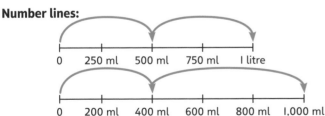

KEY LANGUAGE

There is some key language that children will need to know as part of the learning in this unit:

→ capacity, amount, measurement

→ litres (l), millilitres (ml)

→ scale, number line, interval

→ compare, convert, order

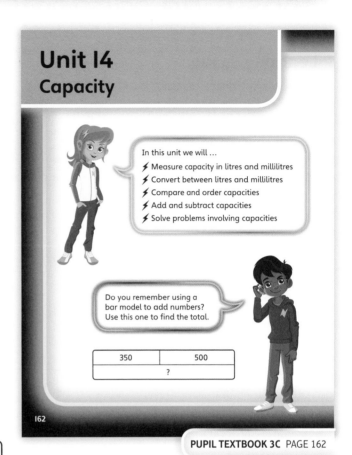

PUPIL TEXTBOOK 3C PAGE 162

PUPIL TEXTBOOK 3C PAGE 163

Measuring capacity ①

Learning focus

In this lesson, children will learn to measure volume in litres and in millilitres. They will learn how to read a variety of scales where only some of the divisions are labelled; drawing on their understanding of number, division and multiplication.

Small steps

→ Previous step: Problem solving – mass
→ **This step: Measuring capacity (1)**
→ Next step: Measuring capacity (2)

NATIONAL CURRICULUM LINKS

Year 3 Measurement

Measure, compare, add and subtract: lengths (m/cm/mm); mass (kg/g); volume/capacity (l/ml).

ASSESSING MASTERY

Children can read a scale in either litres or millilitres in order to determine volume. They will be able to work out the value of intervals not labelled, by applying known multiplication and division facts.

COMMON MISCONCEPTIONS

Children may struggle to determine how the scale is divided up. This could be due to not applying division facts or miscounting the intervals between two labelled measures. Encourage the children to look at the scale as a number line. Draw the scale horizontally, as this may be a more familiar orientation for them. Ask:

• *What is the total amount between these two labelled markers? How many jumps are there between these two labelled markers? How can you work out how much each jump is worth?*

Children may not understand that capacity is the amount a container holds when full, whereas the amount actually in the container is often not its full capacity. Ask:

• *What is the capacity of this jug when it is full? What is the amount of liquid in the jug? How much more will fill it to its capacity?*

STRENGTHENING UNDERSTANDING

Encourage children to use a range of different containers and a variety of scales. Ask children to fill the containers to a given level, discussing how they would find this on the scale and encouraging them to identify the container's capacity.

GOING DEEPER

Children could create their own capacity problems by coming up with their own scales. They could think of different ways to divide multiples of 100 ml or 1,000 ml on their scales.

KEY LANGUAGE

In lesson: capacity, litres (l), millilitres (ml), scale, interval, amount, number line, divided by, half-way between, least, most, approximate, measure, gauge

Other language used by the teacher: volume, add, subtract, divide, multiply, unit of measure

STRUCTURES AND REPRESENTATIONS

number line, bar model

RESOURCES

Optional: number lines, capacity measuring equipment (selection of 100 ml, 500 ml and litre containers)

 In the eTextbook of this lesson, you will find interactive links to a selection of teaching tools.

Before you teach

• Use practical activities to improve understanding.
• Link this to other curriculum areas (i.e. science).
• Can children count in 10s, 2s, 5s?

Discover

Unit 14: Capacity, Lesson 1

WAYS OF WORKING Pair work

ASK

- Question ❶ a): *How many intervals are there between 0 litres and 100 litres?*
- Question ❶ a): *Is the interval the number of markers, or the number of jumps between the markers?*
- Question ❶ a): *How could you work out how much each interval is worth?*
- Question ❶ a): *If the tank was full at the start, how many litres has the elephant drank?*

IN FOCUS The focus is on identifying the intervals between unlabelled markers on two different scales. Modelling the scale as a number line (with arrowed jumps between markers) will help children to see how to work out what each interval (amount between each marker) is worth. Remind children that when counting on, you do not count the start number, so the number of intervals is the same as the number of jumps between marked points. Some children will count just the unlabelled markers and others may include the ones given as well.

PRACTICAL TIPS Give children number lines modelled on the scales to practise counting the number of intervals between marked points. Practise counting in 25s to 200, and in 20s to 200, then count in 10s, 20s, 25s and 50s on each scale to see which works. Discuss how you know you have the right interval.

ANSWERS

Question ❶ a): There are 150 litres of water left in the tank.

Question ❶ b): Each marker is 20 ml. There are 140 ml in the bottle.

Share

WAYS OF WORKING Whole class teacher led

ASK

- Question ❶ a): *How many jumps are there from 0 to 100 litres?*
- Question ❶ a): *How does Astrid's comment help you to work out how much is left in the tank?*
- Question ❶ b): *How else could you divide 100 ml equally?*
- Question ❶ b): *How does Dexter's comment help you to work out the scale on the bottle?*

IN FOCUS The questions show that scales can be divided in different ways. In question ❶ a), the scale is divided into four equal sections, each worth 25 litres; but in question ❶ b), the scale is divided into five, so children need to work out 100 ml divided by 5. Some children may struggle with this. Can they use 10 ÷ 5 to work out 100 ÷ 5? It is important for children to see that they can use their knowledge of counting and calculations within this context.

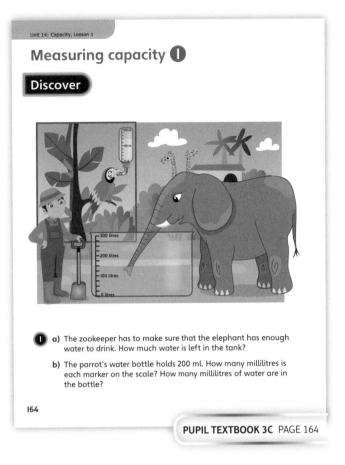

Measuring capacity ❶

Discover

❶ a) The zookeeper has to make sure that the elephant has enough water to drink. How much water is left in the tank?

b) The parrot's water bottle holds 200 ml. How many millilitres is each marker on the scale? How many millilitres of water are in the bottle?

164

PUPIL TEXTBOOK 3C PAGE 164

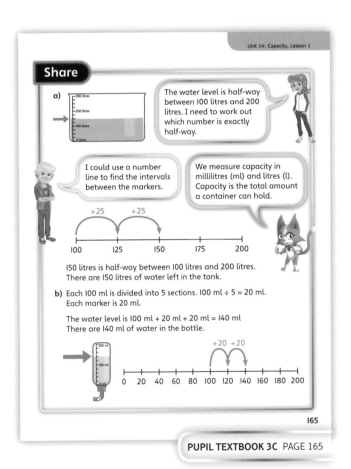

Share

a) The water level is half-way between 100 litres and 200 litres. I need to work out which number is exactly half-way.

I could use a number line to find the intervals between the markers.

We measure capacity in millilitres (ml) and litres (l). Capacity is the total amount a container can hold.

+25   +25

100   125   150   175   200

150 litres is half-way between 100 litres and 200 litres. There are 150 litres of water left in the tank.

b) Each 100 ml is divided into 5 sections. 100 ml ÷ 5 = 20 ml. Each marker is 20 ml.

The water level is 100 ml + 20 ml + 20 ml = 140 ml There are 140 ml of water in the bottle.

+20 +20

0 20 40 60 80 100 120 140 160 180 200

165

PUPIL TEXTBOOK 3C PAGE 165

Think together

Whole class teacher led (I do, We do, You do)

ASK

- Questions ❶, ❷ and ❸ : *How can you calculate what each interval is worth?*
- Questions ❶, ❷ and ❸ : *What number facts can you draw on to help you work out what each interval is worth?*
- Question ❸ : *What number is half-way between 150 and 200?*
- Question ❹ : *What does capacity mean? What knowledge can you use to match the amounts?*

IN FOCUS Question ❸ : This question involves three different scales and an amount that is half-way between two intervals. Once children have worked out each interval, encourage discussion about what the values half-way between markers would be, and how to work this out.

Question ❹ : Children will not know the actual capacities of these items, but encourage logical reasoning to work out the matches, even though the items are not shown to scale.

STRENGTHEN Allow children to experiment with 500 ml and 1 l containers with scales in 100s, 50s and 25s; first working out the in between values to identify the intervals, then partially filling them to read the amounts. Colouring water with a little bit of poster paint can help children to read the quantities. Let children look at a variety of milk and drink bottles to see what each capacity is.

DEEPEN Ask children to create different scales for 1 litre and to identify one(s) that make it easy to measure 250 ml / 200 ml.

ASSESSMENT CHECKPOINT Can children use division or counting strategies to work out the intervals on a millilitre or litre scale?

Children should know that amounts of liquids are measured in millilitres or litres, and be able to give examples of capacities measured in litres and capacities measured in millilitres. Children are beginning to understand that capacity is the amount a container can hold when filled up.

ANSWERS

Question ❶ : The scale is marked in intervals of 5 l.

$$7 \times 5 = 35 \, l$$

There are 35 l of fuel left in the tank.

Question ❷ : Children should indicate 275 ml on the scale (marker just under 300 ml).

Question ❸ a): A 80 ml; B 175 ml C 125 ml

Question ❸ b): A, C, B

Question ❹ : A 5 litres, B 5 ml, C 50 litres, D 500 ml

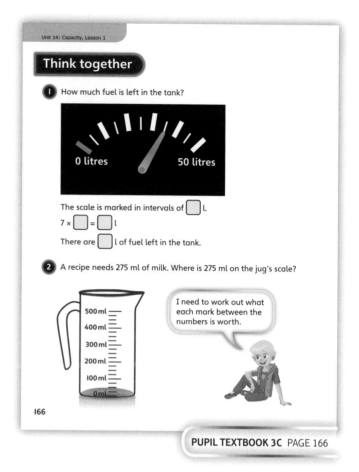

PUPIL TEXTBOOK 3C PAGE 166

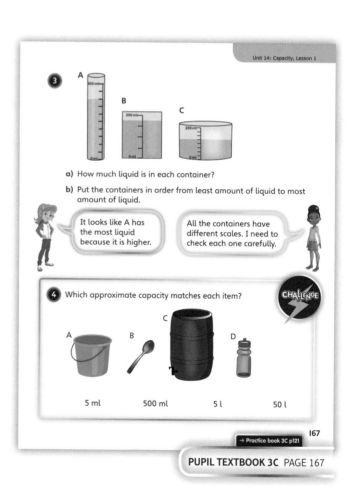

PUPIL TEXTBOOK 3C PAGE 167

Practice

WAYS OF WORKING Independent thinking

IN FOCUS The focus in questions **1**, **3**, and **4** is on reading scales and working out what each interval is worth. A variety of different types of measuring scales are used, including gauges. There is plenty of opportunity to work out the value of each interval, which is a key skill in this unit.

STRENGTHEN Look at scales that children may be more familiar with, such as scales on a ruler. Talk about how the scales have been divided up. Children could use a ruler to draw a line of 10 cm to create a scale that goes up to 100 millilitres in 10s, or up to 1,000 ml in 100s. Ask them to number each marker. Discuss different ways that a 10 cm scale could be divided. Give children the opportunity to explore what 5 ml, 50 ml, 500 ml and 1 litre look like on a 10 cm scale.

DEEPEN Children draw three vertical lines. One is 20 cm, the second is 50 cm and the third is 80 cm. They label the top of each line 100 ml. Can children divide these scales so that each has 10 ml divisions? What strategies did they use to work it out? Can children draw an accurate scale to show 0 – 100 ml with 20 ml or 25 ml intervals?

THINK DIFFERENTLY Question **2** involves children using their general knowledge of the world to decide whether something will be measured in litres or millilitres. An understanding that a litre is quite a lot and 1 millilitre is a very small drop will help.

ASSESSMENT CHECKPOINT Questions **1**, **3** and **4** will determine whether the children are able to read a variety of scales.

Question **2** will determine whether children understand the relative sizes of litres and millilitres.

ANSWERS Answers to the **Practice** part of the lesson appear in a separate **Practice and Reflect answer guide**

Reflect

WAYS OF WORKING Independent thinking

IN FOCUS This section encourages children to think about what information is important when reading scales. They have to consider the value of the labelled divisions, and the number of divisions between each labelled division. Children should reflect on the types of operations they need to carry out, in order to determine how much each division is worth.

ASSESSMENT CHECKPOINT Do children mention the importance of the scale on measuring equipment? Can children explain how to work out the unlabelled parts of the scale?

ANSWERS Answers to the **Reflect** part of the lesson appear in a separate **Practice and Reflect answer guide**

After the lesson

- Can you provide opportunities for children to practise these skills in other curriculum areas?
- Are children secure on how to read a scale where not every interval is labelled?
- Did you draw links with other areas of maths such as number, calculations and other measures?

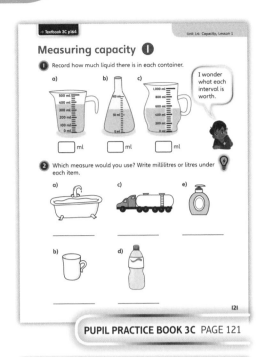

PUPIL PRACTICE BOOK 3C PAGE 121

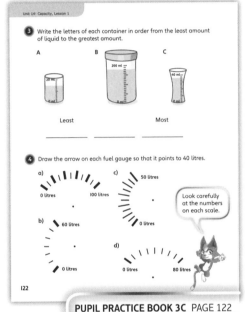

PUPIL PRACTICE BOOK 3C PAGE 122

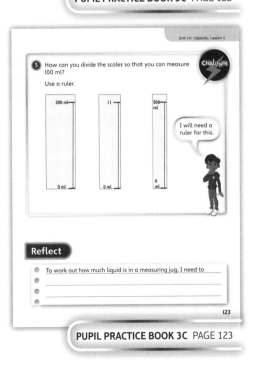

PUPIL PRACTICE BOOK 3C PAGE 123

Measuring capacity ❷

Learning focus

In this lesson, children will learn to read mixed units of capacity given in litres and millilitres and as $\frac{1}{2}$ litres, and convert them to millilitres. They will also read scales showing amounts over 1 litre.

Small steps

→ Previous step: Measuring capacity (1)
→ **This step: Measuring capacity (2)**
→ Next step: Measuring capacity (3)

NATIONAL CURRICULUM LINKS

Year 3 Measurement

Measure, compare, add and subtract: lengths (m/cm/mm); mass (kg/g); volume/capacity (l/ml).

ASSESSING MASTERY

Children can measure amounts greater than 1 litre. They will understand that capacity between whole litres is measured in a mixture of litres and millilitres. Children understand that $\frac{1}{2}$ litre is the same as 500 ml. Children will begin to convert between mixed units and millilitres.

COMMON MISCONCEPTIONS

Children may read only the millilitres and overlook any litres when measuring with mixed units. Ask:
• *Is this amount more than 1 litre? How many whole litres are there?*

STRENGTHENING UNDERSTANDING

Encourage children to create their own amounts with mixed units. First measure 1 litre of water and pour it into a larger container then add 500 millilitres of water. Ask:
• *How much water is in the container altogether?*

Add different amounts to the litre and record as, for example, 1 l 500 ml.

Make links with the previous lesson clear. Encourage children to think of the scale as a number line. Draw the scale horizontally if that helps children to understand it.

GOING DEEPER

Give children a measurement with mixed units. Get children to create their own scale to record the measurement.

KEY LANGUAGE

In lesson: Capacity, litre (l), millilitre (ml), scale, intervals, half ($\frac{1}{2}$), partition, amount, whole, half-way, number line, partition

Other language used by the teacher: mixed unit, greater than (>), less than (<)

STRUCTURES AND REPRESENTATIONS

number line, bar model, column addition

RESOURCES

Optional: capacity measuring equipment

 In the eTextbook of this lesson, you will find interactive links to a selection of teaching tools.

Before you teach

• Are there any children who may need support reading scales?
• Can you provide practical activities to support children's understanding of measuring capacity?
• How will you make the links between measuring capacity and their understanding of number patterns clear to children?

Discover

Measuring capacity ❷

WAYS OF WORKING Pair work

ASK

- Question ❶ a): *What is the same and what is different about the way the capacities have been measured?*

IN FOCUS This lesson introduces the children to capacities over 1 litre given as mixed units of litres and millilitres, including $\frac{1}{2}$ litre and converting these to millilitres. As half of 10 is 5, half of 1,000 is 500 so $\frac{1}{2}$ litre = 500 ml.

PRACTICAL TIPS Allow children to measure out 1 litre 500 millilitres into a 2 litre jug and to record the measurement in litres and millilitres, in millilitres and as $1\frac{1}{2}$ litres. Repeat if appropriate with 2 litres 500 millilitres. Can children record other whole and half litres in these three ways?

ANSWERS

Question ❶ a): Watering can A holds 500 ml, B 1,500 ml and C 2,500 ml.

Question ❶ b): Watering can B holds $1\frac{1}{2}$ litres.

Discover

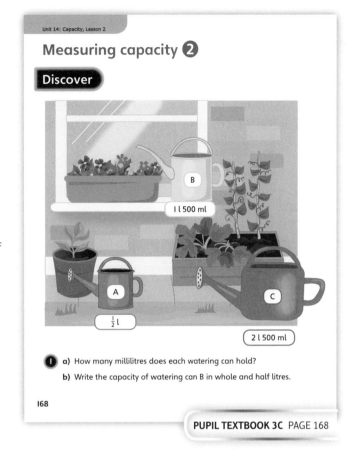

❶ a) How many millilitres does each watering can hold?

b) Write the capacity of watering can B in whole and half litres.

168

PUPIL TEXTBOOK 3C PAGE 168

Share

WAYS OF WORKING Whole class teacher led

ASK

- Question ❶ a): *How can you use the fact box to help you work out how many millilitres is in watering can A?*
- Question ❶ a): *Look at the part-whole model: how has the capacity in watering can B has been partitioned?*
- Question ❶ a): *1,000 ml = 1 litre so how many litres is 2,000 ml? 3,000 ml?*
- Question ❶ a): *Can you use a part-whole model to partition the amount in watering can C?*
- Question ❶ b): *How can you use $\frac{1}{2}$ litre = 500 ml from the first question to help you with this question?*

IN FOCUS

The focus here is on the different ways capacities can be recorded. How that is translated to a scale will be tackled in **Think Together** using the learning from lesson 1.

Share

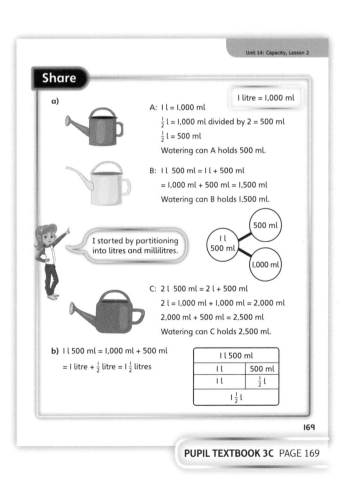

PUPIL TEXTBOOK 3C PAGE 169

Think together

WAYS OF WORKING Whole class teacher led (I do, We do, You do)

ASK

- Question **1** : *What do you need to know in order to work out the value of the intervals?*
- Question **2** : *How do you work out amounts when the liquid is between intervals?*
- Question **3** : *How are the scales the same? How are they different?*

IN FOCUS In question **2** c), help children to think about place value when writing 1 l 50 ml as 1,**0**50 ml.

The focus in question **3** is on estimation, as children are given only 0 and various maximum values. Encourage children to start by working out where the whole litre intervals should be on each scale. Children should then be able to see that the arrows on the second and third scales point to less than 1 litre, and the arrow on the fourth scale points to more than 2 l.

STRENGTHEN Ask children to identify how many whole litres the liquid has gone over, and then how many extra millilitres are above that. Practise counting in 1,000s to convert the litres to millilitres. Write this as an addition and finally as an amount in millilitres. Children could make the amounts using a range of measuring jugs and cylinders.

DEEPEN Look at question **3**. Can children draw other scales that will show 1 l 400 ml? Ask: *Draw three scales to show other amounts (such as 1 l 250 ml).*

ASSESSMENT CHECKPOINT Question **1** : Can children accurately read a scale using mixed litres and millilitres?

Question **2** : Can children read scales where the liquid is between intervals?

Question **3** : Are children able to interpret a range of scales and reason about them in order to estimate a capacity?

ANSWERS

Question **1** : There is 1 whole litre and 500 ml in the jug.
There are 1,500 ml in the jug.

Question **2** a): A 1 l 200 ml; B 3 l 500 ml; C 1 l 50 ml

Question **2** b): A 1,200 ml; B 3,500 ml; C 1,050 ml

Question **3** : A shows 1 l 400 ml because the scale goes up in intervals of 200 ml.

PUPIL TEXTBOOK 3C PAGE 170

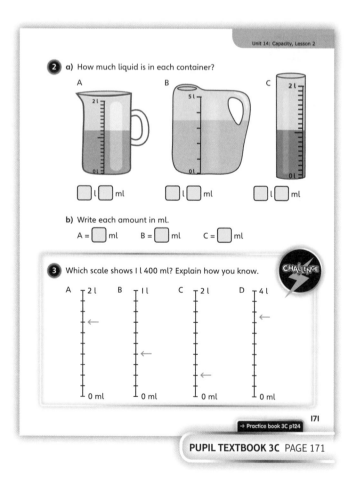

PUPIL TEXTBOOK 3C PAGE 171

Practice

Independent thinking

IN FOCUS The focus in questions **1**, **2** and **3** is on determining the intervals on a variety of scales and writing the amounts shown in mixed units and also in millilitres. Encourage children to realise that the intervals are likely to be 100 ml, 200 ml, 250 ml or 500 ml and that the number of unlabelled intervals (jumps between markers rather than the number of markers) will determine which it is (10 for 100 ml, 5 for 200 ml, 4 for 250 ml and 2 for 500 ml as 10 × 100 ml, 5 × 200 ml, 4 × 250 ml and 2 × 500 ml all equal 1,000 ml = 1 litre).

In question **1**, one amount is 500 ml. Encourage children to write this as 0 l 500 ml.

STRENGTHEN Allow children to label some of the unlabelled intervals in between the whole litre intervals, to make the scale easier to read. Practise counting in 100s, 200s, 250s and 500s to see which work for each scale (does the count result in the next recorded value?).

DEEPEN Ask children to create their own versions of question **5** to try out on their partner, and to discuss how accurate they can be when there is no scale shown.

THINK DIFFERENTLY The focus in question **4** is on measuring an amount in a slightly different context. Encourage children to think about what they need to do to answer the question (Flo's comment: measure the amount in the large jug), then what they need to do first to be able to measure the amount (work out where the whole litre intervals are). Have children fully answered the question by deciding which jug it is?

ASSESSMENT CHECKPOINT Questions **1**, **2** and **3** will determine whether the children are able to read a variety of scales to measure capacity in mixed units. Question **4** will determine whether children can solve a word problem involving scales and mixed units. Question **5** will determine whether children can apply their knowledge of number to read a scale and make an estimation.

ANSWERS Answers to the **Practice** part of the lesson appear in a separate **Practice and Reflect answer guide**.

Reflect

Independent thinking

IN FOCUS Children should be aware that as the number of intervals changes, the amount that they represent also changes. Responses should also include the unit of measurement.

ASSESSMENT CHECKPOINT Is it clear from children's responses that they understand the use of intervals on a scale? Have they also included 0 l and 1 l at either ends of the scale?

ANSWERS Answers for the **Reflect** part of the lesson appear in the separate **Practice and Reflect answer guide**.

After the lesson

- Are children confident in reading a range of scales?
- How could you further support those children who are not secure in measuring amounts using mixed units?
- Can you provide practical opportunities to reinforce children's learning in other curriculum areas?

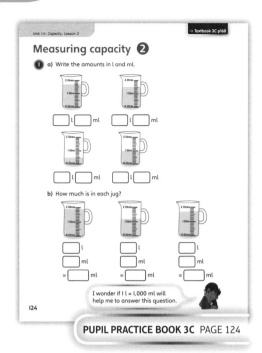

PUPIL PRACTICE BOOK 3C PAGE 124

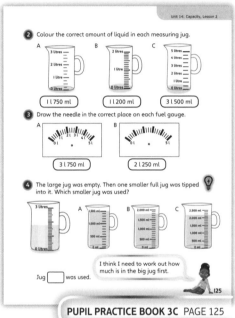

PUPIL PRACTICE BOOK 3C PAGE 125

PUPIL PRACTICE BOOK 3C PAGE 126

203

Measuring capacity ❸

Learning focus

In this lesson, children will continue to learn how to convert between litres and millilitres, including mixed units, in the context of real-life scenarios.

Small steps

→ Previous step: Measuring capacity (2)
→ **This step: Measuring capacity (3)**
→ Next step: Comparing capacities

NATIONAL CURRICULUM LINKS

Year 3 Measurement

Measure, compare, add and subtract: lengths (m/cm/mm); mass (kg/g); volume/capacity (l/ml).

ASSESSING MASTERY

Children will know that 1 litre is the same as 1,000 millilitres and that $\frac{1}{2}$ litre equals 500 millilitres. Children will be able to convert measurements between litres and millilitres, and millilitres in the context of real-life word problems.

COMMON MISCONCEPTIONS

If children are not fully secure in their place value of 4-digit numbers, they may make errors when converting, particularly when the number of millilitres in a mixed unit measure is less than 100. Ask:
• *How do you write the number one thousand and twenty? Three thousand and five?*

STRENGTHENING UNDERSTANDING

Support children by using equipment (such as base 10 equipment, place value cards) or by labelling the place value columns (so they are able to partition and identify the number of thousands and remaining millilitres). Children can represent the partition in a part-whole model: 1 l 250 ml = 1 l and 250 ml = 1,000 ml and 250 ml = 1250 ml.

GOING DEEPER

Provide children with a blank scale, with the bottom labelled 0 litres and the top labelled 10 litres. Children roll dice to generate a 4-digit number. This represents a measurement in millilitres. Children then have to plot that measurement on their scale.

KEY LANGUAGE

In lesson: capacity, litres (l), millilitres (ml), scale, bar model, number line, place value, convert, approximately, thousand

Other language used by the teacher: mixed unit, measure, measurement, compare, interval, partition

STRUCTURES AND REPRESENTATIONS

bar model, number line, part-whole model, column addition

RESOURCES

Optional: base 10 equipment, capacity measuring equipment, place value columns, place value cards, number lines, milk containers with a capacity greater than 1 litre

 In the eTextbook of this lesson, you will find interactive links to a selection of teaching tools.

Before you teach

• Can you make links to previous learning on converting measurements?
• Are there any children who may need support in applying their knowledge of place value?
• Do children know that 1,000 ml = 1 litre?

Discover

WAYS OF WORKING Pair work

ASK

- Question ❶ a): *What do you notice about the scale on the jug? Where would 1,000 ml be on the scale?*
- Question ❶ b): *Can you use the scale to work out how many millilitres 3 litres is?*

IN FOCUS Question ❶ a) involves converting millilitres to mixed units, the inverse of the learning in the previous lesson. Although this is new for this unit, children may be able to draw on their knowledge of converting measurements in mass. Encourage children to look carefully at the scale on the jug to remind themselves that 1 l is equivalent to 1,000 ml. In question ❶ b), encourage children to use the jug scale to help them: although the scale does not go up to 3 litres, they could deduce that 2 l = 2,000 ml so 3 l = 3,000 ml.

PRACTICAL TIPS Use large measuring containers to partially fill and read off the levels, giving the measurements in mixed units and in millilitres. Show some larger milk containers and practise converting the capacities to litres.

ANSWERS

Question ❶ a): The water will be at 1 l and 200 ml on the scale.

Question ❶ b): 3 l 250 ml is 3,250 ml of cream.

PUPIL TEXTBOOK 3C PAGE 172

Share

WAYS OF WORKING Whole class teacher led

ASK

- Question ❶ a): *Look at the bar model. What have the millilitres been partitioned into?*
- Question ❶ a): *Does this remind you of converting between other units of measure?*
- Question ❶ a): *What do you think the prefix 'milli-' in millimetres means?*
- Question ❶ b): *How has 3 l 250 ml been partitioned?*

IN FOCUS The focus in both parts of the question is on partitioning the measurement using bar models. Question ❶ b) shows the 3 litres partitioned into 1 l + 1 l + 1 l first, then into 1,000 ml + 1,000 ml + 1,000 ml. Encourage children to use the number link between 1 + 1 + 1 = 3 and 1,000 + 1,000 + 1,000 = 3,000. Ask: *How many millilitres is 5 l? 8 l?*

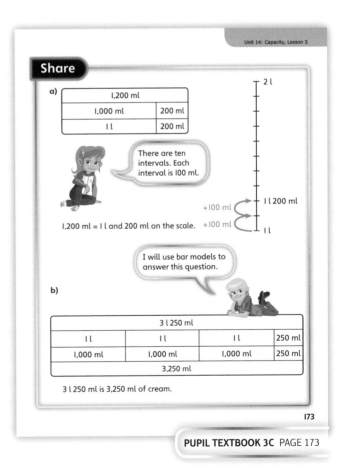

PUPIL TEXTBOOK 3C PAGE 173

Think together

Think together

WAYS OF WORKING Whole class teacher led (I do, We do, You do)

ASK

- Question **1** : *What do you have to partition the millilitres into when converting to litres?*
- Question **1** : *Can you see the relationship between a measurement in millilitres and a measurement in mixed litres and millilitres?*
- Question **2** : *Is there more than one possibility? Which one would you choose and why?*

IN FOCUS Question **3** has a measurement of 1 l and 50 ml. Some children may get confused with how to represent this in millilitres, as it requires a place holder. Children could write the 1,000 ml and the 50 ml as a column addition, making sure to align the digits in the correct columns. This may help them to identify the need for the zero place holder in the hundreds column.

STRENGTHEN Use base 10 equipment to model the conversion between millilitres and mixed units. Using place value columns will help support children in identifying how to partition, in order to convert between units. Practise particularly amounts with less than 100 ml, such as 3 l 60 ml and 2,075 ml.

DEEPEN Children roll dice to create a 4-digit number. Explain that this number represents a measurement in millilitres. Ask: *Can you convert it to mixed units without the support of a bar model? How did you work it out?*

ASSESSMENT CHECKPOINT Question **1** shows whether children are able to convert between mixed units and millilitres. Question **2** shows whether children are able to apply their knowledge of conversion in order to solve a problem. Question **3** shows whether children can securely use their knowledge of place value when converting capacity.

ANSWERS

Question **1** a): 1 l 600 ml = 1,600 ml of orange juice.

Question **1** b): 2 l 750 ml = 2,750 ml of apple juice.

Question **1** c): 4,250 ml = 4 l 250 ml.

Question **2** : The $2\frac{1}{2}$ l bowl and the 4,000 ml bowl are both big enough to hold 2 l 350 ml of water.

Question **3** : He will have 1,050 ml of liquid altogether.

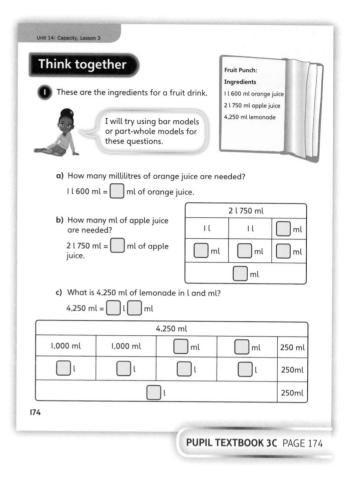

PUPIL TEXTBOOK 3C PAGE 174

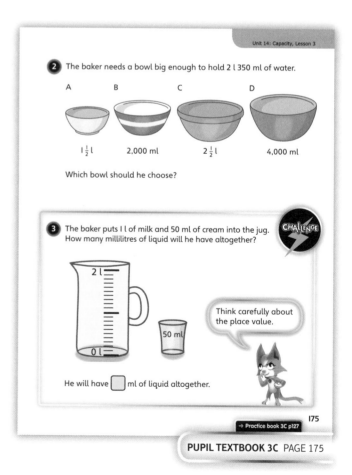

PUPIL TEXTBOOK 3C PAGE 175

Practice

IN FOCUS These questions focus on converting between units of measure. Question ❶ a) is supported with artwork, question ❶ b) with a bar model and a part-whole model. Question ❷ asks children to draw their own model to support the conversion. Question ❹ provides the challenge of working out amounts between markers.

STRENGTHEN Use of base 10 equipment and place value columns can support children with converting between millilitres and mixed units. Get children to spot that numbers are the same and in the same order in the conversion (**3 l 450** ml = **3,450** ml). The exception is when there are no hundreds 3 l 50 ml = 3,**0**50 ml. Practise finding half-way between pairs of numbers (such as 100 and 200, 50 and 100, 1,000 and 2,000).

DEEPEN Can children create their own conversion problems set in a real-life context? Children could also draw and label their own containers, coloured to show a level, and swap with a partner for them to write the amount in two ways.

THINK DIFFERENTLY Question ❺ requires children to record a number on a scale. It combines the skill of reading a scale and of converting between millilitres and mixed measures.

ASSESSMENT CHECKPOINT Can children confidently convert millilitres to mixed litres and millilitres? Can children confidently convert litres and ml to millilitres? Children should now be able to read scales for amounts over 1 litre, given in either millilitres or mixed units.

ANSWERS Answers to the **Practice** part of the lesson appear in a separate **Practice and Reflect answer guide**.

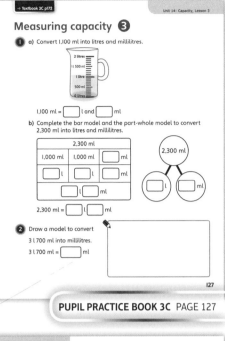

PUPIL PRACTICE BOOK 3C PAGE 127

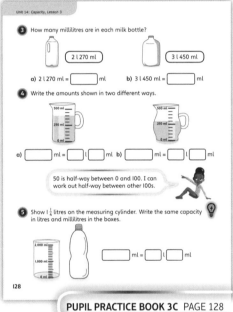

PUPIL PRACTICE BOOK 3C PAGE 128

Reflect

IN FOCUS This section requires children to identify what they need to consider when converting between units. Answering this question will help children secure their understanding of the process.

ASSESSMENT CHECKPOINT Are children able to describe what they need to do in order to convert between millilitres and mixed units?

ANSWERS Answers to the **Reflect** part of the lesson appear in a separate **Practice and Reflect answer guide**.

After the lesson ⏸

- Did the lesson identify any gaps in the way children applied their place value knowledge?
- Were children able to apply their learning from other areas of measurement?
- Have children become fluent in converting between millilitres and mixed units?

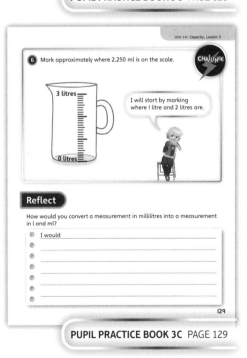

PUPIL PRACTICE BOOK 3C PAGE 129

Comparing capacities

Learning focus

In this lesson, children will learn to compare capacities by first comparing the number of litres then the number of millilitres. Children will also apply their knowledge of converting when comparing capacities given in different units.

Small steps

→ Previous step: Measuring capacity (3)
→ **This step: Comparing capacities**
→ Next step: Adding and subtracting capacities

NATIONAL CURRICULUM LINKS

Year 3 Measurement

Measure, compare, add and subtract: lengths (m/cm/mm); mass (kg/g); volume/capacity (l/ml).

ASSESSING MASTERY

Children can compare and order a range of capacities. Children will be able to convert measures into the same units before making comparisons.

COMMON MISCONCEPTIONS

Children may not consider the number of litres before looking at the number of millilitres. Be sure to emphasise that they must first look at how many litres there are in each measure. Make links to comparing numbers, where you look at the largest place value first. Ask:

• *How many litres is in this measure? And in this one?*

STRENGTHENING UNDERSTANDING

Start by comparing measures that are just in litres, to ensure that the children focus on litres first. Then move to comparing two capacities, where one is in whole litres and the other is in mixed litres and millilitres. This will help children see the importance of looking at the litres first.

GOING DEEPER

Children play a game in pairs or small groups. Each child rolls four dice to generate the largest 4-digit number. This gives them a capacity in millilitres. They each convert their capacity to mixed units and order them largest to smallest. The child who generates the largest capacity in each round wins a point. Children could have other rules: generate a capacity between 2 l and 4 l, or generate capacities as close to 3 litres as possible.

KEY LANGUAGE

In lesson: order, compare, litres (l), millilitres (ml), capacity, more, less, most, least, greater, greatest, greater than (>), less than (<), half ($\frac{1}{2}$)

Other language used by the teacher: place value

STRUCTURES AND REPRESENTATIONS

bar model, number line

RESOURCES

Optional: dice, capacity measuring equipment

 In the eTextbook of this lesson, you will find interactive links to a selection of teaching tools.

Before you teach

• Are children secure at reading capacities of mixed units on a range of scales?
• What practical opportunities can you incorporate in the lesson?
• Are there any children who may need support in place value in order to make comparisons?

Discover

Pair work

ASK

- Question **1** a): *What should you look at first when comparing these measurements?*
- Question **1** b): *What do you need to do before you can compare all these measurements?*
- Question **1** b): *Which holds the most/least of all four jugs?*

IN FOCUS These questions cover the key aspects of comparing two or more capacities. As with place value, the litres have the highest value, so this is the first number to consider. If the litres are the same, then the number of millilitres becomes important. When capacities are in different forms, then one (or more) of the measures will have to be converted so that they are all same. Encourage children to verbalise their reasoning when tackling these questions to ensure that they go through the correct process.

PRACTICAL TIPS Practical experience of using pairs of similar sized containers (where one has measurements in mixed measures and the other just millilitres) would be a helpful way for children to see that, for example: 1 l 500 ml is the same as 1,500 ml. Counting up in steps of 100 ml, 200 ml, 250 ml and 500 ml to 5,000 ml would be useful (800, 1,000, 1,200, 1,400 and so on). This can be repeated immediately with the related mixed measure: … 800 ml, 1 litre, 1 l 200 ml, 1 l 400 ml and so on.

ANSWERS

Question **1** a): The orange juice has 2 litres, the lemon squash has only 1 litre. There is more orange juice.

Question **1** b): The drinks in order of amount from most to least are: water, orange juice, apple juice, lemon squash.

Share

Whole class teacher led

ASK

- Question **1** a): *Why do you compare the litres first?*
- Question **1** b): *What do you do if the number of litres are the same?*
- Question **1** b): *Which is easier, to convert millilitres into mixed litres and millilitres or to convert mixed litres and millilitres into millilitres?*

IN FOCUS These questions highlight the importance of comparing the number of litres first, because they are the larger unit. Only when the litres are different do you need to look at the smaller unit, the millilitres. Question **1** b) encourages children to convert one or more of the measurements so that all the measurements are in the same unit, making a direct comparison easier.

Comparing capacities

Discover

a) Is there more orange juice or more lemon squash? Show how you know.

b) Put the drinks in order of amount, from the most to the least.

176

PUPIL TEXTBOOK 3C PAGE 176

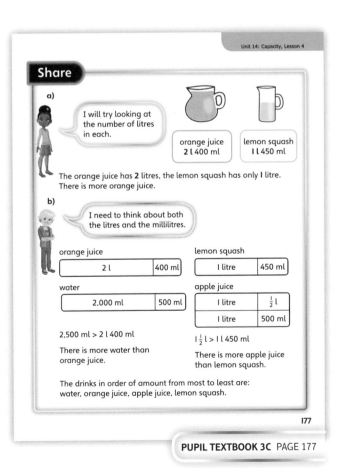

PUPIL TEXTBOOK 3C PAGE 177

Think together

WAYS OF WORKING Whole class teacher led (I do, We do, You do)

ASK

- Question **1** : *What do you have to do before you can compare these capacities?*
- Question **2** : *Is it easy to see which one will hold the least? Why?*
- Question **3** : *Can you draw a picture to help you solve this?*

IN FOCUS Question **3** requires children to carry out a multiplication to solve the problem. They could use repeated addition in order to do this. They will then need to carry out a conversion to compare the capacities. Encourage children to draw or make notes to keep track of their thinking. The fact that the capacities are the same may make some children question whether they calculated correctly.

STRENGTHEN Use capacity equipment so children can physically measure and compare the capacities in the questions.

DEEPEN For question **3** , ask: *What other ways can Reena and Max still have the same capacities?*

ASSESSMENT CHECKPOINT Question **1** will determine whether children can convert and compare capacities that have the same number of litres. Question **2** will determine whether children can convert, compare and order capacities that have different numbers of litres. Question **3** will determine whether children can apply their knowledge of multiplication in order to solve a multi-step problem comparing capacities.

ANSWERS

Question **1** a): $\frac{1}{2}$ l = 500 ml. Car A has the greater capacity.

Question **1** b): 2,850 ml is less than 2 l 900 ml.
2,850 ml = 2 l 850 ml, 850 < 900

Question **1** c): 3,550 ml is more than $3\frac{1}{2}$ litres.
$3\frac{1}{2}$ litres = 3,500 ml, 3,550 ml > 3,500 ml

Question **2** : C: 750 ml, A: 1 l 300 ml, B: 2,050 ml, D: 2 l 200 ml

Question **3** : Reena and Max have the same amount of fizzy drink as they each have 4 litres.
8 × 500 = 4,000 ml = 4 l
$(\frac{1}{2} + \frac{1}{2} + \frac{1}{2} + \frac{1}{2} + \frac{1}{2} + \frac{1}{2} + \frac{1}{2} + \frac{1}{2} = 4)$
2 × 2 l = 4 l.

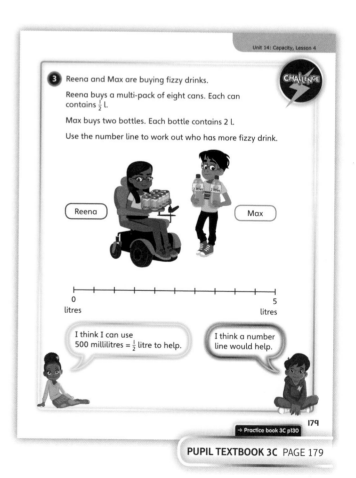

Practice

IN FOCUS In question **7**, some children may just guess, thinking that the tall, thin container is fuller than the short wide container. But the total capacity of the wide one holds 2 litres and it is at least $\frac{3}{4}$ full which is 1 l 500 ml (1,500 ml); whereas the total capacity of the taller container is only 1,500 ml (1 l 500 ml) and it is not full.

STRENGTHEN Children can make comparisons by using capacity equipment. Firstly give each pair two different containers. Ask them to pour 1 or 2 litres of water into them. Ask: *Which looks as if it has more liquid?* Provide two 2 litre jugs, one in litres and one in millilitres. Ask children to pour the same amount in each jug. Then read and record the amounts. Children should then pour more water into one container and record each amount as a comparison: a > b.

DEEPEN Children work in pairs. Give each pair a scale from 0 l to 7 l, marked in 100 millilitre intervals, whole litres labelled. Children take it in turns to roll two dice to generate two numbers. They choose one for the litres and the other for the hundreds of millilitres (for example, 3 and 4 could give 3 l 400 ml or 4 l 300 ml). Children plot their capacity on the scale. The first child to get three in a row wins. To simplify, the first number rolled is litres and the second the hundreds (so that the winning depends more on the roll of the dice than on choosing strategically).

THINK DIFFERENTLY Question **5** combines learning from this and previous lessons. Children need to read the amounts from a variety of vertical line scales and order the amounts. Some may need support reading the intervals on each scale.

ASSESSMENT CHECKPOINT Children should compare by first looking at the number of litres in mixed units, or by using place value to 4 digits for millilitres. Children should realise that they may need to convert units, so that all the measurements are in the same unit of measure. Children can read off a scale where not all intervals are labelled.

ANSWERS Answers to the **Practice** part of the lesson appear in a separate **Practice and Reflect answer guide**.

Reflect

IN FOCUS Children list the steps needed to order a set of capacities. Steps should include: converting to same unit of measure, comparing the litres or thousands of millilitres, converting $\frac{1}{2}$ l to 500 ml, comparing the number of millilitres.

ASSESSMENT CHECKPOINT Do children understand that the number of litres is compared first, as that is the largest unit? Do children mention converting units when the units of measure are different? You only need to compare the millilitres when the units of measure are different.

ANSWERS Answers to the **Reflect** part of the lesson appear in a separate **Practice and Reflect answer guide**.

After the lesson

- Were there any gaps in understanding that hindered children's ability to compare capacities?
- Were children able to convert to the same units in order to compare capacities?
- Were children able to draw on their knowledge from other units on measures to help them in this lesson?

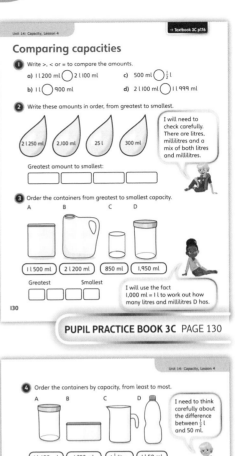

PUPIL PRACTICE BOOK 3C PAGE 130

PUPIL PRACTICE BOOK 3C PAGE 131

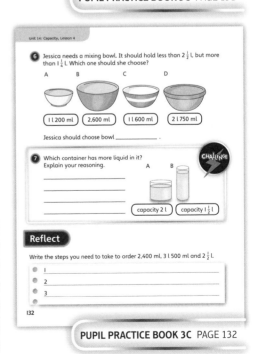

PUPIL PRACTICE BOOK 3C PAGE 132

Adding and subtracting capacities

Learning focus

In this lesson, children will apply what they have learnt about converting between litres and millilitres to add and subtract capacities. They will have to draw on their knowledge of number bonds to 1,000 and their knowledge of partitioning.

Small steps

→ Previous step: Comparing capacities
→ **This step: Adding and subtracting capacities**
→ Next step: Problem solving – capacity

NATIONAL CURRICULUM LINKS

Year 3 Measurement

Measure, compare, add and subtract: lengths (m/cm/mm); mass (kg/g); volume/capacity (l/ml).

ASSESSING MASTERY

Children can add and subtract capacities across a litre boundary. Children will be able to use what they know about converting between litres and millilitres, as well as number bonds to 1,000, to solve addition and subtraction problems in the context of capacity.

COMMON MISCONCEPTIONS

Children may not be able to make the link between bonds to 10 and bonds to 100 and 1,000. Start by asking the children to record their bonds to 10. Then look at bonds to 100 with multiples of 10, and discuss the similarities. Finally, look at bonds to 1,000 with multiples of 100, and discuss the patterns between the three sets of number bonds. Ask:
• *What do you add to 6 to make 10? What do you add to 60 (600) to make 100 (1,000)?*

STRENGTHENING UNDERSTANDING

Where possible, use bar models to illustrate the addition or subtraction. Children could use the scales as number lines to help calculate the addition or subtraction. Ensure children have practise in crossing the litre boundaries, and in partitioning the mixed measure, in order to add or subtract them where appropriate.

GOING DEEPER

Children by posing problems where they have to add or subtract three or more quantities. Include amounts in different units, so that children need to convert as well as cross a litre boundary. Children could make up their own capacity problems to solve.

KEY LANGUAGE

In lesson: add, subtract, total, difference, capacity, millilitres (ml), litres (l), scale, column addition, counting on, subtraction, greater than (>), less than (<), total, number bonds to 1,000

Other language used by the teacher: number bonds to 10/100, mixed measure, pattern

STRUCTURES AND REPRESENTATIONS

bar model, column addition, column subtraction, number line

RESOURCES

Optional: capacity measuring equipment

 In the eTextbook of this lesson, you will find interactive links to a selection of teaching tools.

Before you teach

• Can you provide practical opportunities for children to add and subtract quantities?
• How secure are children in addition and subtraction with up to three digits?
• How will you link this lesson to previous units on addition and subtraction?

Discover

Unit 14: Capacity, Lesson 5

WAYS OF WORKING Pair work

ASK

- Question **1** a): *Which containers have less than 1 litre? Less than 500 ml?*
- Question **1** a): *Is it possible to answer the question without adding the amounts?*
- Question **1** b): *What do you need to do first to answer this question?*

IN FOCUS In question **1** a), bar models should help children to answer the question, rather than adding the amounts. As both of Professor Smith's amounts are less than 500 ml, their total must be less than 1,000 ml, which is 1 litre. Similarly, Doctor Crawford's amounts are both more than 500 ml, so their total must be over 1 litre. Question **1** b) requires column addition, but children can use a counting on method (using a number line) for subtraction.

PRACTICAL TIPS Allow children to act out the scene. They can physically measure out the amounts and pour them in together in a clearly labelled container, to find the totals. Children could also use the scale as a counting-up number line for the subtraction.

ANSWERS

Question **1** a): Professor Smith has less than 1 litre of liquid altogether.

Question **1** b): The doctor has 750 ml more liquid than the professor.

Share

WAYS OF WORKING Whole class teacher led

ASK

- Question **1** a): *How do the bar models show that Professor Smith has less than 1 litre in total?*
- Question **1** b): *What do you need to remember when doing column addition?*
- Question **1** b): *Can you answer this question without adding or subtracting?*
- Question **1** b): *Do you need to do addition or subtraction first?*
- Question **1** b): *Which method is being shown for the subtraction?*

IN FOCUS Although question **1** a) could be answered using addition, the bar models show that it is not necessary. However, it is necessary to add and subtract to answer question **1** b). Children may suggest other known methods for addition and subtraction to the ones modelled, which could be used to check the answers given.

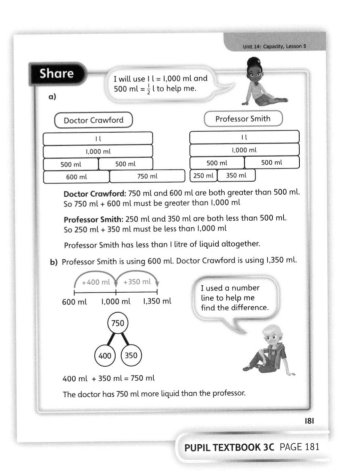

Think together

Whole class teacher led (I do, We do, You do)

ASK

- Questions **1** and **2** : *Which addition facts could help you?*
- Question **3** : *Do you need to convert between units? Why not?*

IN FOCUS Question **4** involves crossing the litre boundary when adding and also when subtracting. Discuss some strategies for adding the amounts, including using bonds to 1,000 then adding on, or adding the litres and millilitres separately and converting the units. Ask: *Which do you find easier?* Steps for this question are modelled using bar models, but number lines marked as scales could also be used.

STRENGTHEN Model the additions and subtractions using the part-whole model and the bar model. It may support some children's understanding of adding and subtracting capacities to explore the questions practically.

DEEPEN Set children word problems to deepen learning. Ask: *What three quantities could you add together to make a total of 2 l 200 ml? Each quantity must be a multiple of 100 ml. How many different combinations can you find?*

ASSESSMENT CHECKPOINT Questions **1** and **2** show whether the children are able to use number bonds to 1,000. Question **3** shows whether children can add mixed units by partitioning the litres and millilitres. Question **4** shows whether children can add and subtract capacities involving crossing litre boundaries.

ANSWERS

Question **1** : A 600 ml + 400 ml = 1 l, B 200 ml + 800 ml = 1 l, C 550 ml + 450 ml = 1 l, D 350 ml + 650 ml = 1 l

Question **2** : 750 ml is left in the jug.

Question **3** : Total capacity = 3 l 650 ml

Question **4** : The total is 2 l 200 ml. 800 ml more liquid is needed to fill the 3 l jug.

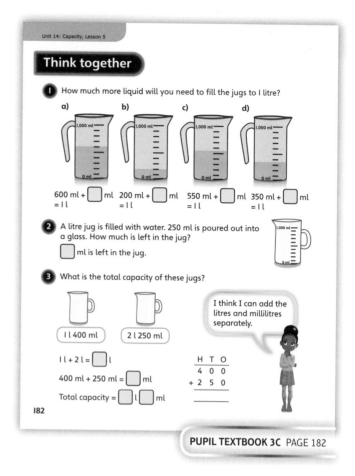

PUPIL TEXTBOOK 3C PAGE 182

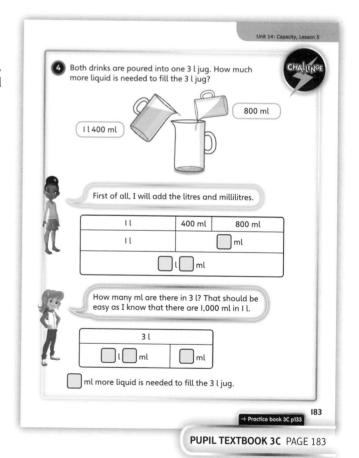

PUPIL TEXTBOOK 3C PAGE 183

Practice

WAYS OF WORKING Independent thinking

IN FOCUS Question **4** is a two-step problem requiring addition then subtraction, and a knowledge of how to convert between litres and millilitres. Some children may need extra guidance to identify the calculations that need to be done. Encourage children to draw a bar model of the problem to help them identify the steps.

Question **5**, the challenge question, is a multi-step problem. Some children may need to physically act it out, then draw bar models or number lines to realise they need to add the first two amounts and subtract that from 2 l (2,000 ml) to then work out what must be in cylinder C.

STRENGTHEN Children should use bar models or number lines to represent each problem. They can use base 10 equipment to help calculate with the 1,000 cubes representing litres. Practise multiple of 10 and multiple of 100 bonds to 1,000.

DEEPEN Ask children to develop their own addition and subtraction 2-step problems. Their problems need to require the crossing of a litre boundary.

ASSESSMENT CHECKPOINT Questions **1**, **2** and **3** assess whether children can add or subtract amounts without crossing a litre boundary. Questions **4** and **5** assess whether children can solve multi-step word problems involving crossing litre boundaries and converting between units.

ANSWERS Answers to the **Practice** part of the lesson appear in a separate **Practice and Reflect answer guide**.

Reflect

WAYS OF WORKING Independent thinking

IN FOCUS Children are asked to explain how they would add together two amounts, given in different units of measure.

ASSESSMENT CHECKPOINT Can children identify strategies such as converting between units, adding the litres and millilitres separately, or using knowledge of number bonds to 1,000?

ANSWERS Answers to the **Reflect** part of the lesson appear in a separate **Practice and Reflect answer guide**.

After the lesson ⏸

- Were there any gaps in children's knowledge and application of place value, number bonds or partitioning that acted as barriers to their learning?
- Were you able to make the links between this lesson and previous lessons in this unit?

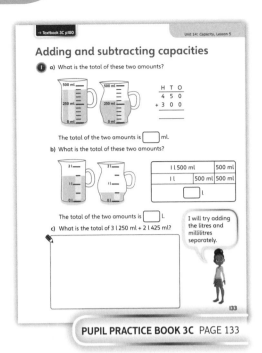

PUPIL PRACTICE BOOK 3C PAGE 133

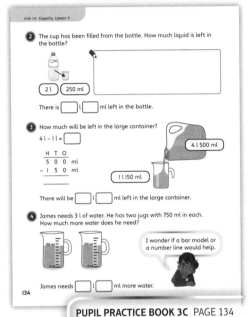

PUPIL PRACTICE BOOK 3C PAGE 134

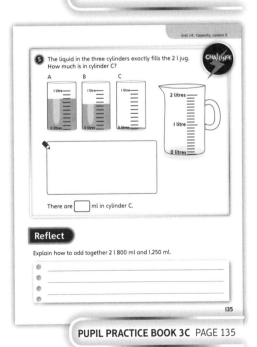

PUPIL PRACTICE BOOK 3C PAGE 135

Problem solving – capacity

Learning focus

In this lesson, children will apply their learning from this unit to solve problems involving all four operations.

Small steps

→ Previous step: Adding and subtracting capacities
→ **This step: Problem solving – capacity**

NATIONAL CURRICULUM LINKS

Year 3 Measurement

Measure, compare, add and subtract: lengths (m/cm/mm); mass (kg/g); volume/capacity (l/ml).

ASSESSING MASTERY

Children can carry out multi-step capacity problems involving all four operations. Children will be able to apply their knowledge of multiplication, division, subtraction and addition, as well as converting between litres and millilitres.

COMMON MISCONCEPTIONS

Children may need support to identify what calculations they need to do, particularly if it is a multi-step problem. Encourage children to draw a picture of the problem and use bar models in order to identify what operations are required. Ask:
• *What is the question asking you to do? What do you need to do first? What could you draw to show what the problem is asking?*

STRENGTHENING UNDERSTANDING

Where possible, represent the problem using concrete apparatus. Encourage children to talk the problem through with a partner or an adult and to say the problem in their own words. It can help model children's thinking process by thinking out loud whilst solving the problem with them.

GOING DEEPER

Ask children to adapt some of the problems in order to change the type of operations required. For example, they could adapt a problem that requires addition, so that it requires subtraction instead.

KEY LANGUAGE

In lesson: capacity, millilitres (ml), litres (l), add (+), subtract (–), multiply (×), divide (÷), difference, total, convert, equivalent
Other language to be used by the teacher: calculation, scale, division

STRUCTURES AND REPRESENTATIONS

bar model, number line, part-whole model

RESOURCES

Optional: capacity measuring equipment, base 10 equipment

 In the eTextbook of this lesson, you will find interactive links to a selection of teaching tools.

Before you teach

• Are there any children who may need support with calculating?
• How can you model the problems for children to help them identify the calculations required?

Discover

WAYS OF WORKING Pair work

ASK

- Question ❶ a: *What do you need to do to solve this?*
- Question ❶ b): *What could you draw to show a picture of the problem?*
- Question ❶ b): *What calculation do you need to do to solve the problem?*

IN FOCUS Both questions involve division, but question ❶ a) is modelled as a repeated addition, whereas question ❶ b) shows the problem as a division. Both parts are shown using bar models. Children need to draw on their knowledge of converting 1 litre to millilitres.

PRACTICAL TIPS You can support children by drawing a scale for 1 litre with five divisions. This will help children apply their learning from reading scales to solve the problem. Children could physically enact the questions by using a 200 ml measure and a litre jug.

ANSWERS

Question ❶ a): Holly uses three 200 ml cartons of milk for the pancake recipe.

Question ❶ b): There will be 200 ml of juice in each cup.

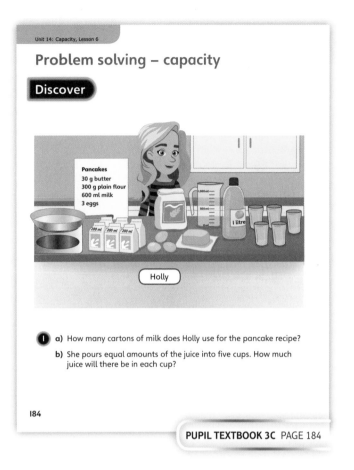

PUPIL TEXTBOOK 3C PAGE 184

Share

WAYS OF WORKING Whole class teacher led

ASK

- Question ❶ a): *What addition facts did you use to find the solution?*
- Question ❶ b): *What multiplication facts did you use to find the solution? Is there another way of finding the solution? How else could you share 1,000 ml equally between cups?*

IN FOCUS Known multiplication facts can be used to work out related division facts. These can be used to solve problems with much larger numbers. Draw attention to the relationship between 10 ÷ 5 = 2, and 100 ÷ 5 = 20 and therefore 1,000 ÷ 5 = 200. Discuss how to divide 100 between 2, 4 and 10, relating that to dividing 1,000 between 2, 4 and 10.

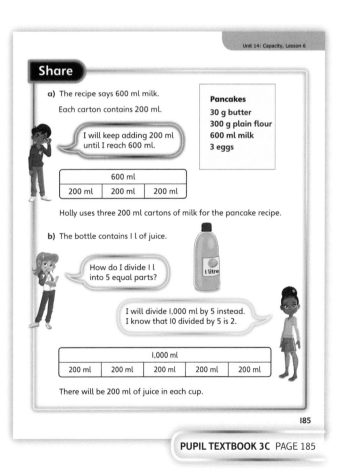

PUPIL TEXTBOOK 3C PAGE 185

Think together

Whole class teacher led (I do, We do, You do)

ASK

- Question **①** : *What addition or multiplication facts are going to help you?*
- Question **③** : *Have you solved it the same way as your partner? If not, which way do you think is easier?*
- Question **③** : *Can you draw a picture of the problem?*

IN FOCUS Question **③** requires children to first convert from litres to millilitres and then carry out a division. Children may overlook that it is 2 l and only divide 1 l. They should remember that 250 ml is a quarter of 1,000 ml (from previous lessons), so they will get four cups from each litre. You could encourage them to draw a scale on a white board for 2 l and to put in 250 ml divisions, so children can link the calculation to the learning they did on reading scales in previous lessons.

STRENGTHEN Ask children to draw a picture of the problem to help understand what is required. If possible, use equipment to replicate the problem, so children can see the calculations needed.

DEEPEN Can children adapt question **③** so that the answer will be: 4 cups? 10 cups? 16 cups? 20 cups?

ASSESSMENT CHECKPOINT Can children solve word problems involving millilitres and litres, choosing the correct operation(s), and using their knowledge of the relationship between litres and millilitres?

ANSWERS

Question **①** a): Francesca uses 30 ml each day.

Question **①** b): 200 − 180 = 20 ml. No, it is not enough for one day.

Question **②** : Francesca drinks 3 l 500 ml altogether.

Question **③** a): Leon can fill 8 cups.

Question **③** b): 6 cups = 1 l 500 ml. There are 500 ml left.

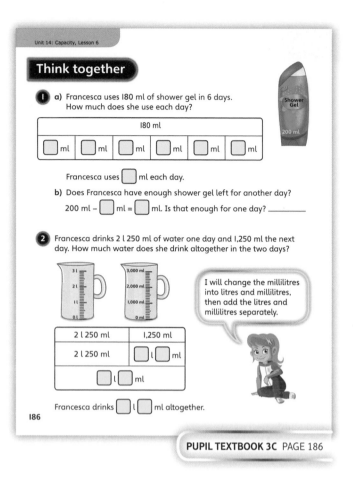

PUPIL TEXTBOOK 3C PAGE 186

PUPIL TEXTBOOK 3C PAGE 187

Practice

WAYS OF WORKING Independent thinking

IN FOCUS Questions from ❸ onwards are 2- or multi-step problems with the challenge question ❼ requiring a number of steps. Children may need support through diagrams to start. A common error is not working all the way through a question. Children may only do the first calculation or miss one of the calculations out. Encourage children to go back and read the problem after they have their answer, in order to check that they have answered it.

STRENGTHEN Encourage children to talk through the problem with a partner or adult. As they are talking it through, the adult or partner can draw a picture of the problem. It may also help to read the problem to the child and get them to repeat it back in their own words. The use of bar models can aid children in identifying the calculations that are needed. You can adapt question ❼ with fewer plants and/or less days.

DEEPEN Ask children to develop their own multi-step problems. You could challenge them further by specifying what operations children have to include in the problem. A good starting point is to write similar problems to those on these pages, with different contexts, values or operations.

THINK DIFFERENTLY Question ❺ is a multi-step problem. Encourage children to look back at other questions to help them work out how many glasses each child needs. Ensure they actually answer the question: *How many more?*

ASSESSMENT CHECKPOINT Can children solve a single-step capacity problem without crossing a litre boundary? Can children solve a single-step capacity problem crossing a litre boundary? Can children solve a 2- or multi-step capacity problem? Are children completing a multi-step problem or only partially completing it?

ANSWERS Answers to the **Practice** part of the lesson appear in a separate **Practice and Reflect answer guide**.

Reflect

WAYS OF WORKING Independent thinking

IN FOCUS This section encourages children to verbalise how they solved one of the problems on these pages. You may wish to specify the question they are to explain. Children should mention the steps they took in the correct order and which calculations they had to work out to answer the question fully.

ASSESSMENT CHECKPOINT Are children able to explain clearly how they solved a capacity problem with more than one step? Did children show the calculations needed in the correct order?

ANSWERS Answers to the **Reflect** part of the lesson appear in a separate **Practice and Reflect answer guide**.

After the lesson ⏸

- How confident were children in identifying the calculations within the problems?
- Did children apply any strategies that could be helpful to others?
- How successful were you and children in making the links between this lesson and previous lessons in this unit?

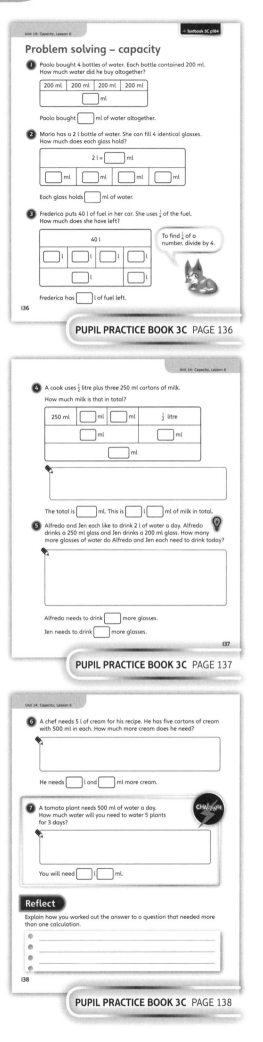

PUPIL PRACTICE BOOK 3C PAGE 136

PUPIL PRACTICE BOOK 3C PAGE 137

PUPIL PRACTICE BOOK 3C PAGE 138

End of unit check

> Don't forget the *Power Maths* unit assessment grid on p26.

WAYS OF WORKING Group work adult led

IN FOCUS

- Question **1** assesses children's ability to read a range of scales involving millilitres.
- Question **2** assesses children's ability to read scales and convert from millilitres to mixed units.
- Question **3** assesses children's ability to convert from mixed units to millilitres.
- Question **4** assesses children's ability to compare capacities involving mixed units.
- Question **5** assesses children's ability to add capacities of mixed units crossing the litre boundary.
- Question **6** assesses children's ability to subtract capacities of mixed units crossing the litre boundary.
- Question **7** assesses children's ability to solve multi-step capacity problems.

ANSWERS AND COMMENTARY

Children who have mastered the concepts in this unit will be able to read and measure amounts in litres and millilitres. They will be able to add, subtract and convert between the units and use this knowledge with the four operations in problem solving.

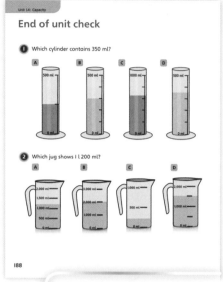

PUPIL TEXTBOOK 3C PAGE 188

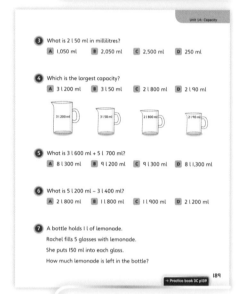

PUPIL TEXTBOOK 3C PAGE 189

Q	A	WRONG ANSWERS AND MISCONCEPTIONS	STRENGTHENING UNDERSTANDING
1	D	A suggests an error in halving 500 ml; B suggests misreading the target capacity as 300ml; C suggests that the total capacity has been ignored when interpreting the scale.	Do not forget to make the links to understanding of number and calculating clear to children. The scale should be seen as a number line and children can use this to support their calculations. Providing opportunities for children to engage in practical exploration of capacity can help them in their understanding of the context. Practice writing numbers (such as one thousand and fifty, two thousand and seventy, three thousand and fifteen), stressing the importance of the 0 as a place holder in the 100s.
2	A	C suggests children have looked at ml only.	
3	B	A suggests incorrect conversion of the whole litres; C and D suggest an error in place value.	
4	A	B suggests an error in place value; C suggests ignoring the whole litres; D suggests ignoring the whole litres and an error in place value.	
5	C	A suggests forgetting the extra litre gained from adding the millilitres; B suggests an addition error when crossing the litre boundary. D suggests forgetting to convert 1,000 ml to 1 litre.	
6	B	A or C suggest an error when crossing the litre boundary; D suggests incorrect subtraction of 400 −200.	
7	250 ml	An answer of 750 ml suggests forgetting to subtract.	

My journal

WAYS OF WORKING Independent thinking

ANSWERS AND COMMENTARY

Children should be able to use the bar models provided to support their understanding of converting between mixed units and millilitres. Remind children that each litre is the same as 1,000 ml. The use of base 10 equipment can support children's understanding.

Question ① a): 4,250 ml

Question ① b): 2,500 ml

Question ① c): 3 l 750 ml

Children should be confident in their understanding that there are 1,000 ml in 1 l.

Power check

WAYS OF WORKING Independent thinking

ASK

• How confident are you in converting between mixed litres and millilitres to millilitres?
• Do you think you can understand a range of scales to work out capacity?
• How happy are you in adding and subtracting capacities?

Power play

WAYS OF WORKING Pair work

IN FOCUS Use this **Power play** to determine how confident children are in reading scales as they add and subtract millilitres across the litre boundaries.

ANSWERS AND COMMENTARY The less confident of the pair could start by being the player who adds. They could use the scale as a number line to count on. Encourage the children to try solving the calculation and finding the answer on the scale before moving their counter, recording their addition or subtraction in both ml and in mixed units. For example, 2 litres: (score of 4) 2 l + 400 ml = 2 l 400 ml = 2,400 ml, or 2 l – 400 ml = 1 l 600 ml = 1,600 ml.

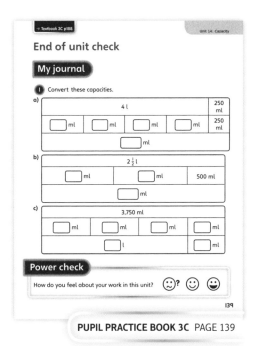

PUPIL PRACTICE BOOK 3C PAGE 139

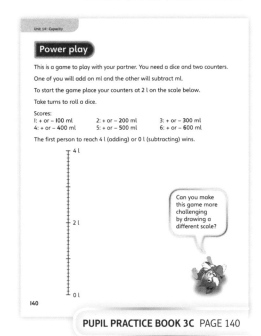

PUPIL PRACTICE BOOK 3C PAGE 140

After the unit ⏸

• The most obvious practical application for capacity is cooking. Could you provide an opportunity for the children to apply their skills by following up with a cooking activity?
• The skills in this unit are transferable to other units of measure. Ask the children what is the same or different about their learning in this unit and their learning in the length and mass units.

Strengthen and **Deepen** activities for this unit can be found in the *Power Maths* online subscription.

Published by Pearson Education Limited, 80 Strand, London, WC2R 0RL.

www.pearsonschools.co.uk

Text © Pearson Education Limited 2018
Edited by Pearson, Little Grey Cells Publishing Services and Haremi Ltd
Designed and typeset by Kamae Design
Original illustrations © Pearson Education Limited 2018
Illustrated by Fran and David Brylewski, Virginia Fontanabona, Adam Linley and Paul Moran at Beehive Illustration; Emily Skinner at Graham-Cameron Illustration; and Kamae.
Cover design by Pearson Education Ltd
Back cover illustration © Diago Diaz and Nadene Naude at Beehive Illustration.

Series Editor: Tony Staneff
Consultants: Professor Liu Jian and Professor Zhang Dan

The rights of Josh Lury, David Board, Belle Cottingham, Neil Jarrett and Paul Wrangles to be identified as authors of this work have been asserted by them in accordance with the Copyright, Designs and Patents Act 1988.

First published 2018

21 20 19
10 9 8 7 6 5 4 3 2

British Library Cataloguing in Publication Data
A catalogue record for this book is available from the British Library

ISBN 978 0 435 19017 0

Printed in Slovakia by Neografia

www.activelearnprimary.co.uk

Note from the publisher
Pearson has robust editorial processes, including answer and fact checks, to ensure the accuracy of the content in this publication, and every effort is made to ensure this publication is free of errors. We are, however, only human, and occasionally errors do occur. Pearson is not liable for any misunderstandings that arise as a result of errors in this publication, but it is our priority to ensure that the content is accurate. If you spot an error, please do contact us at resourcescorrections@pearson.com so we can make sure it is corrected.